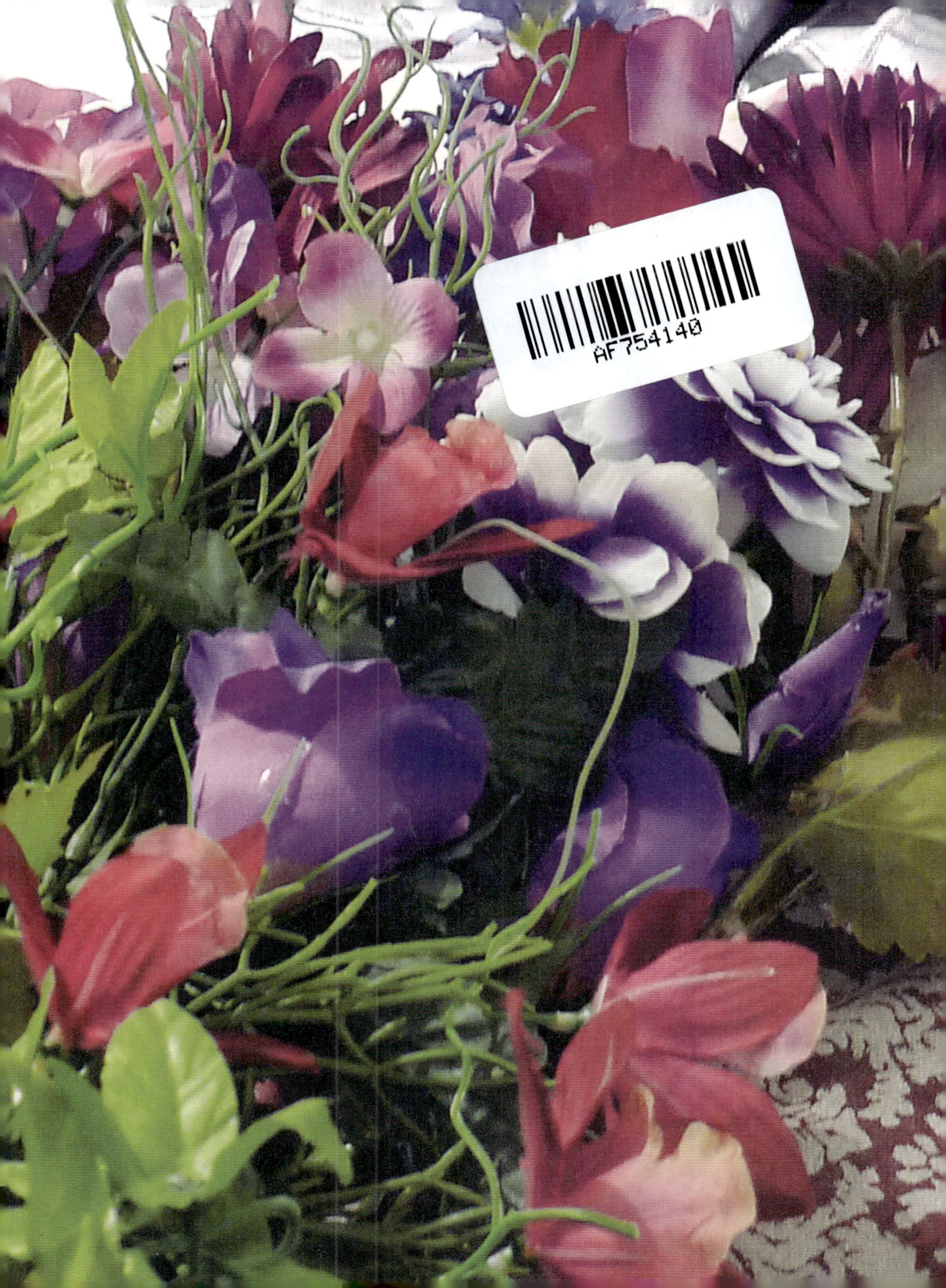

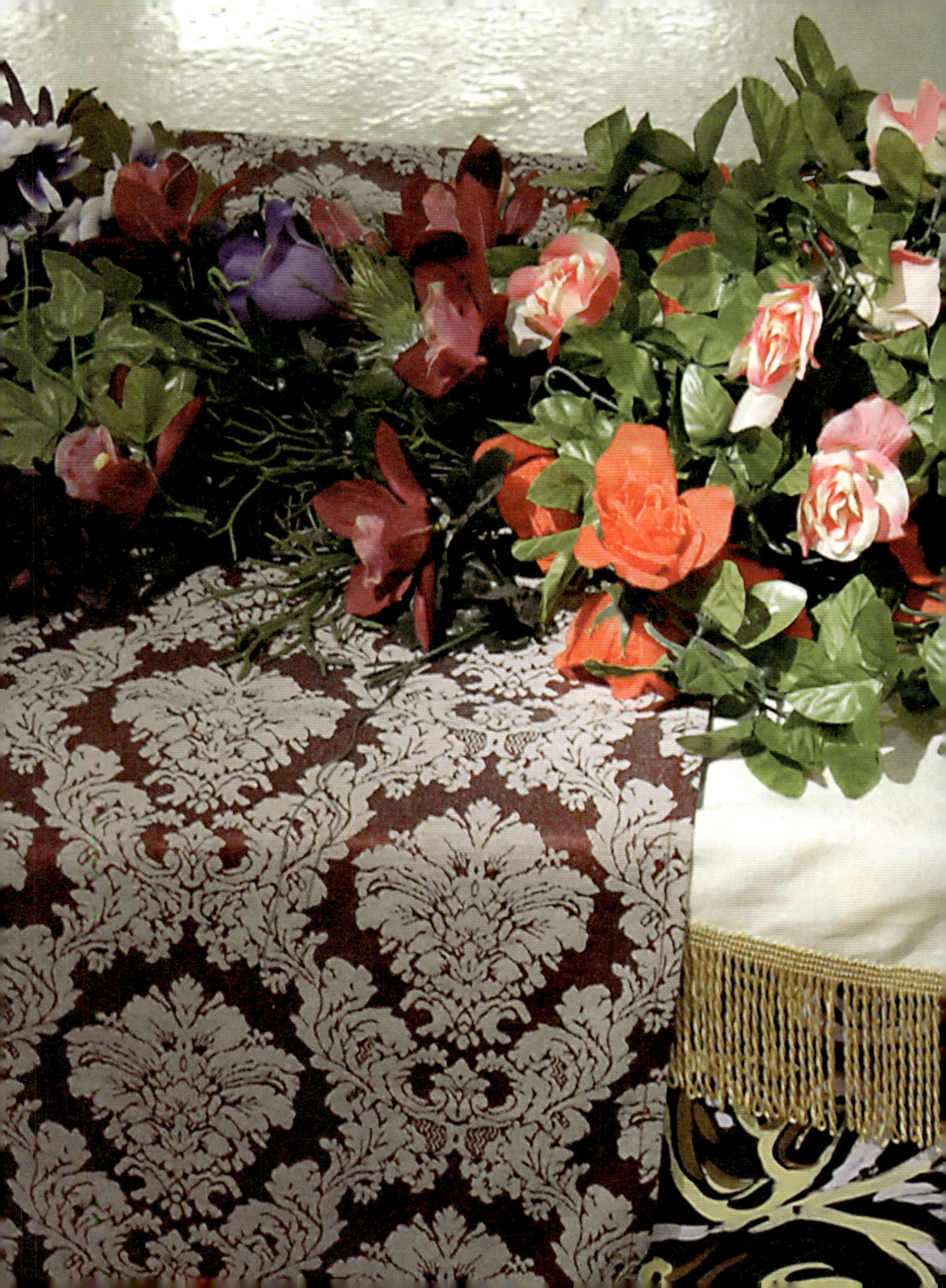

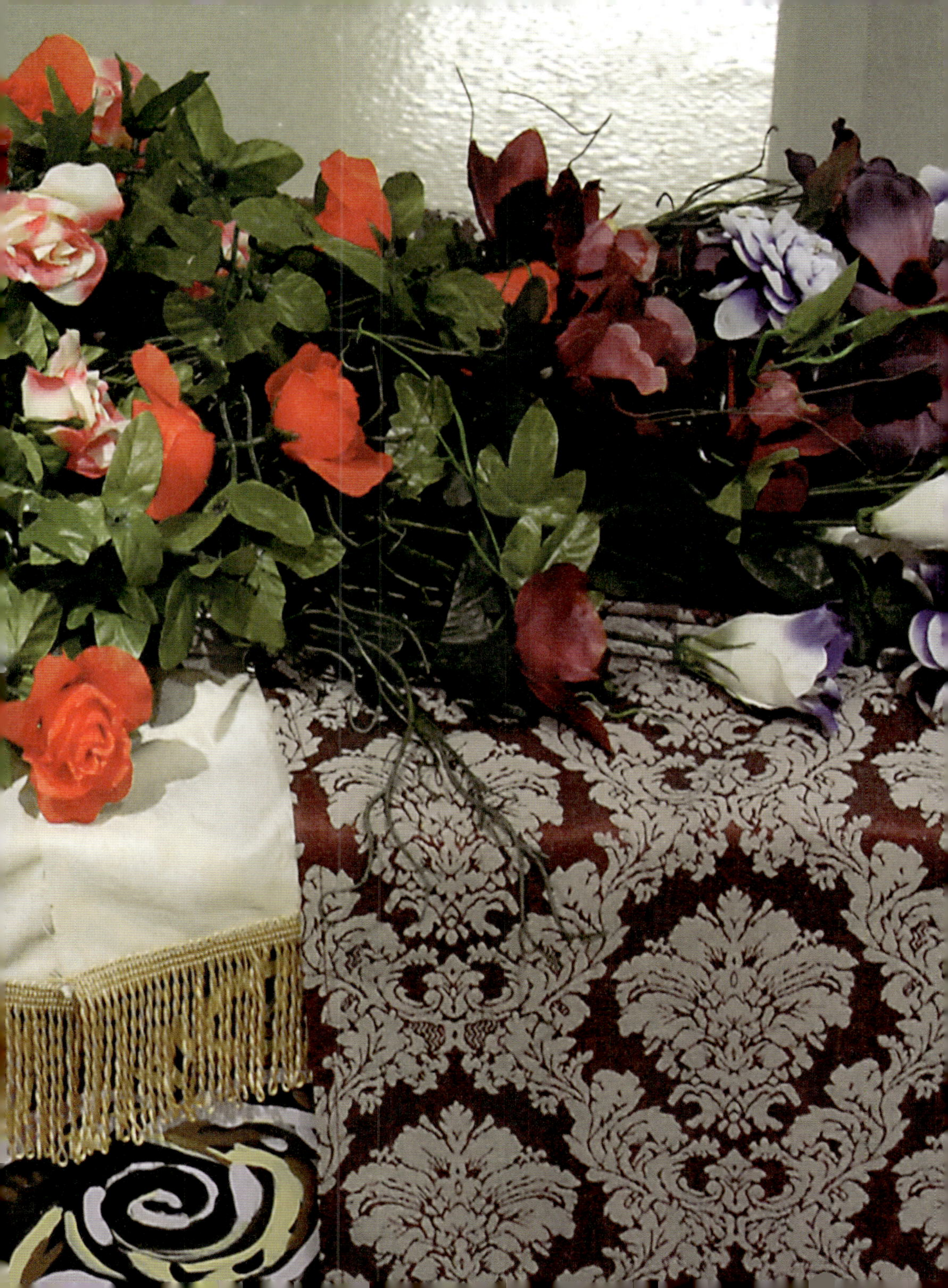

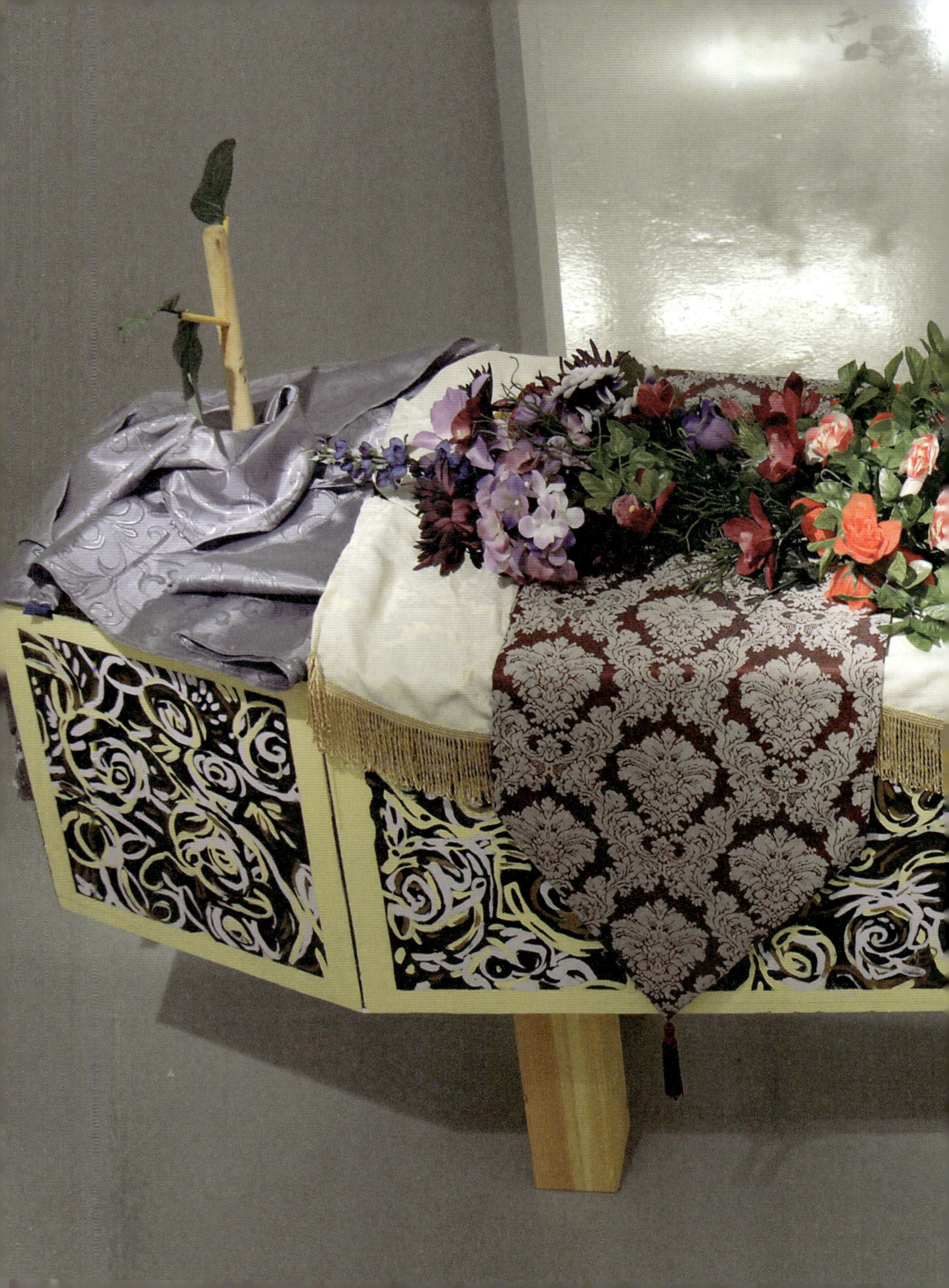

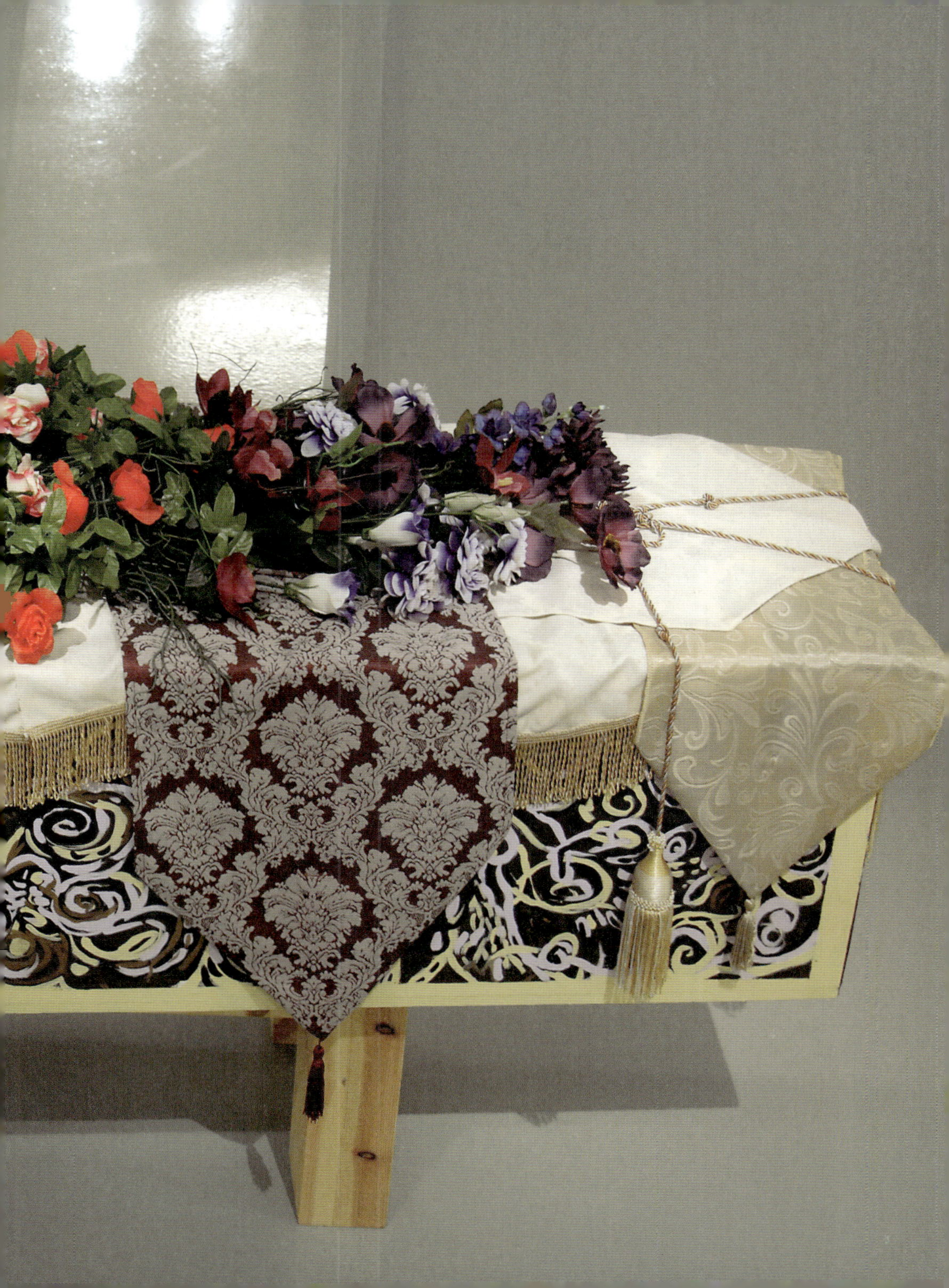

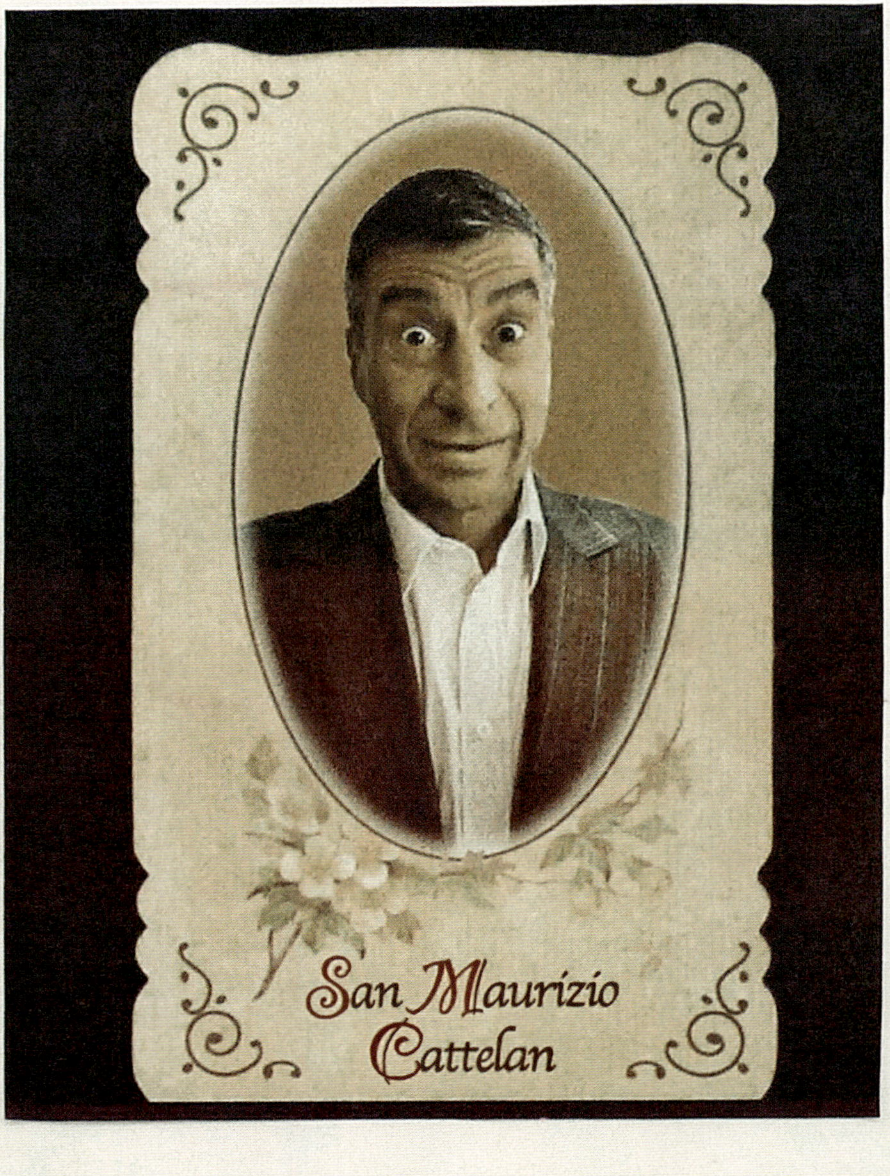
San Maurizio
Cattelan

MAURIZIO
Cattelan is Dead

Life & Work, 1960–2009

Curated, designed, and edited by Triple Candie

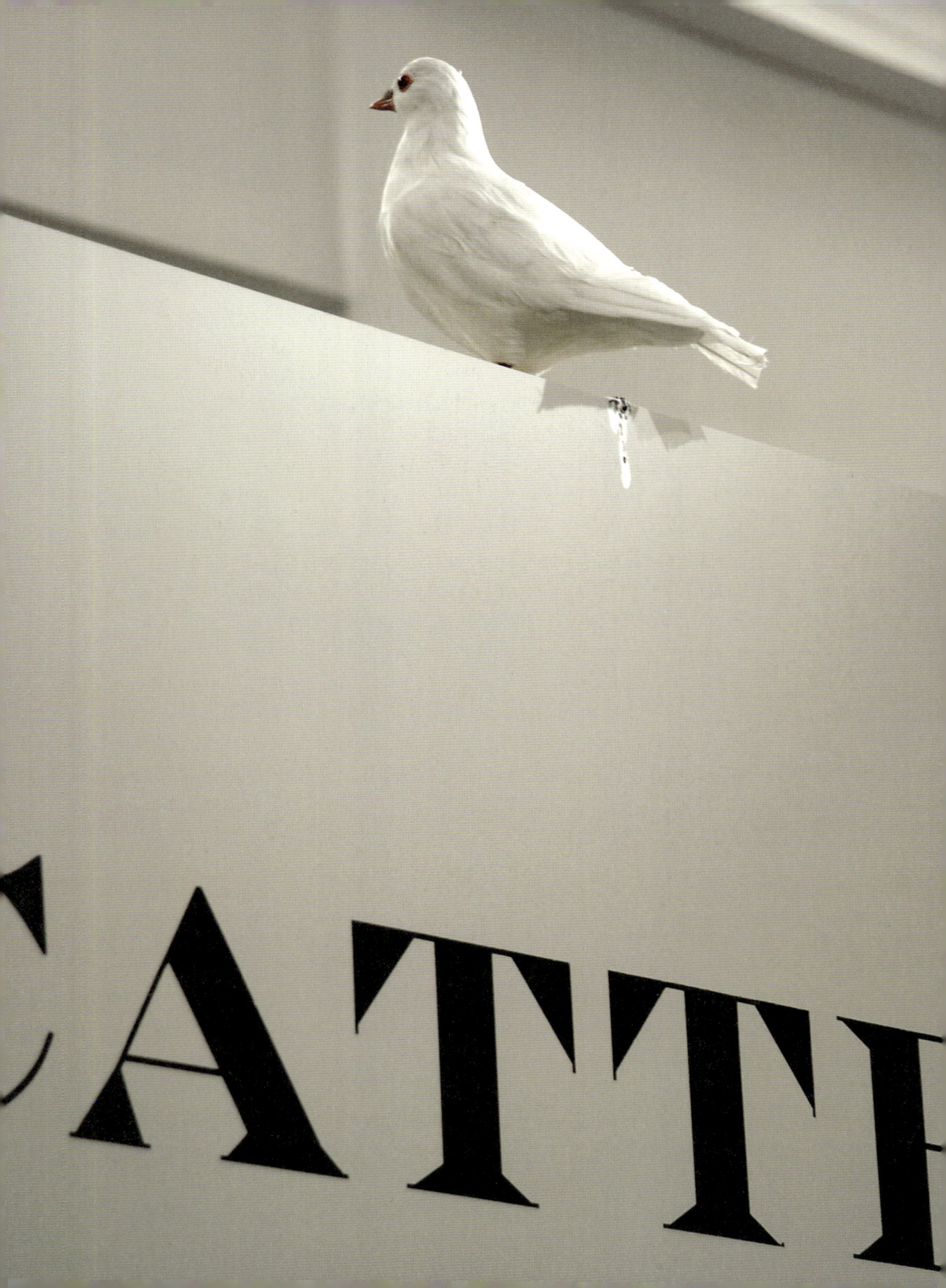
CATT

Maurizio Cattelan (Italian, 1960–2009) was a con artist and a populist philosopher who espoused what might be called a comic existentialism. He began his life in a small city in northeastern Italy, worked briefly as a furniture designer, but quickly abandoned that to become an artist. Through a mix of savvy resourcefulness and puckish deceit, he propelled himself to great heights in the international art world. His rise to fame and fortune began in the mid-1990s. A mere three years into his career, he was invited to exhibit in the prestigious Venice Biennale. A decade later, a New York auction house sold one of his sculptures for three million dollars.

Despite his extraordinary critical and financial success, Maurizio lived a life full of guilt and doubt. He repeatedly tried to do himself in through his art. On one occasion, he dressed himself as a squirrel (an appropriate mascot for a man both frugal in habit and darting in spirit), then shot himself in the head at his parents' kitchen table. Wearing a Pinocchio suit (by his own admission Maurizio was not to be trusted), he leapt from the upper reaches of the Solomon R. Guggenheim Museum's spiral ramp into the tear-drop-shaped reflecting pool below. Though these attempts were unsuccessful, he knew one day he would get it right and he prepared dutifully for that occasion. He dug himself a grave, built himself a coffin, and designed his tombstone with the epitaph "Why Me?"

Triple Candie killed Maurizio in 2009. Then, while his corpse was still warm, we presented the first retrospective on his life and work—a full two years before the Guggenheim Museum ended his career with their own very public hanging. We suspected at the time that the artist would have never permitted a conventional survey—he generally exhibited no more than one piece at a time and showing so much of it together risked reducing his career to a litany of sight gags. Still, as trained art historians, Sunday anthropologists, and practicing curatorial critics, we thought that this time-bound approach was the best way of getting at the fundamental paradoxes of his art. We put his oeuvre on display like one of his taxidermied animals, forever fixed, impotent, to pay homage and to bid adieu.

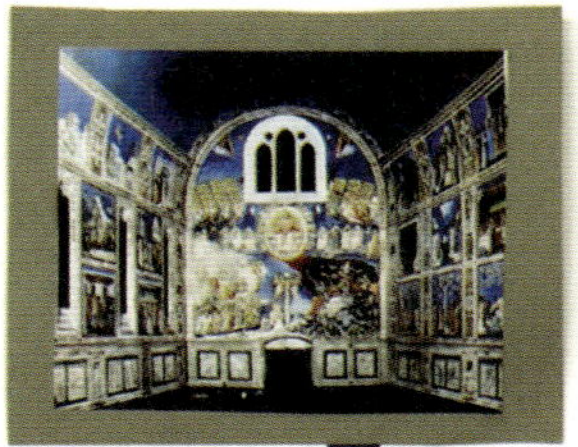

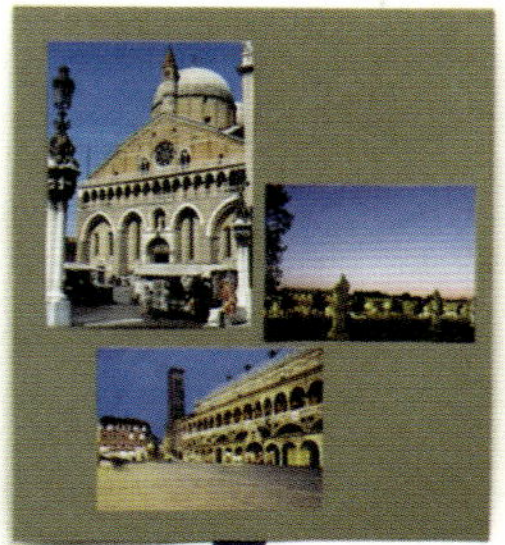

In the Shadow of Venice

Maurizio was born and raised in the city of Padua, in northeastern Italy. The city is widely celebrated for Giotto's frescos in the Arena Chapel (ca. 1305) — groundbreaking because of Giotto's ability to infuse his figures with life. Padua is also home to the oldest anatomical theater in Europe; it was here that corpses were first used for teaching purposes.

In the public imagination, Padua has always existed in the shadow of its more illustrious neighbor Venice — located just 40 miles to its east. Known for its expansive canal system, its palaces, and its art, Venice is also home to the Venice Biennale — the oldest and largest international art festival in the world. Maurizio would participate in six Biennales before his death.

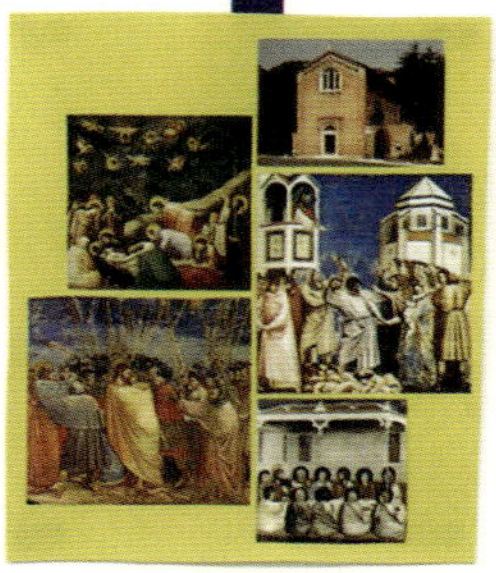

Maurizio was born in 1960

In the Shadow of Venice

Maurizio was born and raised in the city of Padua, in northeastern Italy. The city is widely celebrated for Giotto's frescos in the Arena Chapel (ca. 1305)—groundbreaking because of Giotto's ability to infuse his figures with life. Padua is also home to the oldest anatomical theater in Europe; it was here that corpses were first used for teaching purposes.

In the public imagination, Padua has always existed in the shadow of its more illustrious neighbor, Venice, located just 40 miles to its east. Known for its expansive canal system, its palaces, and its art, Venice is also home to the longest-running international art biennial in the world. Maurizio would participate in six Venice Biennales before his death.

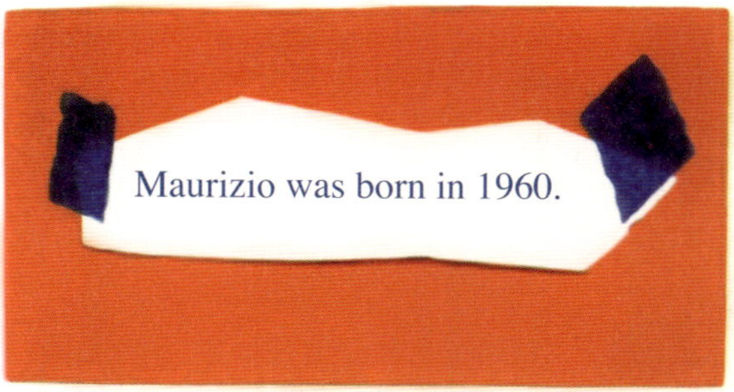
Maurizio was born in 1960.

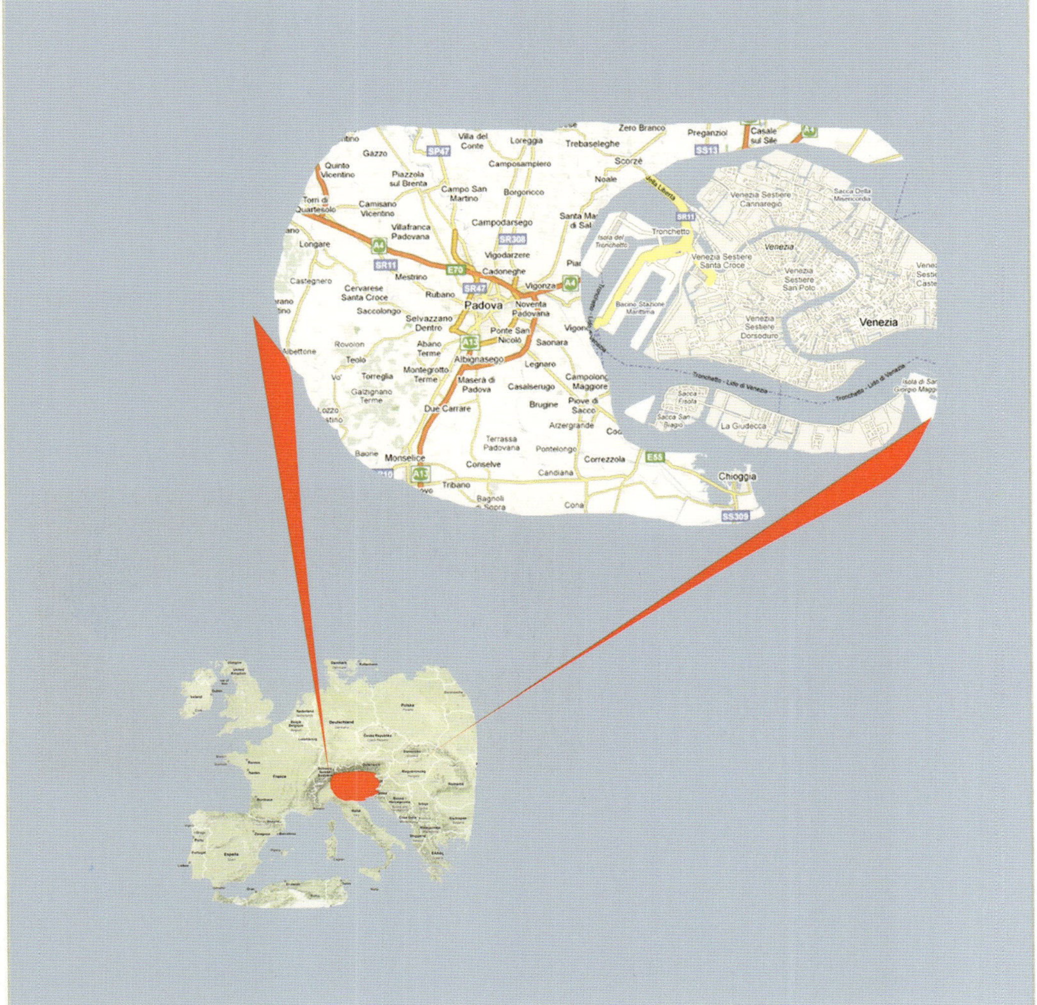

Villa del Conte
Loreggia
Trebaseleghe
Zero Branco
Preganziol
Casale sul Sile
Gazzo
SP47
Camposampiero
SS13
Quinto Vicentino
Piazzola sul Brenta
Scorzè
Noale
Campo San Martino
Borgoricco
Torri di Quartesolo
Camisano Vicentino
Campodarsego
Villafranca Padovana
SR308
Longare
A4
SR11
Vigodarzere
Cadoneghe
Mestrino
E70
Castegnero
Cervarese Santa Croce
Rubano
SR47
Vigonza
Padova
Noventa Padovana
Saccolongo
Selvazzano Dentro
Ponte San Nicolò
Abano Terme
A13
Saonara
Rovolon
Teolo
Albignasego
Legnaro
Torreglia
Montegrotto Terme
Maserà di Padova
Galzignano Terme
Casalserugo
Brugine
Piove di Sacco
Due Carrare
Arzergrande
Terrassa Padovana
Pontelongo
Baone
Monselice
Correzzola
E55
Conselve
Candiana
Chioggia
Tribano
Bagnoli di Sopra
Cona
SS309
SR11
Tronchetto
Isola del Tronchetto
Venezia Sestiere Cannaregio
Sacca Della Misericordia
Venezia
Venezia Sestiere Santa Croce
Venezia Sestiere San Polo
Bacino Stazione Marittima
Venezia Sestiere Dorsoduro
Tronchetto - Lido di Venezia
Sacca Fisola
Sacca San Biagio
La Giudecca

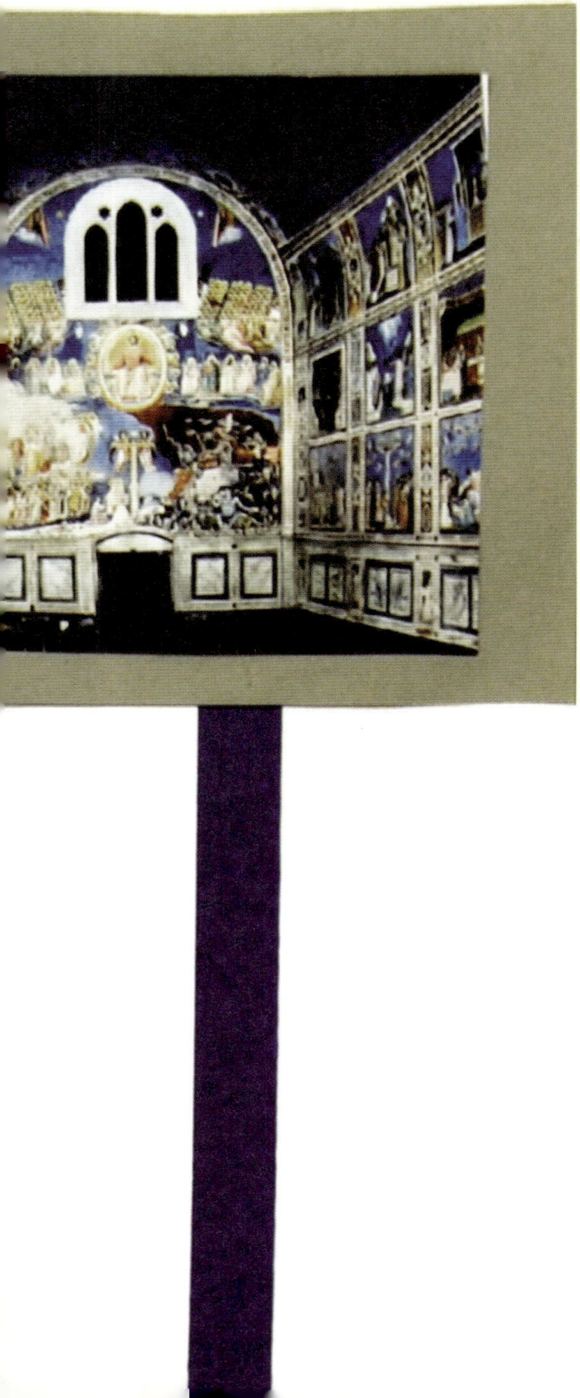

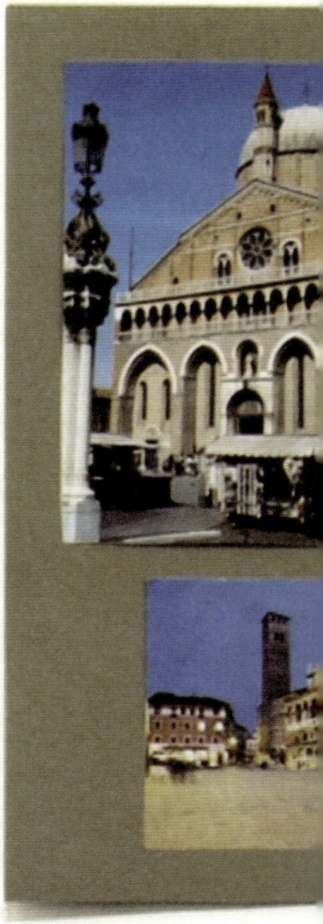

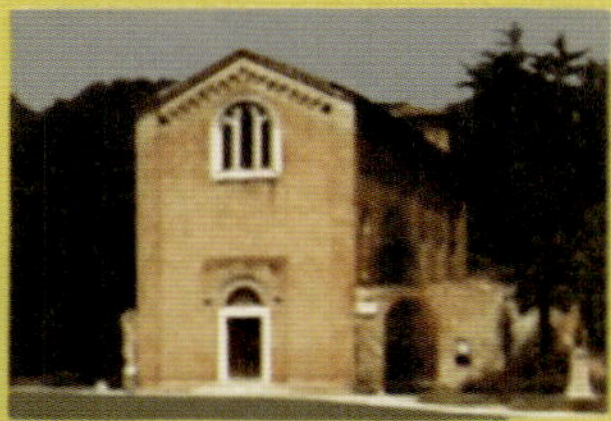

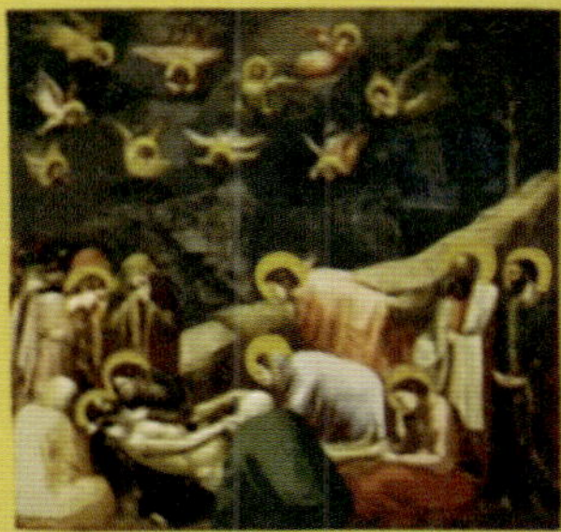

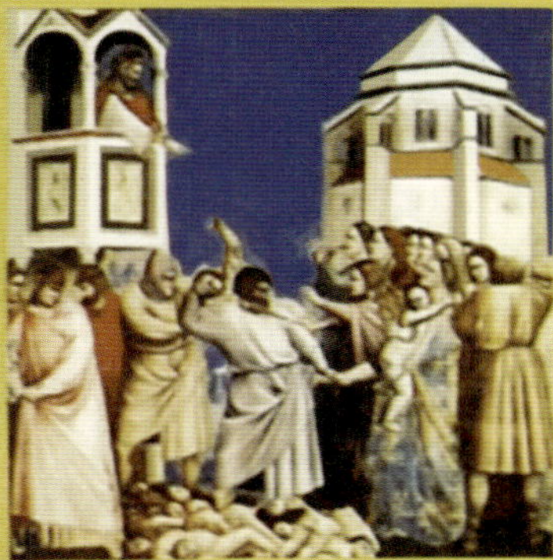

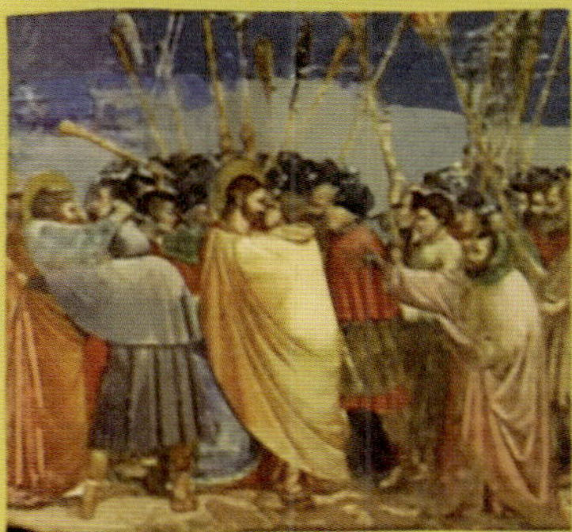

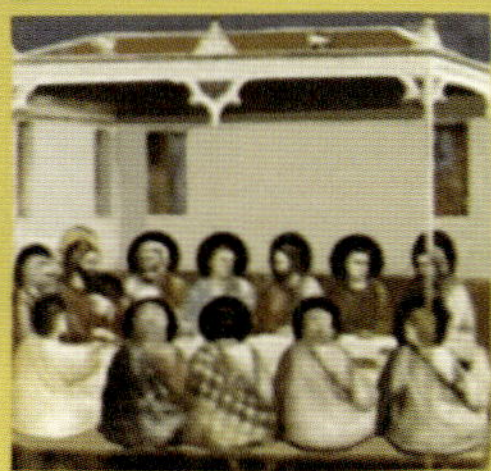

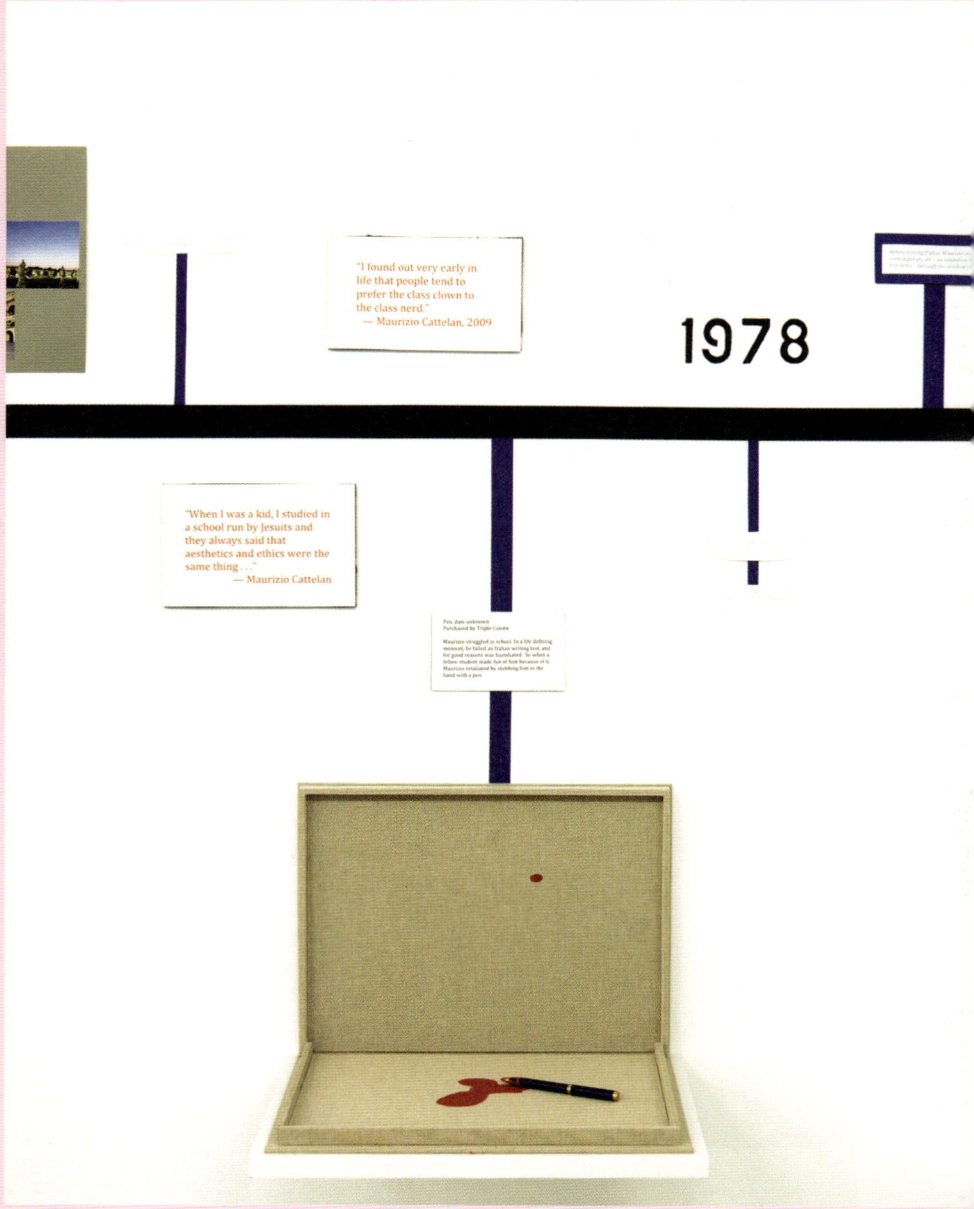
"When I was a kid, I studied in a school run by Jesuits and they always said that aesthetics and ethics were the same thing . . ."
— Maurizio Cattelan
"I found out very early in life that people tend to prefer the class clown to the class nerd."
— Maurizio Cattelan, 2009
1978
Pen, date unknown
Purchased by Triple Candie
Maurizio struggled in school. In a life defining moment, he failed an Italian writing test, and for good reasons was humiliated. So when a fellow student made fun of him because of it, Maurizio retaliated by stabbing him in the hand with a pen.

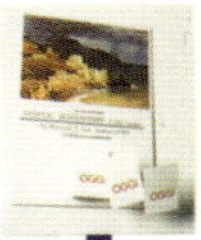

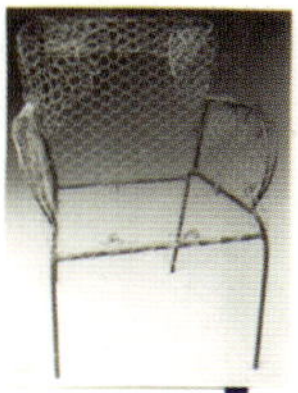

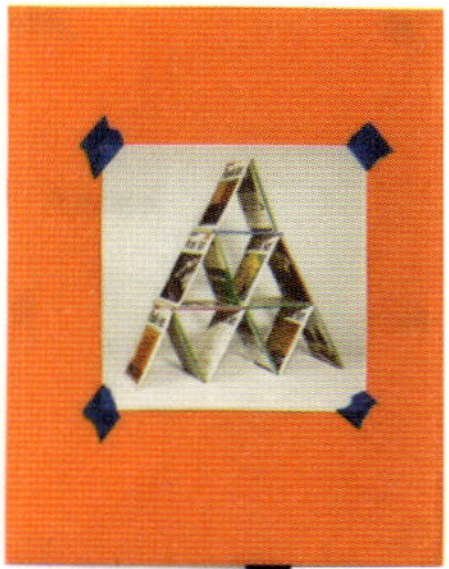

Calendar with tear off sheets, each reading "Oggi" (Italian for "Today")

1990

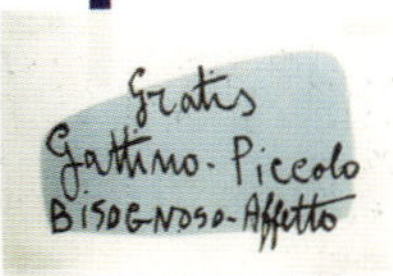

A very early print. The text reads "Free, Small Kitten, Needs Affection"

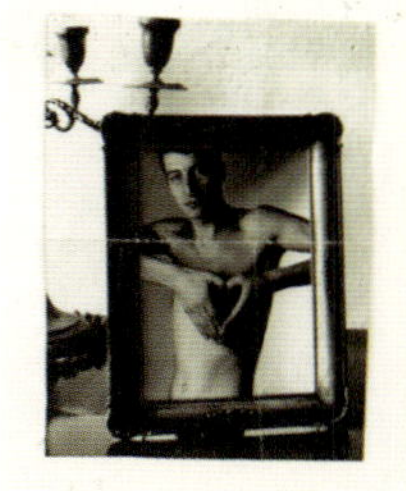

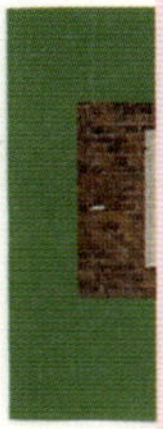

His father worked as a truck driver, his mother did housework for other people.

"I found out very early in life that people tend to prefer the class clown to the class nerd."
—Maurizio Cattelan, 2009

"When I was a kid, I studied in a school run by Jesuits and they always said that aesthetics and ethics were the same thing . . . ."
—Maurizio Cattelan

Maurizio struggled in school. In a life-defining moment, he failed an Italian writing test, and for good reasons was humiliated. When a fellow student made fun of him because of it, Maurizio retaliated by stabbing him in the hand with a pen.

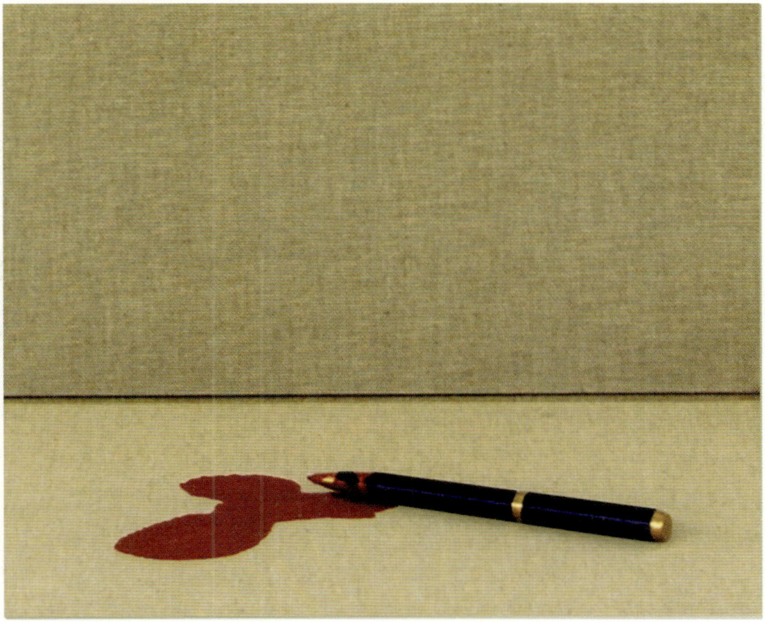

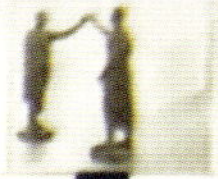

Before leaving Padua, Maurizio saw his first contemporary art—an exhibition by Michelangelo Pistoletto—through the window of a local gallery.

1978

His mother, who had lived with lymphatic cancer for twenty years, died.

Maurizio moved out from his family home to live on his own, in Padua.

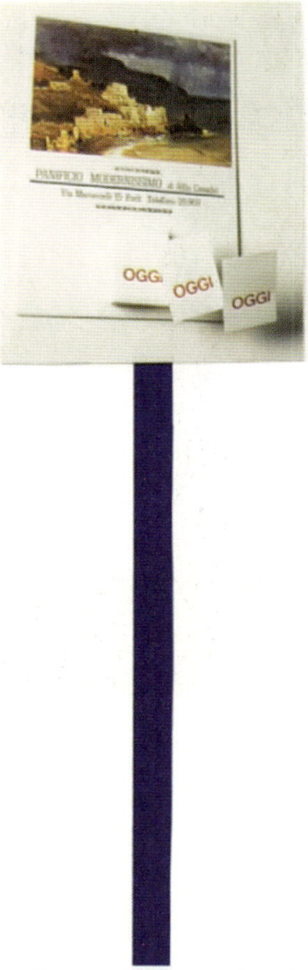

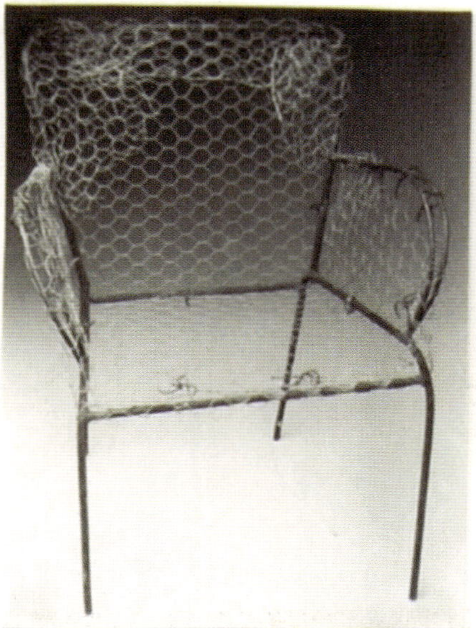

Moved to Forti (near Bologna) to live with his girlfriend. Decided he would never again work for anybody else. Began making furniture.

Calendar with tear-off sheets, each reading "Oggi" (Italian for "today")

As a teenager, Maurizio held a variety of jobs—he worked as a nurse, and at a morgue. One of his jobs was selling religious effigies for a church. He was fired for drawing a mustache on a figurine of a saint.

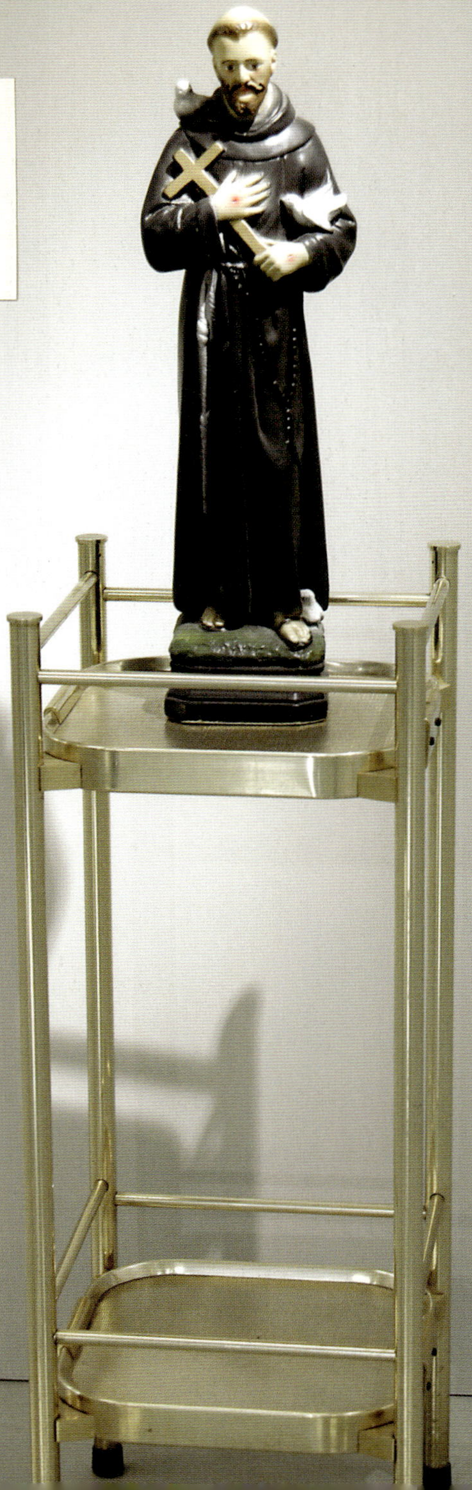

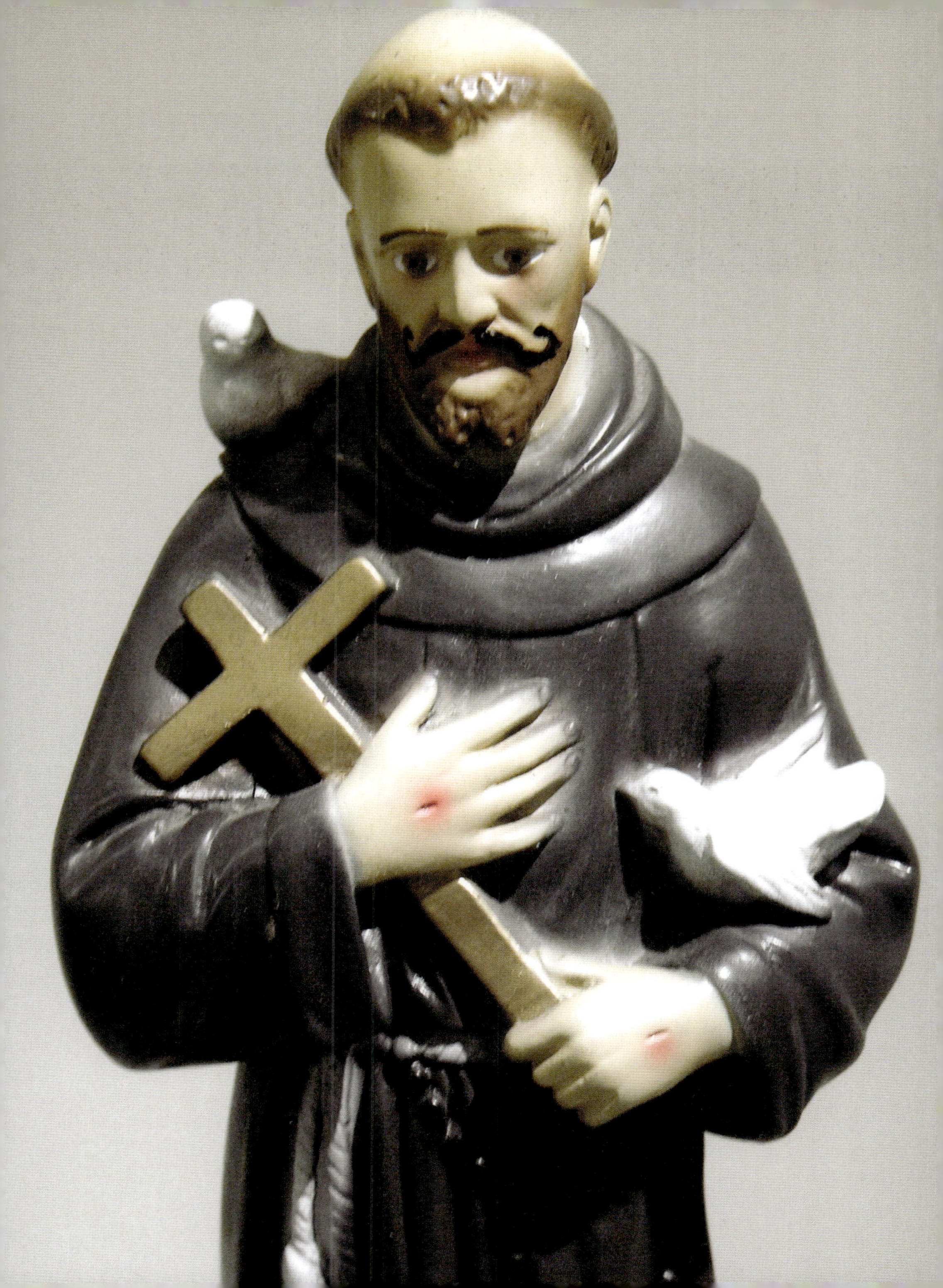

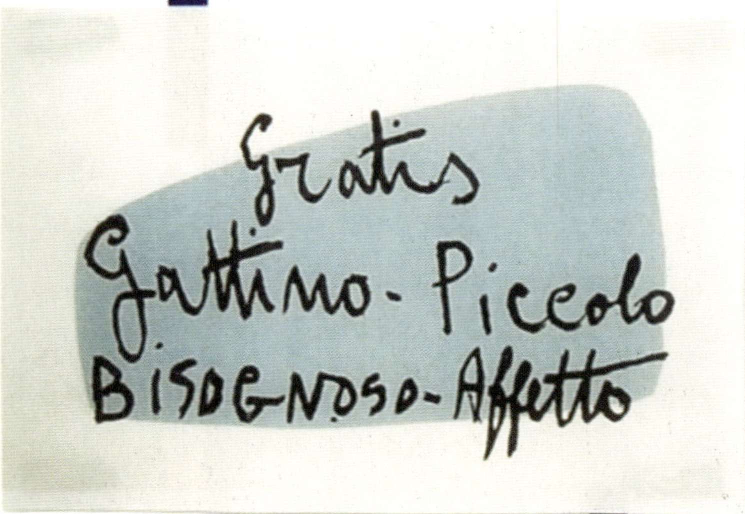

A very early print. The text reads “Free, Small Kitten, Needs Affection.”

Moved to Milan, and began to tentatively consider himself an artist.

Maurizio made his first legitimate "art piece."

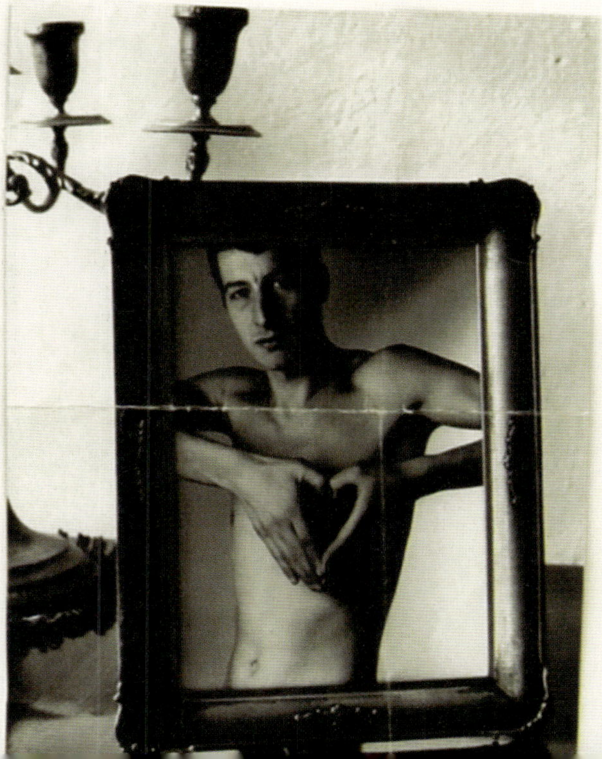

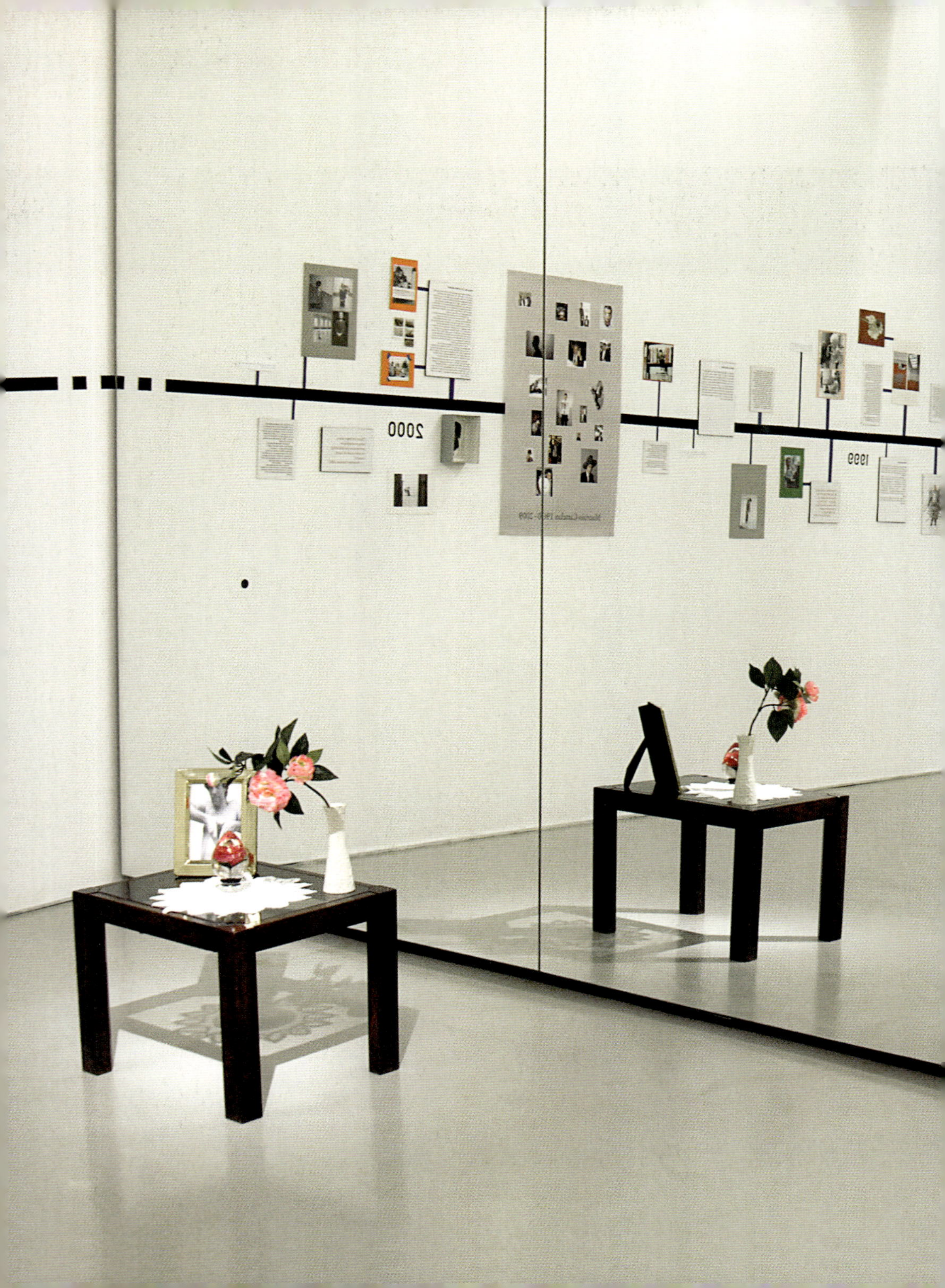
2000

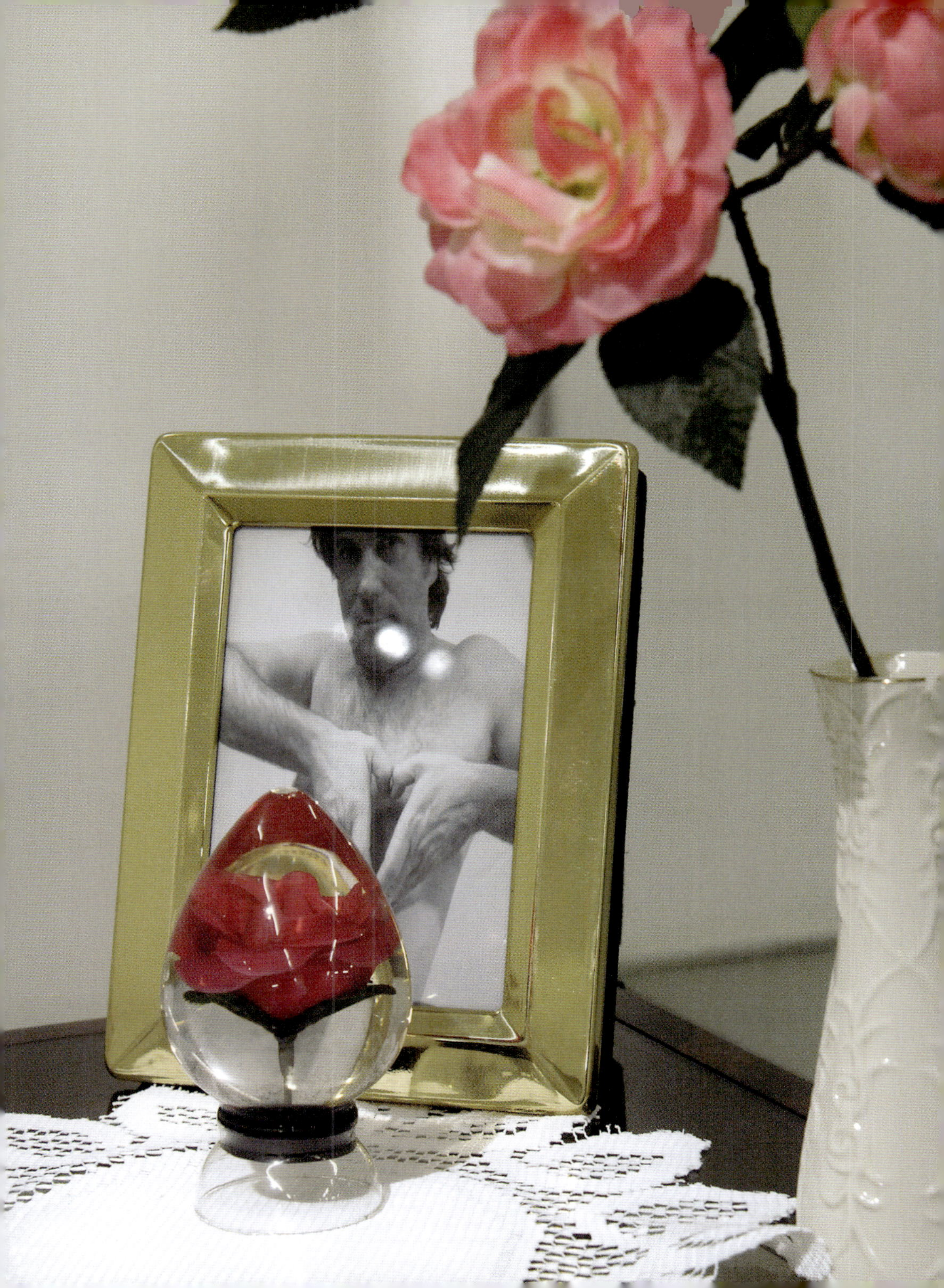

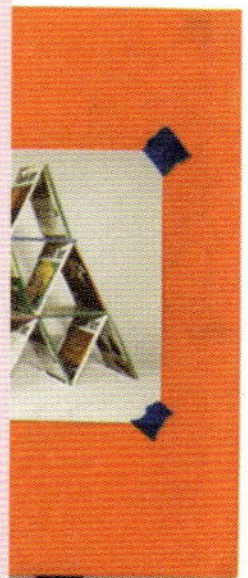

In 1992, Maurizio started the Oblomov Foundation to subsidize an artist's career for one year, but not in the standard sense. Maurizio's idea was to give an artist $50,000 to not make art for one year. Surprisingly, no one would take him up on his offer.

Maurizio eventually awarded the prize to himself, pocketing the $10,000 he had raised to date. To commemorate those he had persuaded to donate to his cause, he used a small portion of the money to fabricate a glass plaque, which he affixed to the façade of the Accademia di Brera in Milan. The plaque stayed there for a year before it was noticed by the authorities and removed.

The name Oblomov comes from a satirical novel by the Russian writer Ivan Goncharov (published in 1859). The book's protagonist is unable to make decisions or undertake any significant actions and spends the first 150 pages of the book in bed.

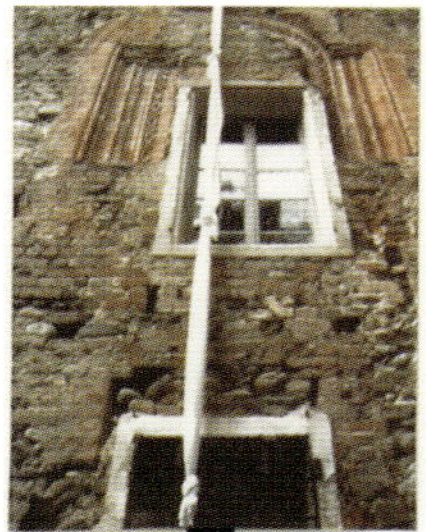

990

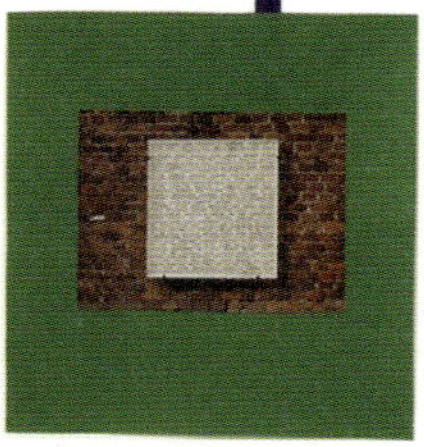

In 1992, Maurizio created *Fast Nichts/Almost Invisible* (later titled *A Sunday in Rivara*) for a gallery in Singen, Germany. For it, he tied together bed sheets and hung them — like a prisoner's escape rope — from the gallery's upper window. When visitors arrived for the show's opening reception, Maurizio was nowhere in sight.

Like much of Maurizio's early work (not all on view here), this piece dealt with the idea of performance anxiety. He often talked about the challenge of coming up with ideas for exhibitions and his fear of failure. Ironically, pieces like this — in which he seemed to skirt his responsibilities as an artist — often had more resonance than if he had installed a "real" exhibition.

199

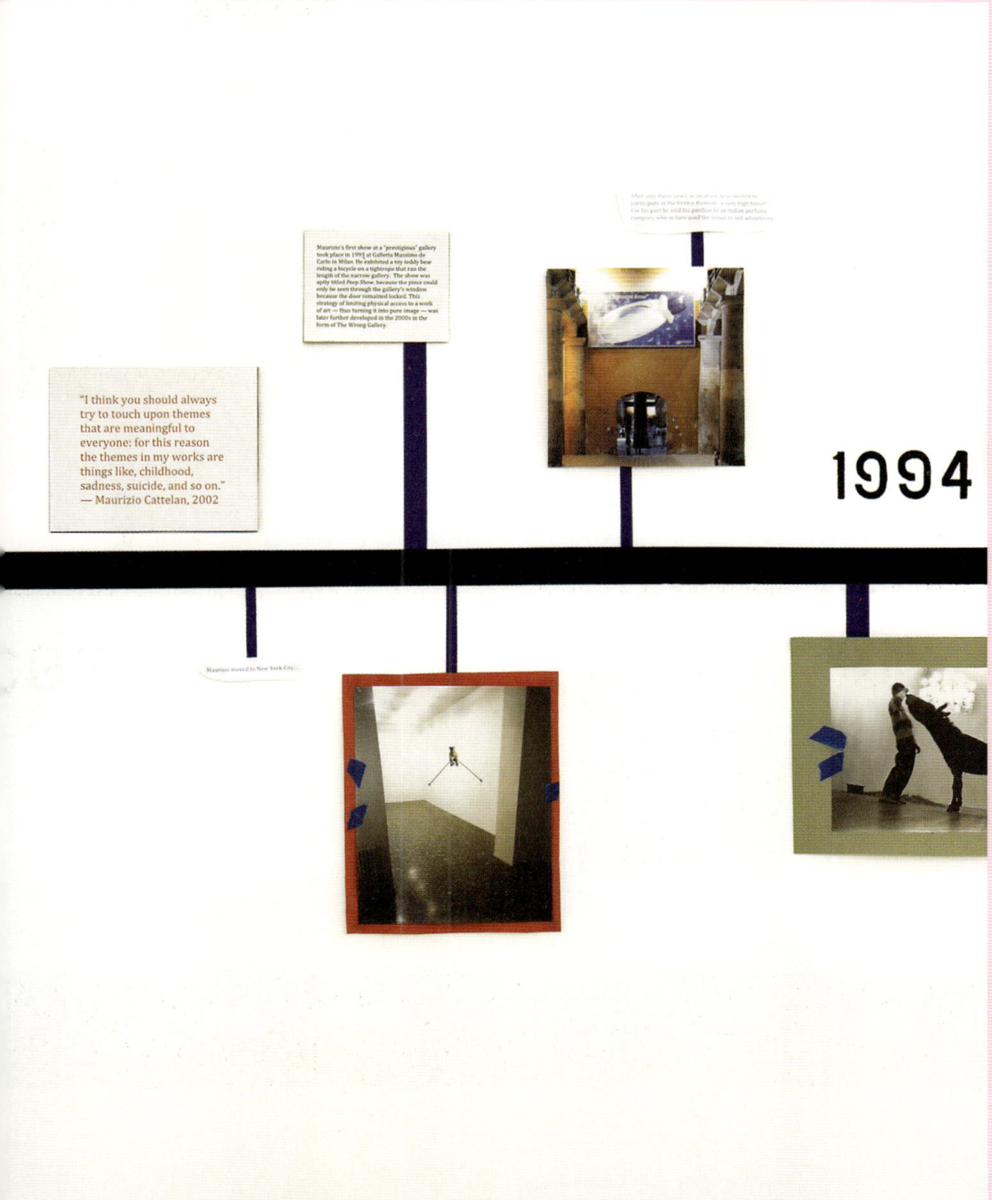

After only three years as an artist he is invited to participate in the Venice Biennale, a very high honor. For his part he sold his pavilion to an Italian perfume company who in turn used the venue to sell advertising
Maurizio's first show at a "prestigious" gallery took place in 1991 at Galleria Massimo de Carlo in Milan. He exhibited a toy teddy bear riding a bicycle on a tightrope that ran the length of the narrow gallery. The show was aptly titled Peep Show, because the piece could only be seen through the gallery's window because the door remained locked. This strategy of limiting physical access to a work of art — thus turning it into pure image — was later further developed in the 2000s in the form of The Wrong Gallery.
"I think you should always try to touch upon themes that are meaningful to everyone: for this reason the themes in my works are things like, childhood, sadness, suicide, and so on." — Maurizio Cattelan, 2002
1994
Maurizio moved to New York City.

In 1992, Maurizio started the Oblomov Foundation to subsidize an artist's career for one year, but not in the standard sense. His idea was to give an artist $50,000 to not make art. Surprisingly, no one would take him up on his offer.

So, Maurizio awarded the prize to himself, pocketing the $10,000 he had raised to date. To commemorate those he had persuaded to donate to his cause, he used a small portion of the money to fabricate a glass plaque, which he affixed to the façade of the Accademia di Brera in Milan. The plaque stayed there for one year before it was noticed by the authorities and removed.

The name Oblomov comes from a satirical novel by the Russian writer Ivan Goncharov (published in 1859). The book's protagonist is unable to make decisions or undertake any significant actions and spends the first 150 pages of the book in bed.

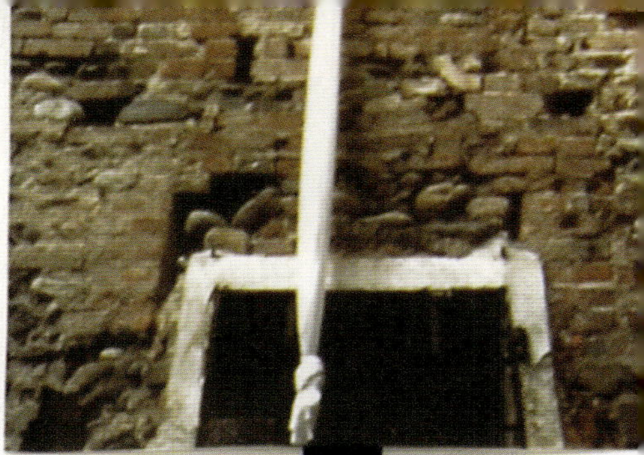

Maurizio had an affair with the artist Vanessa Beecroft, who was working for an Italian gallery. More than a decade later she accused him of stealing many of her ideas.

19

Maurizio made *Fast Nichts/Almost Invisible* (later titled *Sunday in Rivera*) for a gallery in Singern, Germany. He tied together bed sheets and hung them—like a prisoner's escape rope—from the gallery's upper window. When visitors arrived for the show's opening reception, Maurizio was nowhere to be found.

Like much of his early work (not all on view here), this piece dealt with the idea of performance anxiety. He often talked about the challenge of coming up with ideas for exhibitions and his fear of failure. Ironically, pieces like this—in which he seemed to skirt his responsibilities as an artist—often had more resonance than if he had installed a "real" exhibition.

Maurizio's first show at a "prestigious" gallery took place in 1993 at Galleria Massimo de Carlo in Milan. He exhibited a toy teddy bear riding a bicycle on a tightrope that ran the length of the narrow gallery. The show was aptly titled "Peep Show" because the piece could only be seen through the gallery's window, as the door was locked. This strategy of limiting physical access to a work of art—thus turning it into a pure image—was later further developed by Maurizio in the 2000s in the form of The Wrong Gallery.

"I think you should always try to touch upon themes that are meaningful to everyone: For this reason the themes in my works are things like childhood, sadness, suicide, and so on."
—Maurizio Cattelan, 2002

Maurizio moved to New York City.

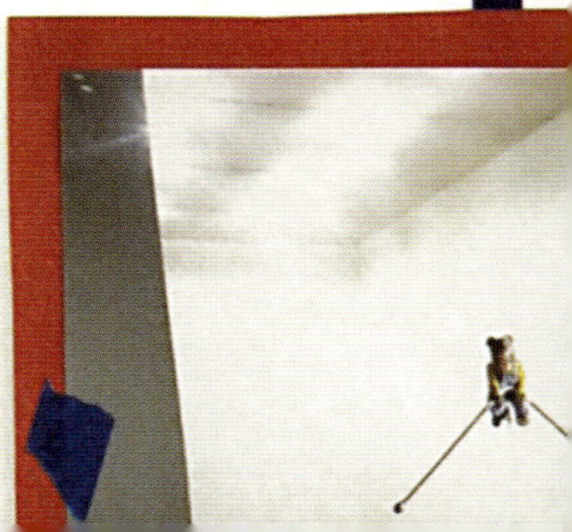

After only three years as an artist, he was invited to participate in the Venice Biennale, a very high honor. For his part, Maurizio sold his pavilion to an Italian perfume company who in turn used the venue to sell advertising.

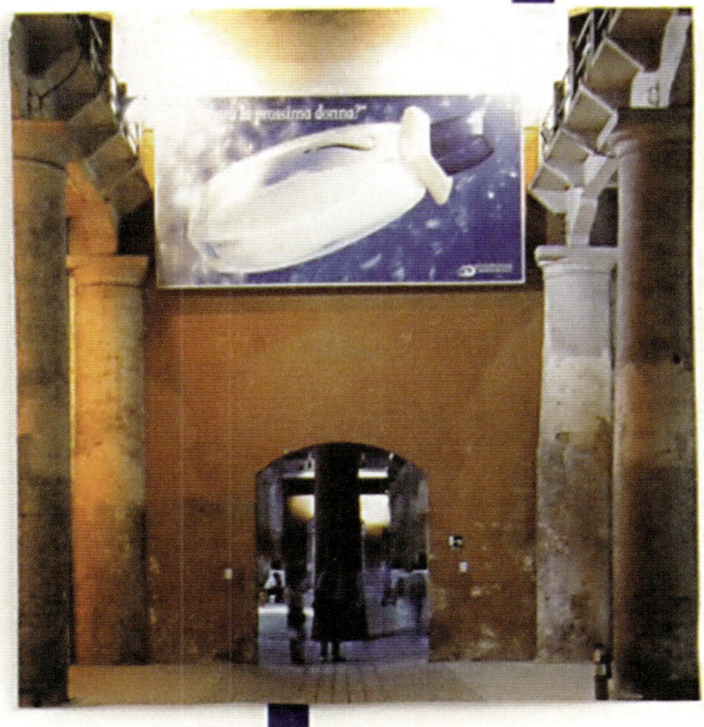

After only three years as an artist, he is invited to participate in the Venice Biennale, a very high honor. For his part he sold his pavilion to an Italian perfume company who in turn used the venue to sell advertising.

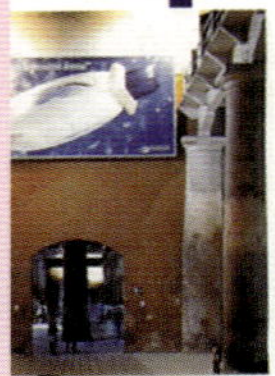

On Being Italian

By some, Maurizio was considered the Roberto Benigni of the art world — the token Italian wit with an international following. Maurizio struggled with such associations throughout his life. "I have started to think about the difficulty of being Italian," he once said, "having a heritage, relationships with other artists, being a member of a community with a history." For an exhibition of contemporary Italian art in London in the 1990s, he made his most explicit statement on the subject: he spray-painted "Bloody Wops" on the gallery's façade to protest the show's nationalistic organizing concept.

Nevertheless, their remains something unmistakingly Italian in Maurizio's work. Francesco Bonami, a prominent Italian curator, has interpreted it as follows: "Catellan draws on his own biography and links this to an Italian attitude to life that continuously swings from banality to extreme devoutness and holy veneration."

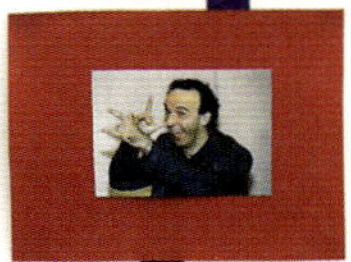

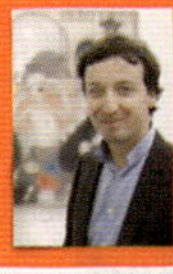

In a video interview, Emmanuel Perrotin claimed that Maurizio made up the story that he was a womanizer but that the rumor has stuck.

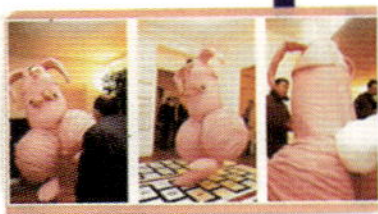

1994

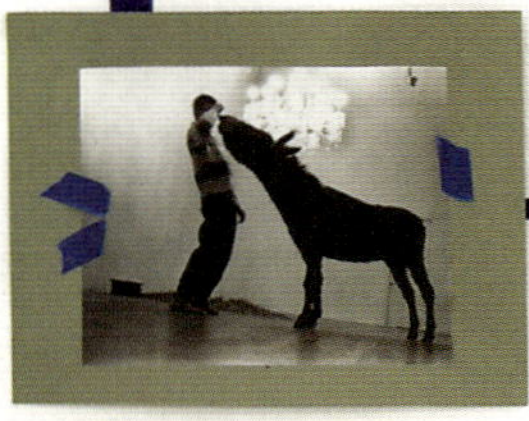

Maurizio had his first solo show in New York in 1994 at the Daniel Newburg Gallery. Titled *Warning . . . Enter at Your Own Risk*, it lasted only one day. The show contained three elements: a chandelier; a string of sausages; and the thing that caused the show's demise, a live donkey, who brayed and honked continuously throughout the night.

1995

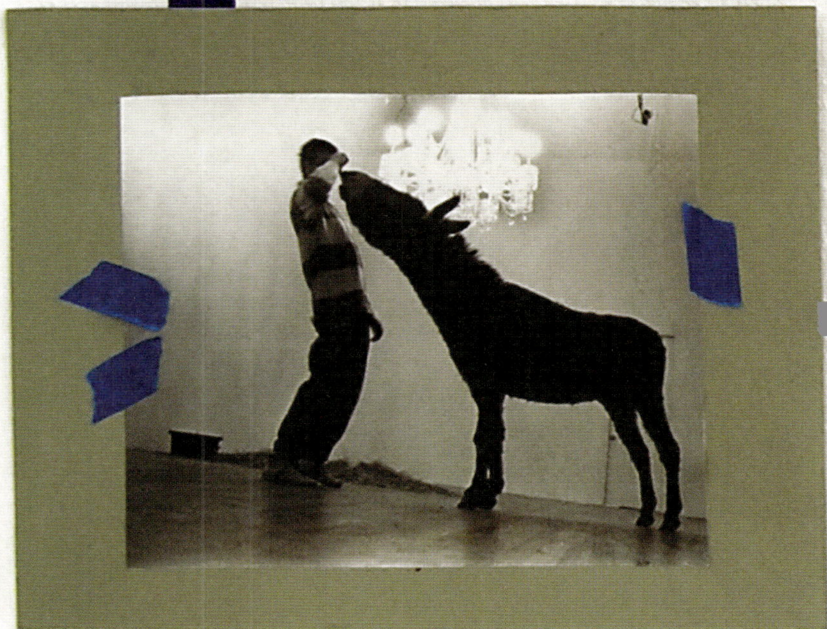

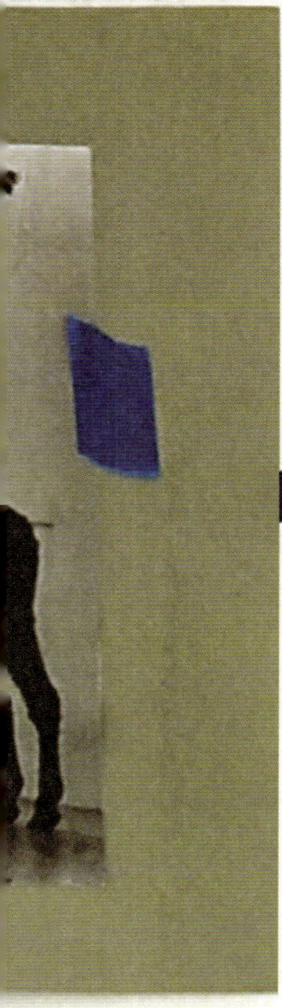

Maurizio had his first solo show in New York in 1994 at the Daniel Newburg Gallery. Titled "Warning . . . Enter at Your Own Risk," it lasted only one day. The show contained three elements: a chandelier, a string of sausages, and the thing that caused the show's demise: a live donkey, who brayed and honked continuously throughout the night.

On Being Italian

By some, Maurizio was considered to be the Roberto Benigni of the art world—the token Italian wit with an international following. Maurizio struggled with such associations throughout his life. “I have started to think about the difficulty of being Italian,” he once said, “having a heritage, relationships with other artists, being a member of a community with a history.” For an exhibition of contemporary Italian art in London in the 1990s, he made his most explicit statement on the subject: He spray-painted “Bloody Wops” on the gallery’s façade to protest the show’s nationalistic organizing concept.

Nevertheless, their remains something unmistakingly Italian in Maurizio’s work. Francesco Bonami, a prominent curator, has interpreted it as follows: “Cattelan draws on his own biography and links this to an Italian attitude to life that continuously swings from banality to extreme devoutness and holy veneration.”

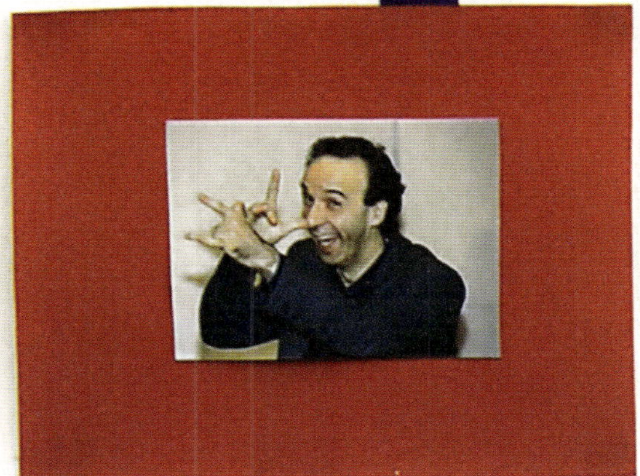

04

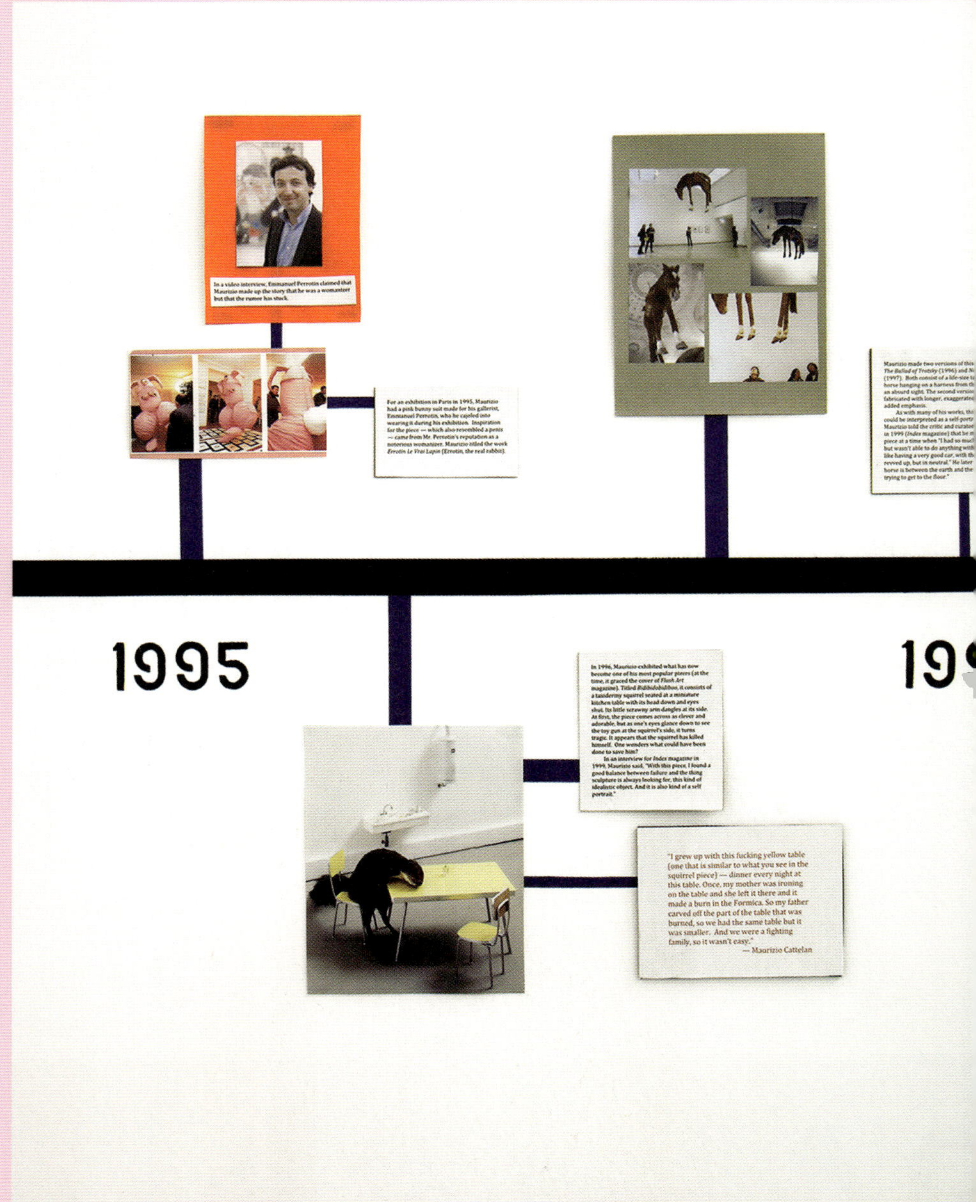
In a video interview, Emmanuel Perrotin claimed that Maurizio made up the story that he was a womanizer but that the rumor has stuck.
For an exhibition in Paris in 1995, Maurizio had a pink bunny suit made for his gallerist, Emmanuel Perrotin, who he cajoled into wearing it during his exhibition. Inspiration for the piece — which also resembled a penis — came from Mr. Perrotin's reputation as a notorious womanizer. Maurizio titled the work Errotin Le Vrai Lapin (Errotin, the real rabbit).
Maurizio made two versions of
The Ballad of Trotsky (1996) and
(1997). Both consist of a life-size
horse hanging on a harness from
an absurd sight. The second
fabricated with longer,
added emphasis.
As with many of his works,
could be interpreted as a
Maurizio told the critic and
in 1999 (Index magazine) that he
piece at a time when "I had so
but wasn't able to do anything
like having a very good car,
revved up, but in neutral." He later
horse is between the earth and the
trying to get to the floor."
1995
19
In 1996, Maurizio exhibited what has now become one of his most popular pieces (at the time, it graced the cover of Flash Art magazine). Titled Bidibidobidiboo, it consists of a taxidermy squirrel seated at a miniature kitchen table with its head down and eyes shut. Its little scrawny arm dangles at its side. At first, the piece comes across as clever and adorable, but as one's eyes glance down to see the toy gun at the squirrel's side, it turns tragic. It appears that the squirrel has killed himself. One wonders what could have been done to save him?
In an interview for Index magazine in 1999, Maurizio said, "With this piece, I found a good balance between failure and the thing sculpture is always looking for, this kind of idealistic object. And it is also kind of a self portrait."
"I grew up with this fucking yellow table (one that is similar to what you see in the squirrel piece) — dinner every night at this table. Once, my mother was ironing on the table and she left it there and it made a burn in the Formica. So my father carved off the part of the table that was burned, so we had the same table but it was smaller. And we were a fighting family, so it wasn't easy."
— Maurizio Cattelan

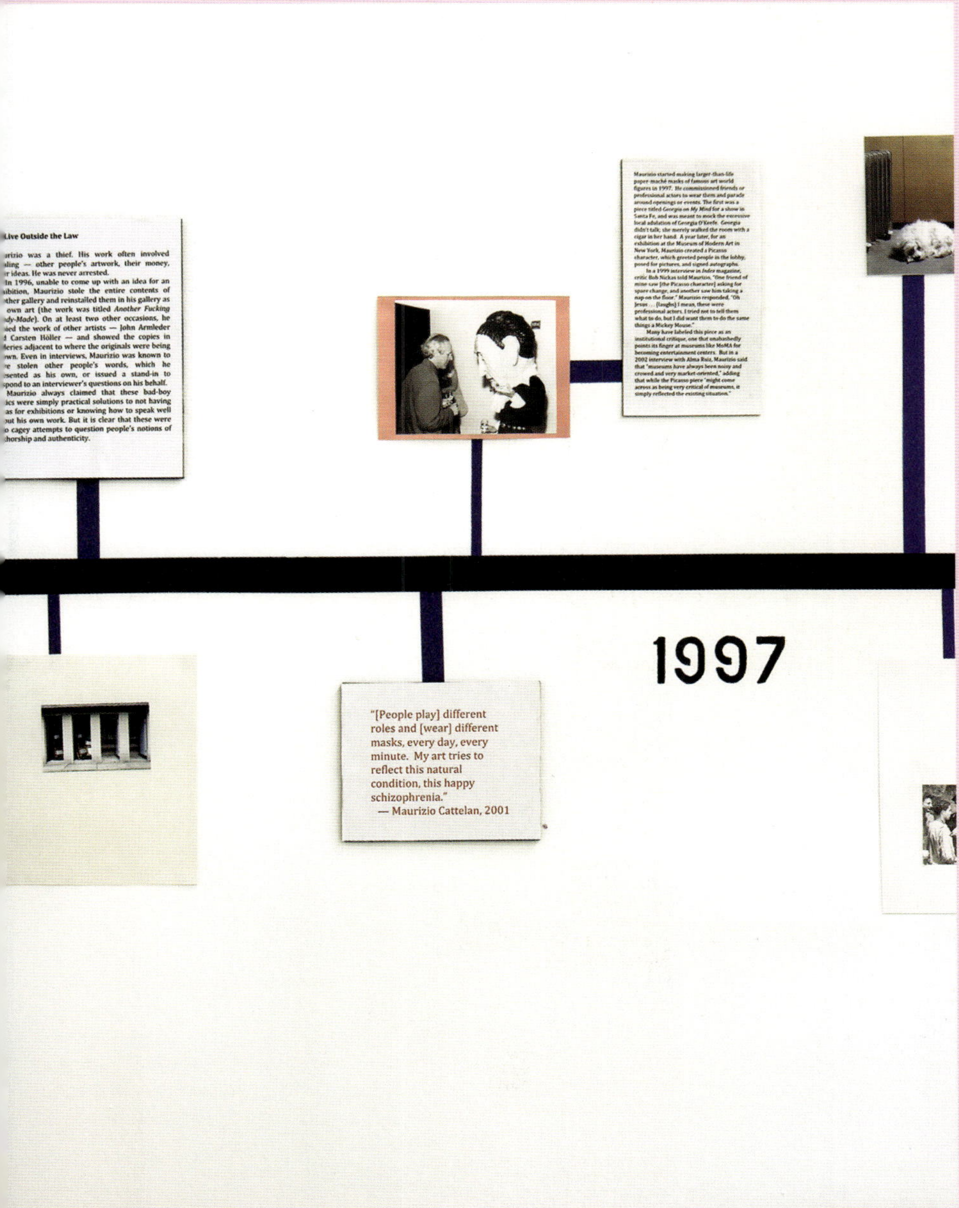
Live Outside the Law
rizio was a thief. His work often involved aling — other people's artwork, their money, r ideas. He was never arrested.
In 1996, unable to come up with an idea for an ibition, Maurizio stole the entire contents of ther gallery and reinstalled them in his gallery as own art (the work was titled Another Fucking dy-Made). On at least two other occasions, he ied the work of other artists — John Armleder Carsten Höller — and showed the copies in leries adjacent to where the originals were being wn. Even in interviews, Maurizio was known to e stolen other people's words, which he sented as his own, or issued a stand-in to pond to an interviewer's questions on his behalf.
Maurizio always claimed that these bad-boy ics were simply practical solutions to not having as for exhibitions or knowing how to speak well out his own work. But it is clear that these were o cagey attempts to question people's notions of horship and authenticity.
Maurizio started making larger-than-life paper-maché masks of famous art world figures in 1997. He commissioned friends or professional actors to wear them and parade around openings or events. The first was a piece titled Georgia on My Mind for a show in Santa Fe, and was meant to mock the excessive local adulation of Georgia O'Keefe. Georgia didn't talk; she merely walked the room with a cigar in her hand. A year later, for an exhibition at the Museum of Modern Art in New York, Maurizio created a Picasso character, which greeted people in the lobby, posed for pictures, and signed autographs.
In a 1999 interview in Index magazine, critic Bob Nickas told Maurizio, "One friend of mine saw [the Picasso character] asking for spare change, and another saw him taking a nap on the floor." Maurizio responded, "Oh Jesus . . . [laughs] I mean, these were professional actors. I tried not to tell them what to do, but I did want them to do the same things a Mickey Mouse."
Many have labeled this piece as an institutional critique, one that unabashedly points its finger at museums like MoMA for becoming entertainment centers. But in a 2002 interview with Alma Ruiz, Maurizio said that "museums have always been noisy and crowed and very market-oriented," adding that while the Picasso piece "might come across as being very critical of museums, it simply reflected the existing situation."
1997
"[People play] different roles and [wear] different masks, every day, every minute. My art tries to reflect this natural condition, this happy schizophrenia."
— Maurizio Cattelan, 2001

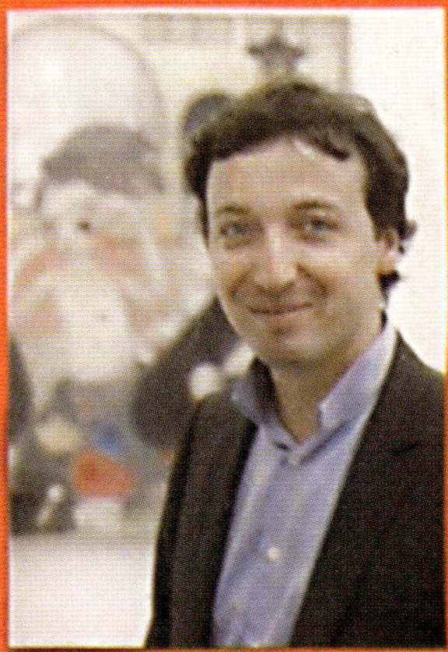

In a video interview, Emmanuel Perrotin claimed that Maurizio made up the story that he was a womanizer but that the rumor had stuck.

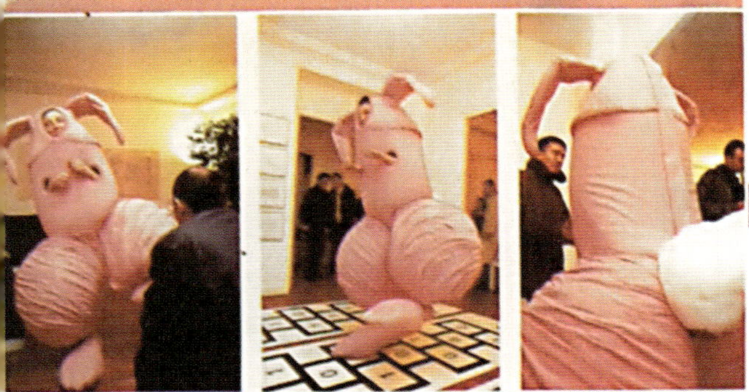

For an exhibition in Paris in 1995, Maurizio had a pink bunny suit made for his gallerist Emmanuel Perrotin, whom he cajoled into wearing it. Inspiration for the costume—which also looked like a penis—came from Mr. Perrotin's reputation as a notorious womanizer. Maurizio titled the work *Errotin Le Vrai Lapin* [Errotin, the true rabbit].

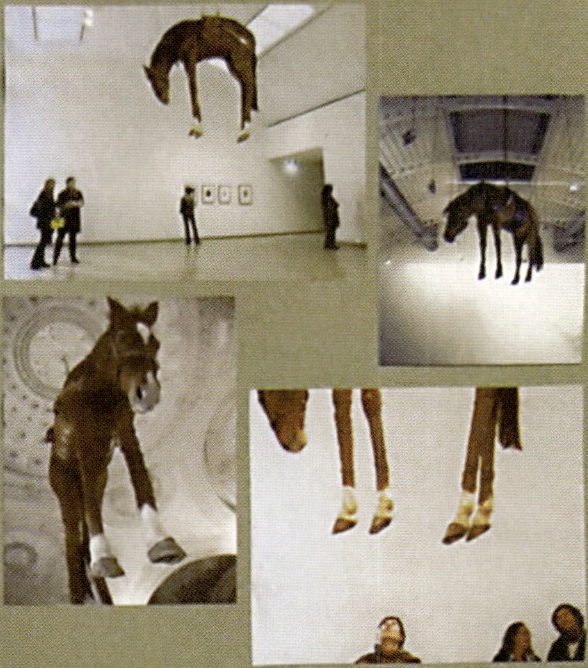

Maurizio made two versions of this piece—*The Ballad of Trotsky* (1996) and *Novecento* (1997). Each consists of a life-size taxidermied horse hanging on a harness from the ceiling, an absurd sight. The second version was fabricated with longer, exaggerated legs for added emphasis.

As with many of his works, this piece could be interpreted as a self-portrait. Maurizio told the critic and curator Bob Nickas in 1999 (*Index* magazine) that he made this piece at a time when "I had so much energy but wasn't able to do anything with it. It was like having a very good car, with the engine revved up, but in neutral." He later said, "The horse is between the earth and the sky and is trying to get to the floor." One can also interpret it as a sexual pun, a bold admission that the artist is "hung like a horse."

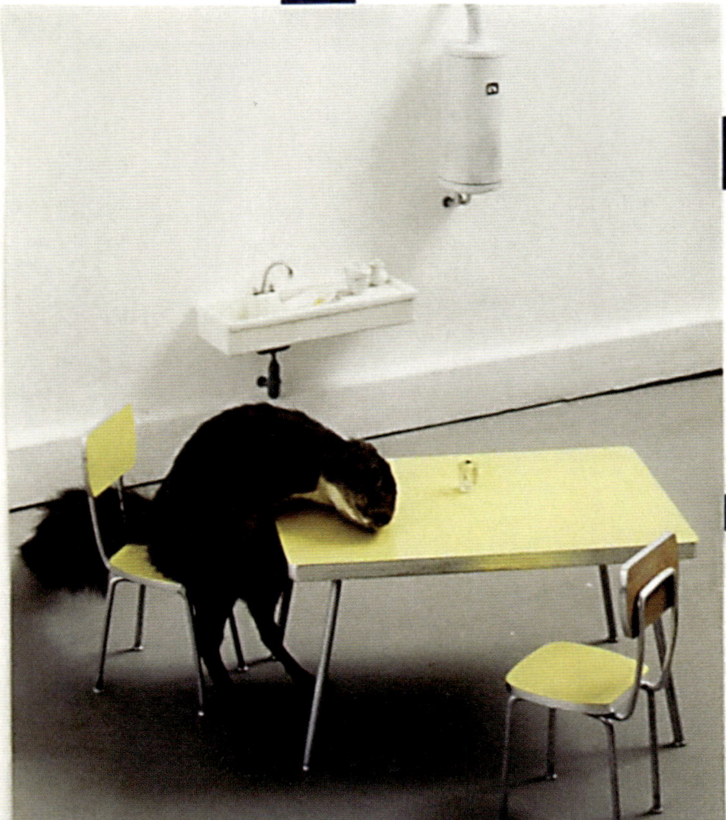

In 1996, Maurizio exhibited what has now become one of his most popular pieces (at the time, it graced the cover of *Flash Art* magazine). Titled *Bidibidobidiboo*, it consists of a taxidermied squirrel seated at a miniature kitchen table with its head down and eyes shut. Its little scrawny arm dangles at its side. At first, the piece comes across as clever and adorable, but upon looking closer one notices a little gun lying at the squirrel's feet, and the scene turns tragic. It appears that the squirrel has killed himself. And one wonders what could have been done to save it.

In a interview for *Index* magazine in 1999, Maurizio said, "With this piece, I found a good balance between failure and the thing sculpture is always looking for, this kind of idealistic object. And it is also kind of a self-portrait."

"I grew up with this fucking yellow table (one similar to that in the 'squirrel' piece)—dinner every night at this table. Once, my mother was ironing on the table and she left it there and it made a burn in the Formica. So my father carved off the part of the table that was burned, so we had the same table but it was smaller. And we were a fighting family, so it wasn't easy."

—Maurizio Cattelan

In 1997, Maurizio started making larger-than-life paper-maché masks of famous art-world figures. He commissioned friends or professional actors to wear them and parade around openings or events. The first was a piece titled *Georgia on My Mind* for a show in Santa Fe, and was meant to mock the excessive local adulation of Georgia O'Keeffe. Georgia didn't talk; she merely walked the room with a cigar in her hand. A year later, for an exhibition at the Museum of Modern Art in New York, Maurizio created a Picasso character who greeted people in the lobby, posed for pictures, and signed autographs.

In a 1999 interview in *Index* magazine, critic Bob Nickas told Maurizio, "One friend of mine saw [the Picasso character] asking for spare change, and another saw him taking a nap on the floor." Maurizio responded, "Oh Jesus . . . [laughs] I mean, these were professional actors, I tried not to tell them what to do, but I did want them to do the same things as Mickey Mouse."

Many have labeled this piece as an institutional critique, one that unabashedly points its finger at museums like MoMA for becoming entertainment centers. But in a 2002 interview with Alma Ruiz, Maurizio said that "museums have always been noisy and crowded and very market-oriented," adding that while the Picasso piece "might come across as being critical of museums, it simply reflected the existing situation."

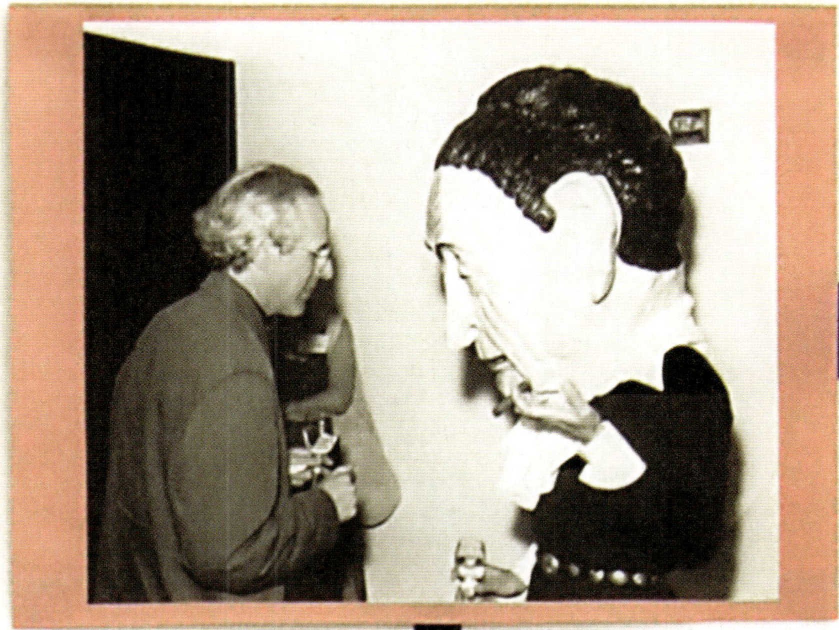

To Live Outside the Law

Maurizio was a thief. His work often involved stealing—other people's artwork, their money, their ideas. He was never arrested.

In 1996, unable to come up with an idea for an exhibition, Maurizio stole the entire contents of another gallery and installed them as his own work (the piece was titled *Another Fucking Ready-Made*). On separate occasions, he copied the work of other artists—John Armleder and Carsten Höller, among them—and showed the copies as his work in galleries adjacent to the ones in which the originals were being shown. And in interviews, Maurizio was known to have stolen other people's words, which he presented as his own, or issued a stand-in to respond to an interviewer's questions on his behalf.

Maurizio always claimed that these bad-boy antics were simply practical solutions to not having ideas for exhibitions or knowing how to speak well about his own work. But it is apparent that these were also cagey attempts to question people's notions of authorship and authenticity.

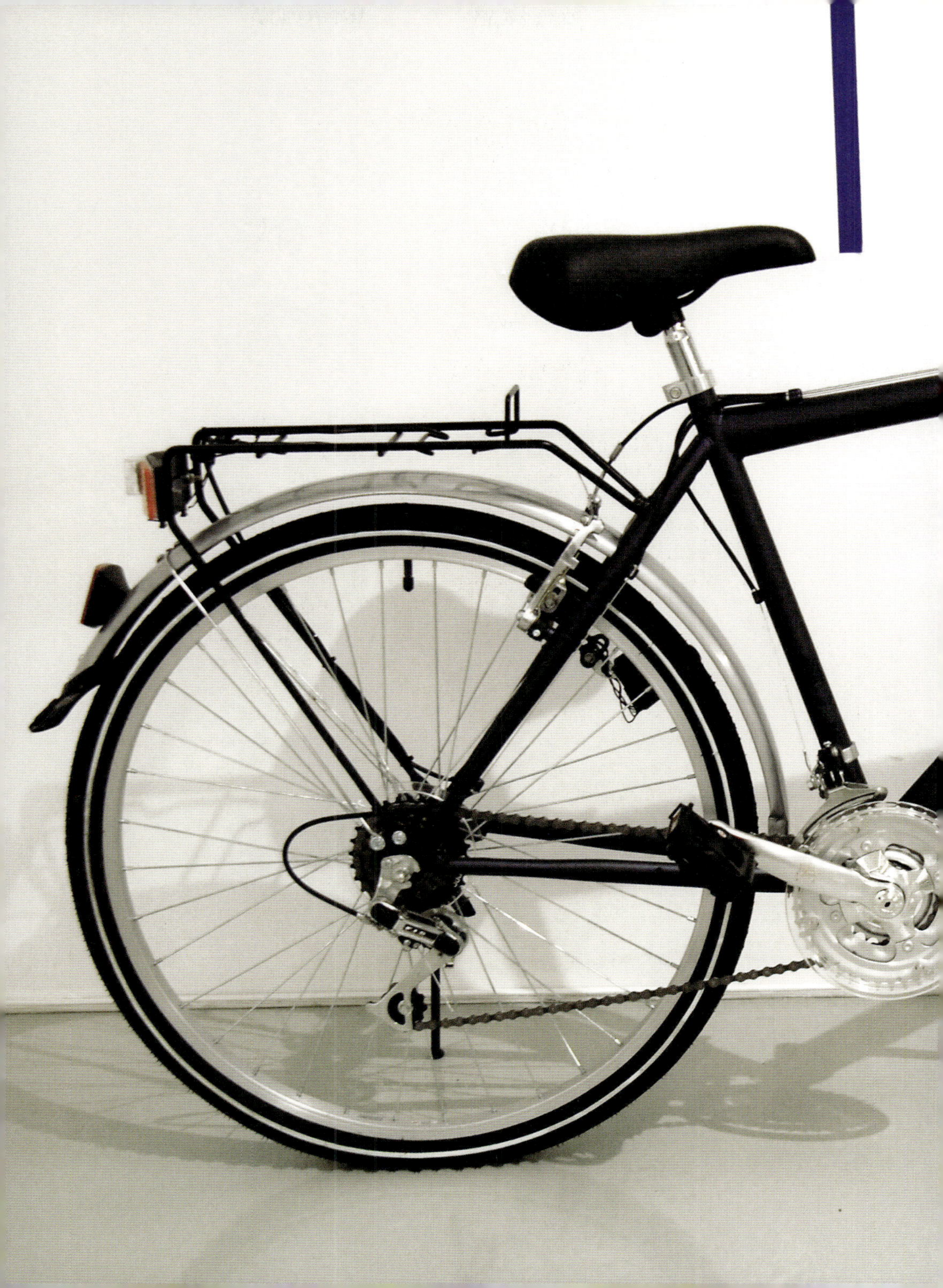

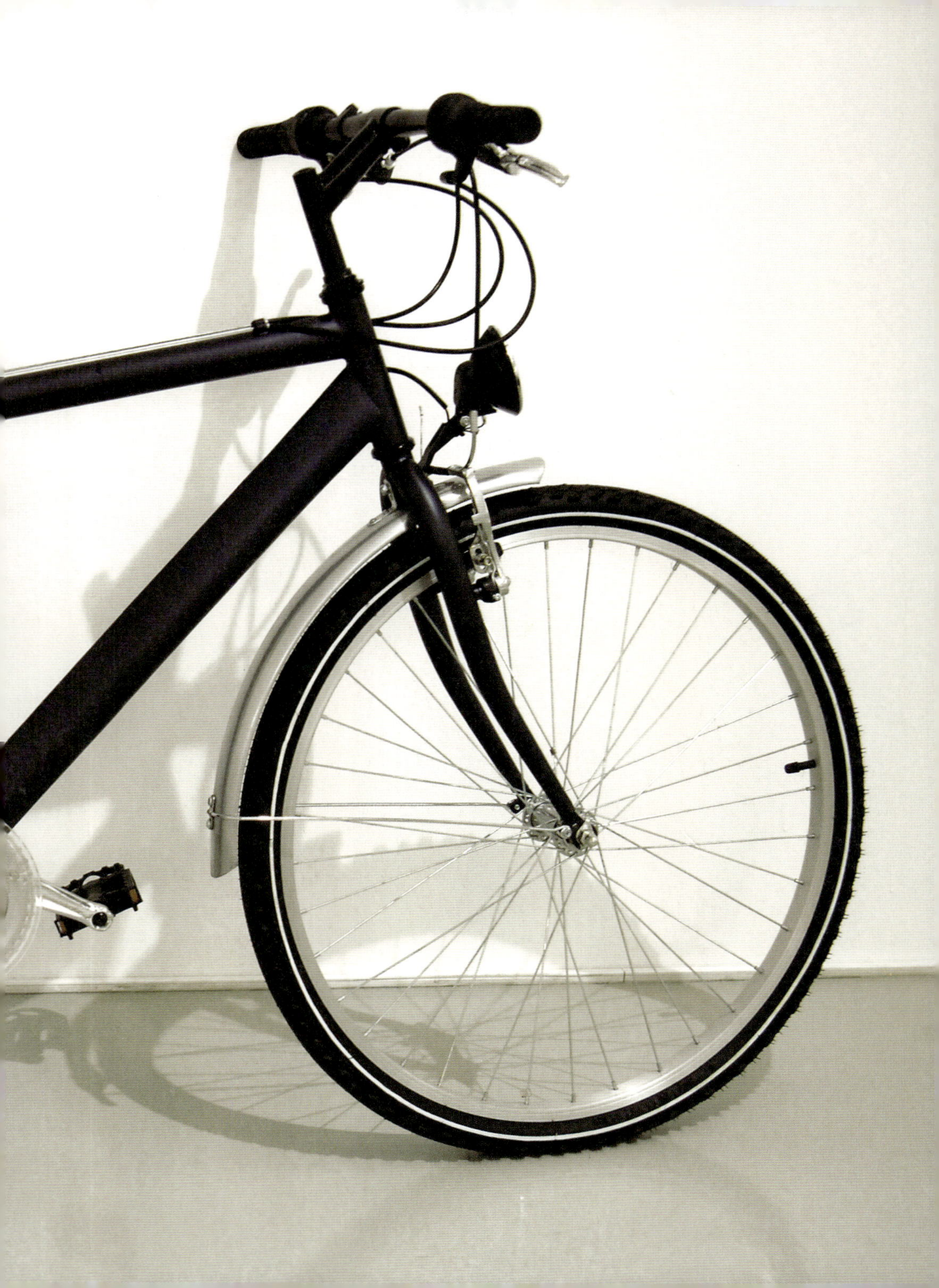

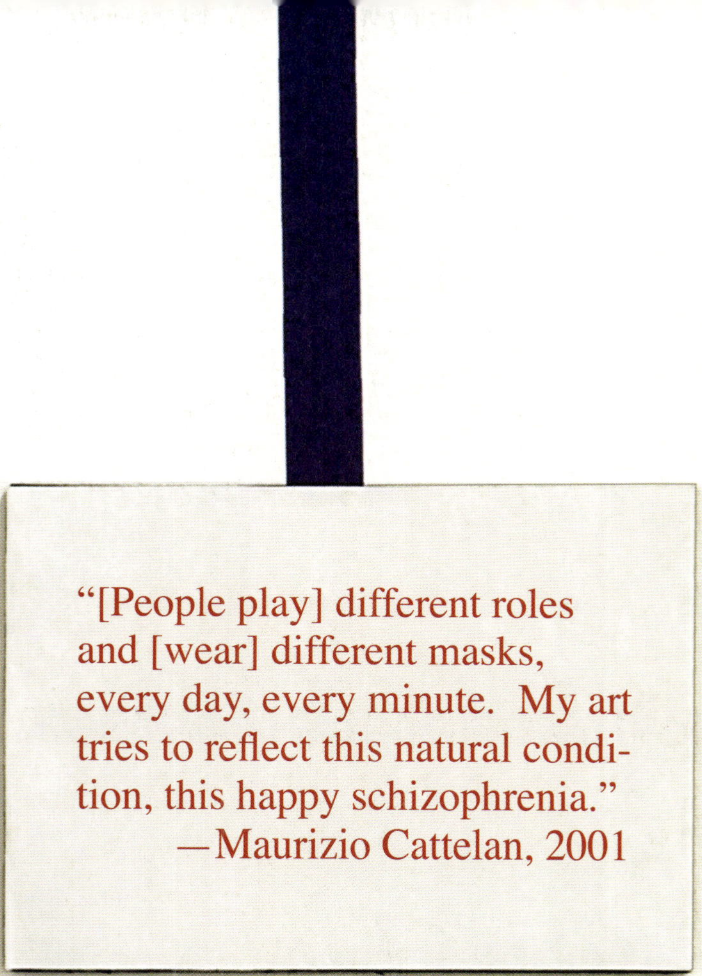
"[People play] different roles and [wear] different masks, every day, every minute. My art tries to reflect this natural condition, this happy schizophrenia."
—Maurizio Cattelan, 2001

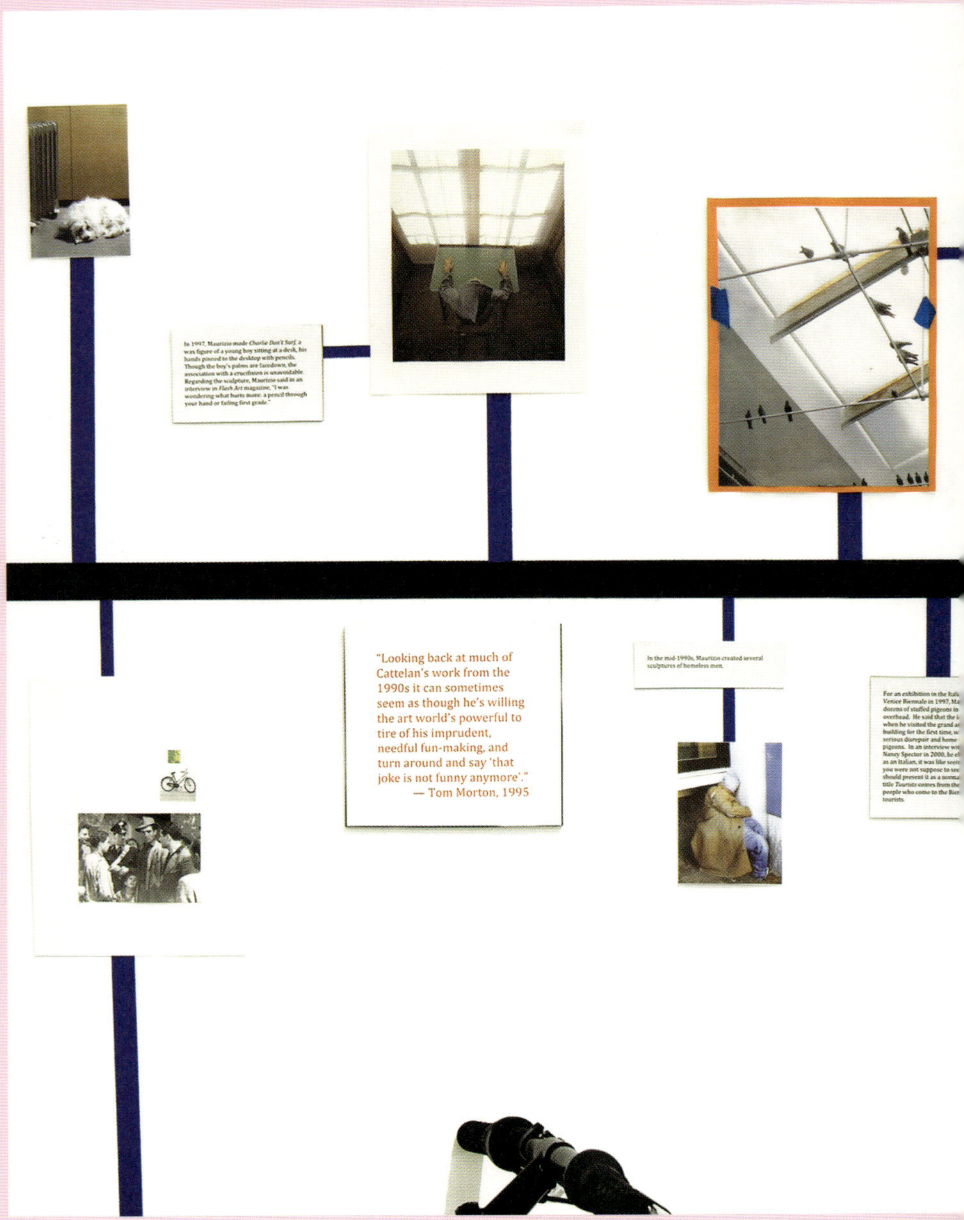
In 1997, Maurizio made Charlie Don't Surf, a wax figure of a young boy sitting at a desk, his hands pinned to the desktop with pencils. Though the boy's palms are facedown, the association with a crucifixion is unavoidable. Regarding the sculpture, Maurizio said in an interview in Flash Art magazine, "I was wondering what hurts more: a pencil through your hand or failing first grade."
"Looking back at much of Cattelan's work from the 1990s it can sometimes seem as though he's willing the art world's powerful to tire of his imprudent, needful fun-making, and turn around and say 'that joke is not funny anymore'."
— Tom Morton, 1995
In the mid-1990s, Maurizio created several sculptures of homeless men.
For an exhibition in the Ital
Venice Biennale in 1997, Ma
dozens of stuffed pigeons in
overhead. He said that the
when he visited the grand a
building for the first time, w
serious disrepair and home
pigeons. In an interview wi
Nancy Spector in 2000, he e
as an Italian, it was like seei
you were not suppose to se
should present it as a norma
title Tourists comes from the
people who come to the Bie
tourists.

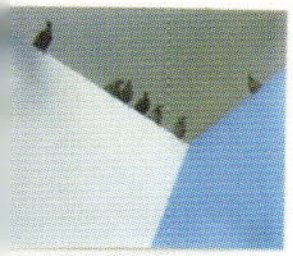

998

Maurizio must have had enjoyed torturing his dealers. Several of his works commented on the power relationship between an artist and his dealer by turning the tables, so to speak, and placing the artist in control. In 1999, for an exhibition, Maurizio duct-tapped his dealer Massimo De Carlo to the gallery wall. (Given the dealer's girth, this could not have been an easy feat.) As fate would have it, De Carlo fainted from exhaustion during the opening and paramedics were called in to revive him.

While these works were realized in good fun, they are also emblematic of a time. Since the late 1990s, the power of the artist in the art world has grown exponentially. And successful artists like Maurizio have increasingly called the shots, with dealers bending over backwards to remain in the artist's good graces.

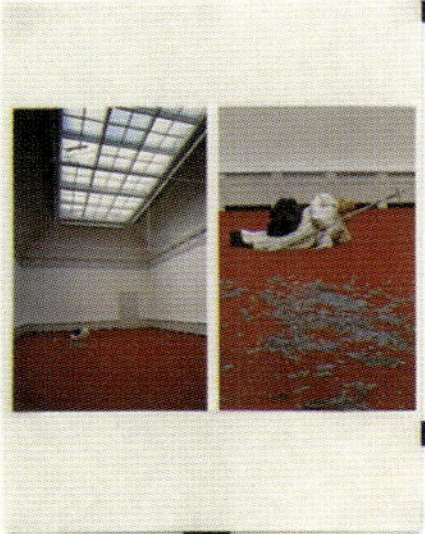

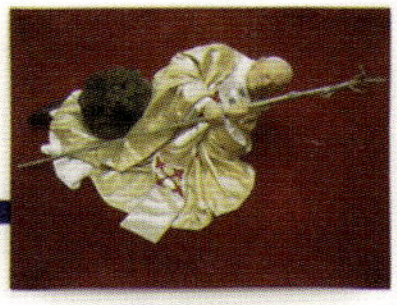

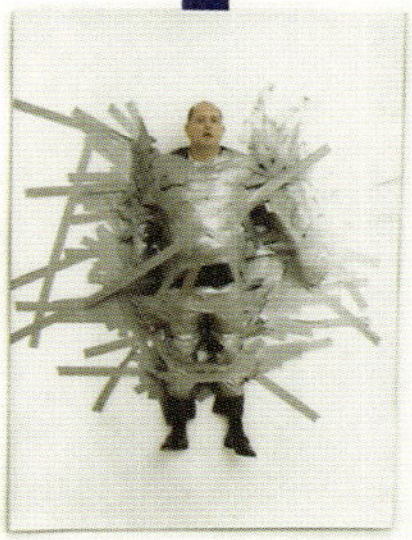

One of Maurizio's most famous pieces depicts the Pope in the moments after being struck by a meteorite. The sculpture, titled *La Nona Ora* (The Ninth Hour), was fabricated in 1999 and shown initially at the Kunsthalle Basel in Switzerland. In an interview with the *New Art Examiner* in 2002, Maurizio said, "The Pope is the authority. When I was in Basel to install the piece it took me two days to decide to put my hands on his body."

When the sculpture was later shown at the state-funded Warsaw Museum in Poland — the Pope's homeland — an uproar ensued. Members of Parliament sent a letter to the prime minister demanding the resignation of the exhibition's curator on the grounds that she, Anda Rottenberg, was "a civil servant of Jewish origin and should not be spending the Roman Catholic's money on disgusting works of art. Ms. Rottenberg should move to Israel where she could commission a wax sculpture of a chief Rabbi knocked down by Yasir Arafat." In an attempt to calm tempers, Poland's president issued a statement saying that he thought the piece served as an allegory for the Pope's heavenly burden. Rottenberg, who refused to step down or remove the artwork, was eventually forced to resign.

In 2001, a version of the sculpture sold at Christies auction house for $886,000; only three years later, it sold for $3,000,000.

Working Methods

Maurizio spent a large portion of his adult life trying to escape his working class roots. In an interview in 2002 he said, "I am trying to solve problems that probably my parents gave me or that I got when I was little."

Massimiliano Gioni cited this as one reason Maurizio made none of his work himself, instead farming out fabrication to specialists — mask-makers, marble-carvers, etc.: "This refusal of any form of physical labor — with all its romantic subtexts — [was] profoundly connected to Cattelan's proletarian upbringing . . . work stands as a synonym for abuse, alienation, blood, sweat and tears."

Maurizio did not have studio. He realized his work much like an executive might, via phone, fax, and email.

1999

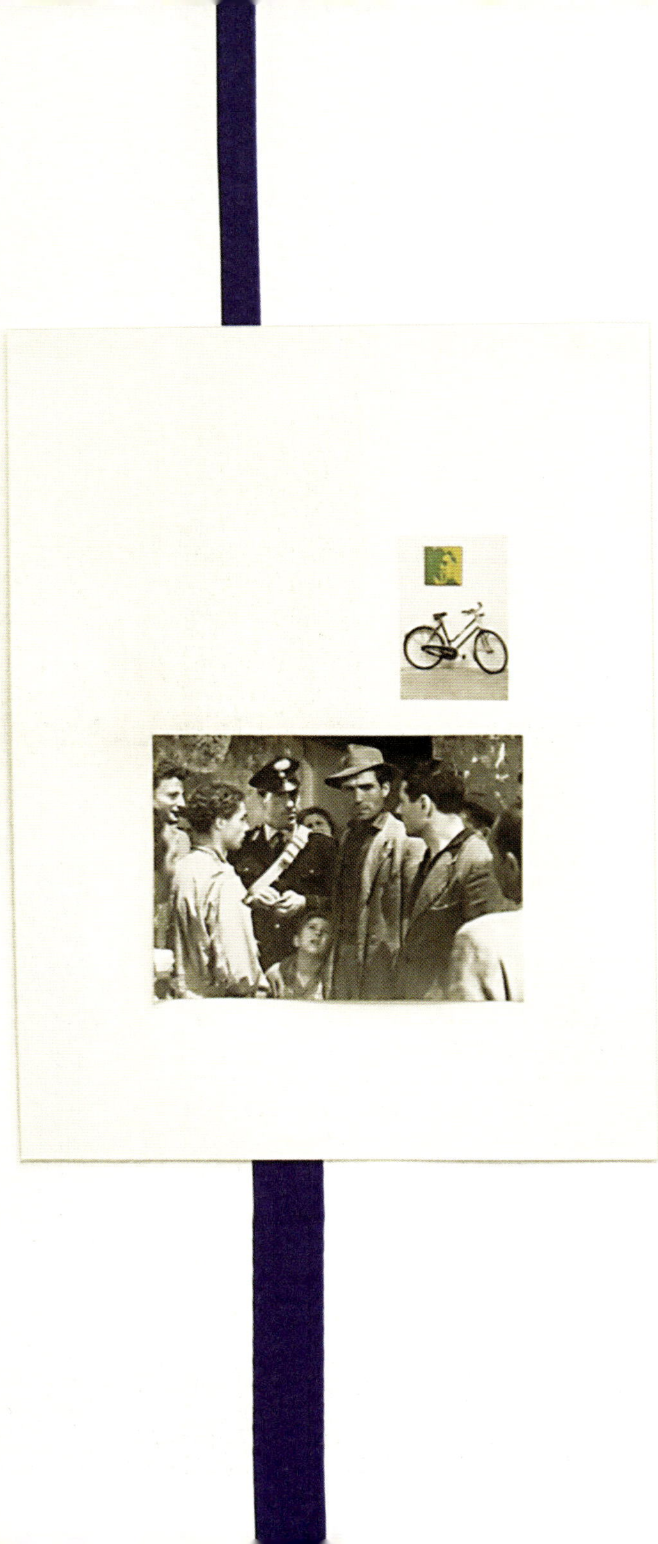

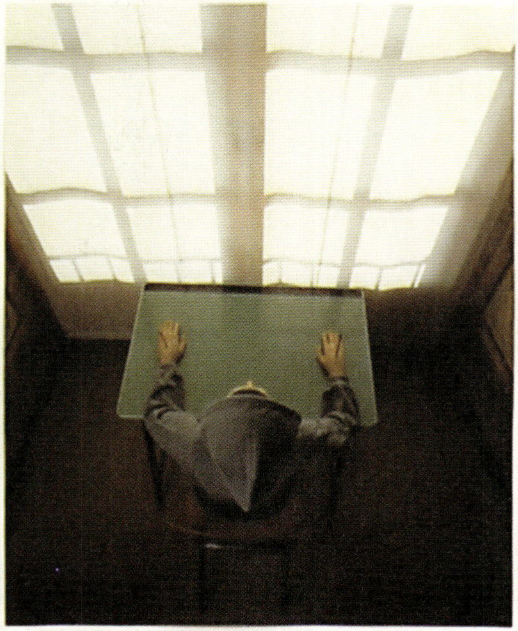

In 1997, Maurizio made *Charlie Don't Surf*, a wax figure of a young boy sitting at a desk, his hands pinned to the surface with pencils. Though the boy's palms are facedown, the association with the crucifixion is unavoidable. Regarding the sculpture, Maurizio said in an interview in *Flash Art* magazine, "I was wondering what hurts more: a pencil through your hand or failing first grade."

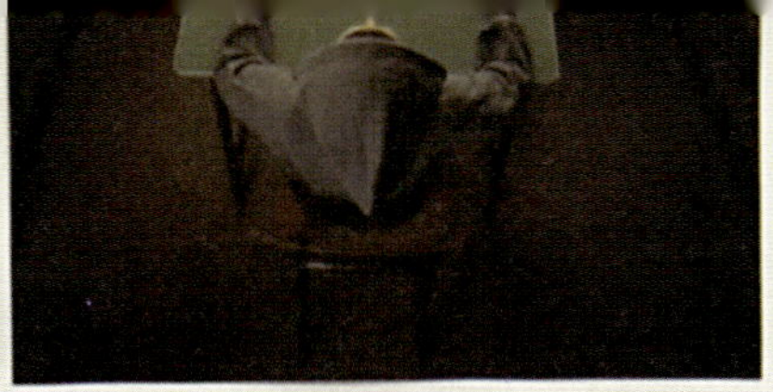

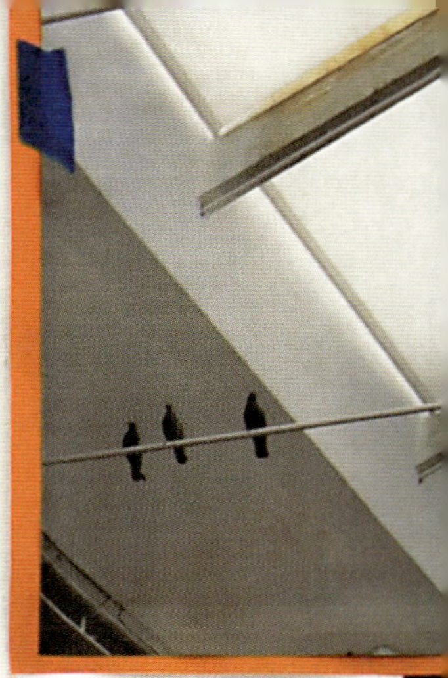

“Looking back at much of Cattelan’s work from the 1990s it can sometimes seem as though he’s willing the art world’s powerful to tire of his impudent, needful fun-making, and turn around and say ‘that joke is not funny anymore.’ ”
—Tom Morton, 1995

In the mid-1990s, Maurizio created several sculptures of homeless men.

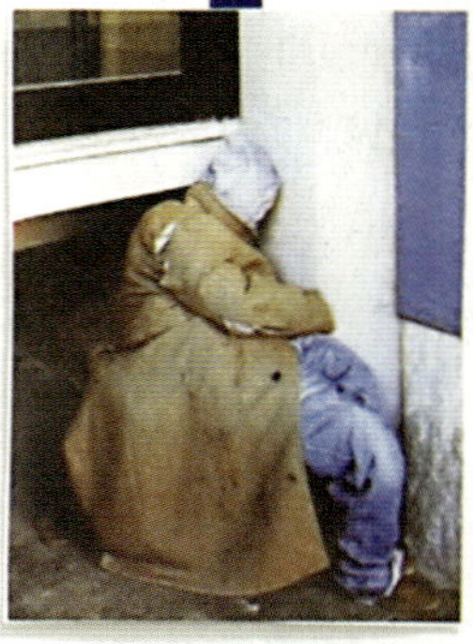

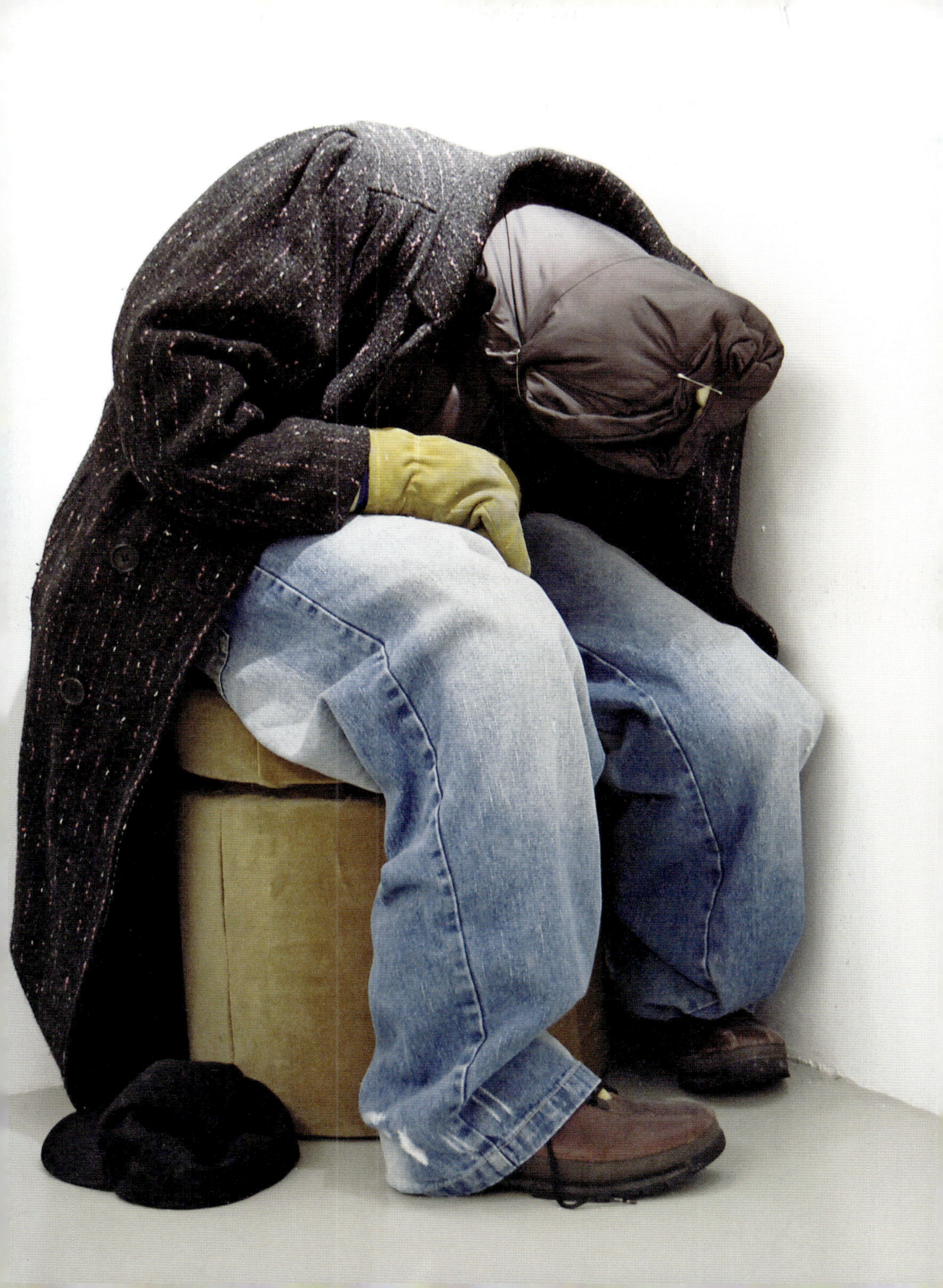

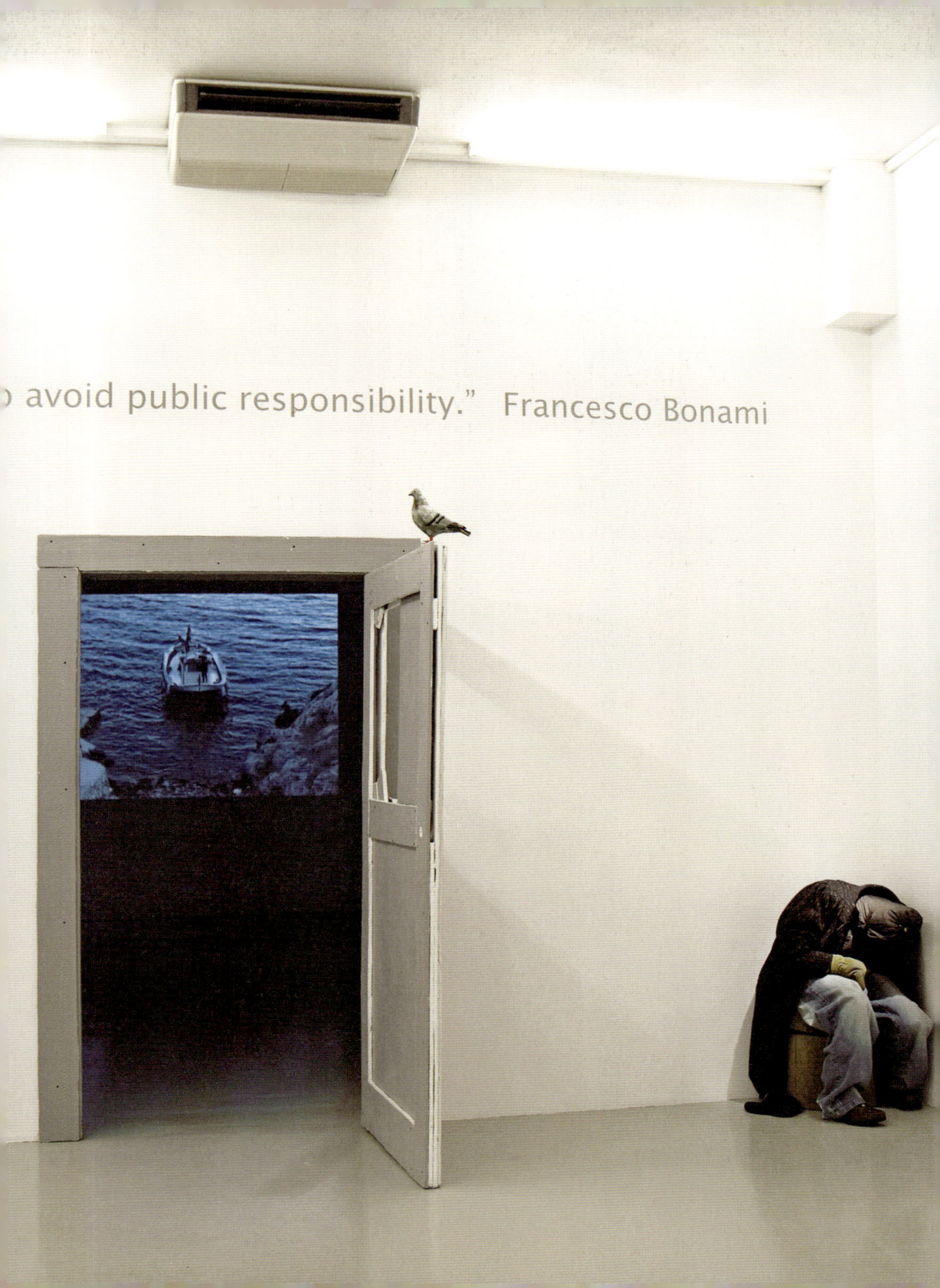
avoid public responsibility.” Francesco Bonami

For an exhibition in the Italian Pavilion at the Venice Biennale in 1997, Maurizio installed dozens of stuffed pigeons in the rafters overhead. He said that the idea came to him when he visited the grand and sprawling building for the first time, which was then in serious disrepair and home to scores of the birds. In an interview with the curator Nancy Spector in 2000, he elaborated, "For me, as an Italian, it was like seeing something that you were not suppose to see . . . so I thought I should present it as a normal situation." The title *Tourists* is meant, perhaps, to equate the city's ever-present pigeons to its largest demographic group.

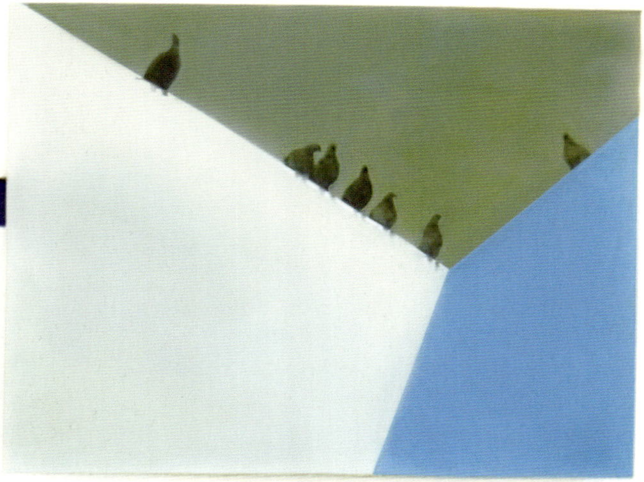

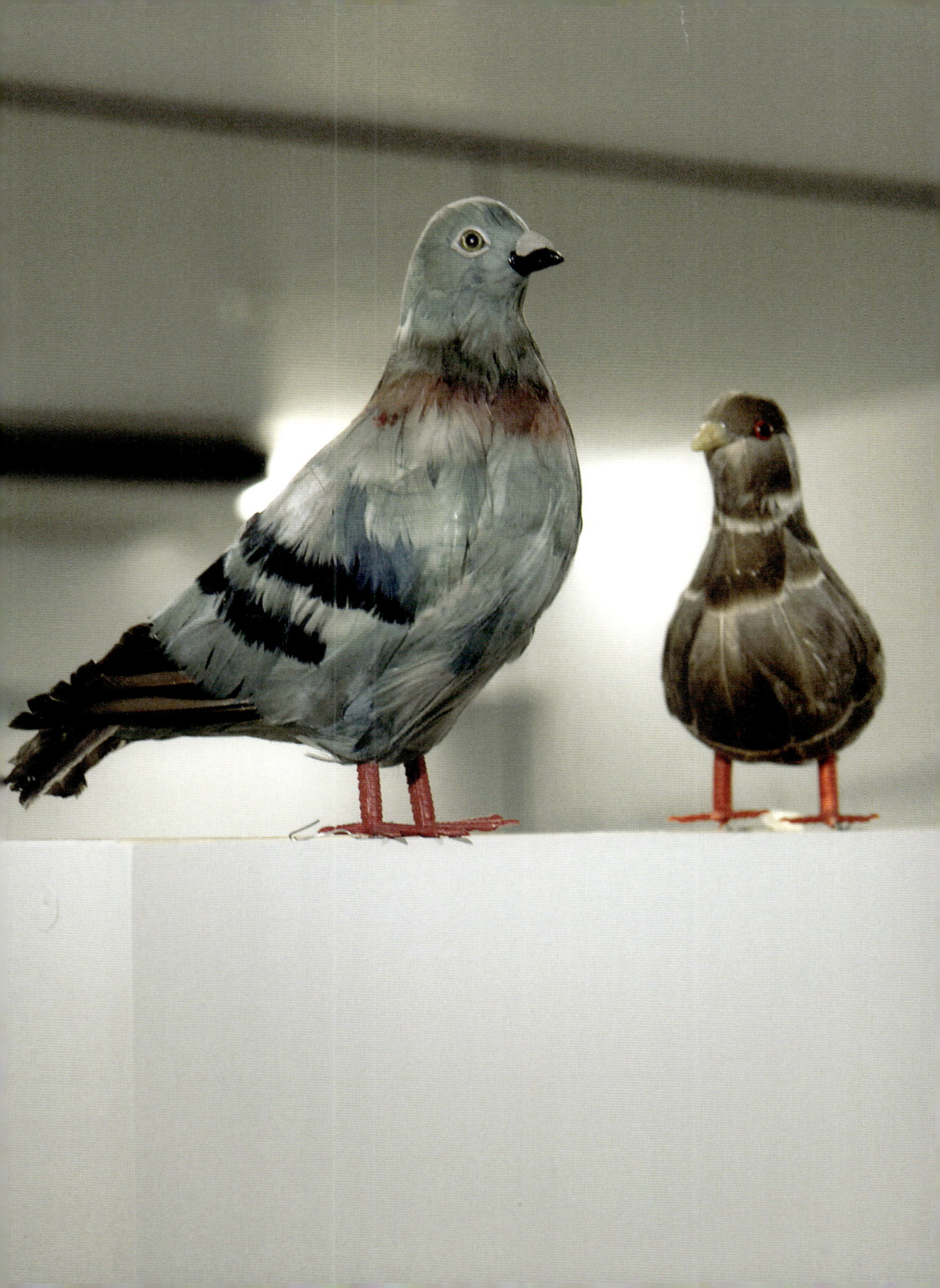

Maurizio must have enjoyed torturing his dealers. Several of his works commented on the power relationship between an artist and his dealer by turning the tables and placing the artist in control. For an exhibition in 1999, Maurizio duct-taped his dealer Massimo De Carlo to the gallery wall. (Given the dealer's girth, this could not have been an easy feat.) As fate would have it, De Carlo fainted from exhaustion during the opening and paramedics were called in to revive him.

While these works were realized in good fun, they are also emblematic of a time. Since the late 1990s, the power of the artist in the art world has grown exponentially. Successful artists like Maurizio have increasingly called the shots, with dealers bending over backwards to remain in their good graces.

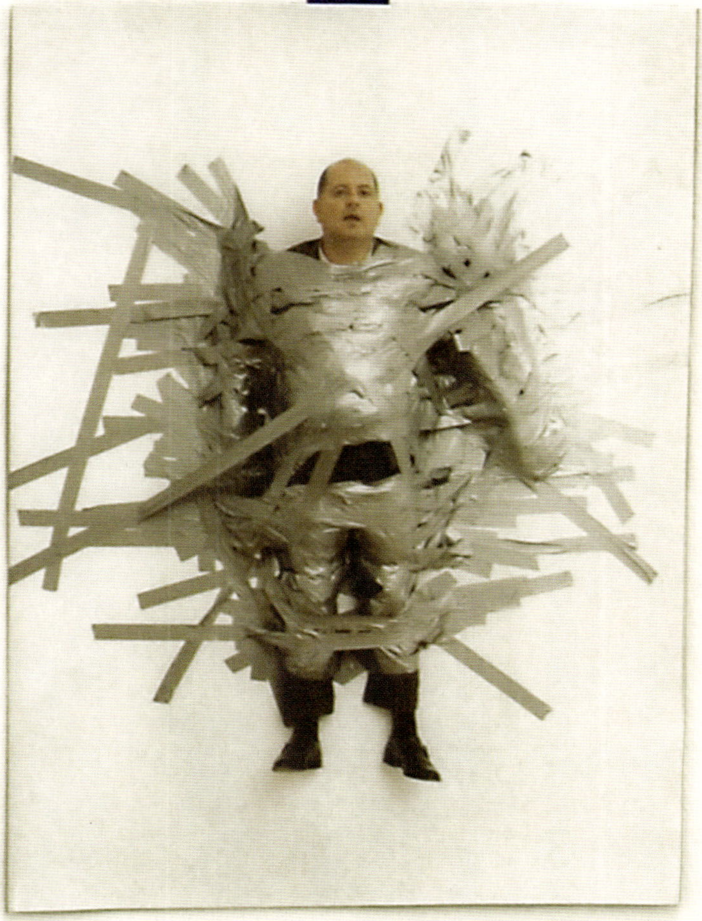

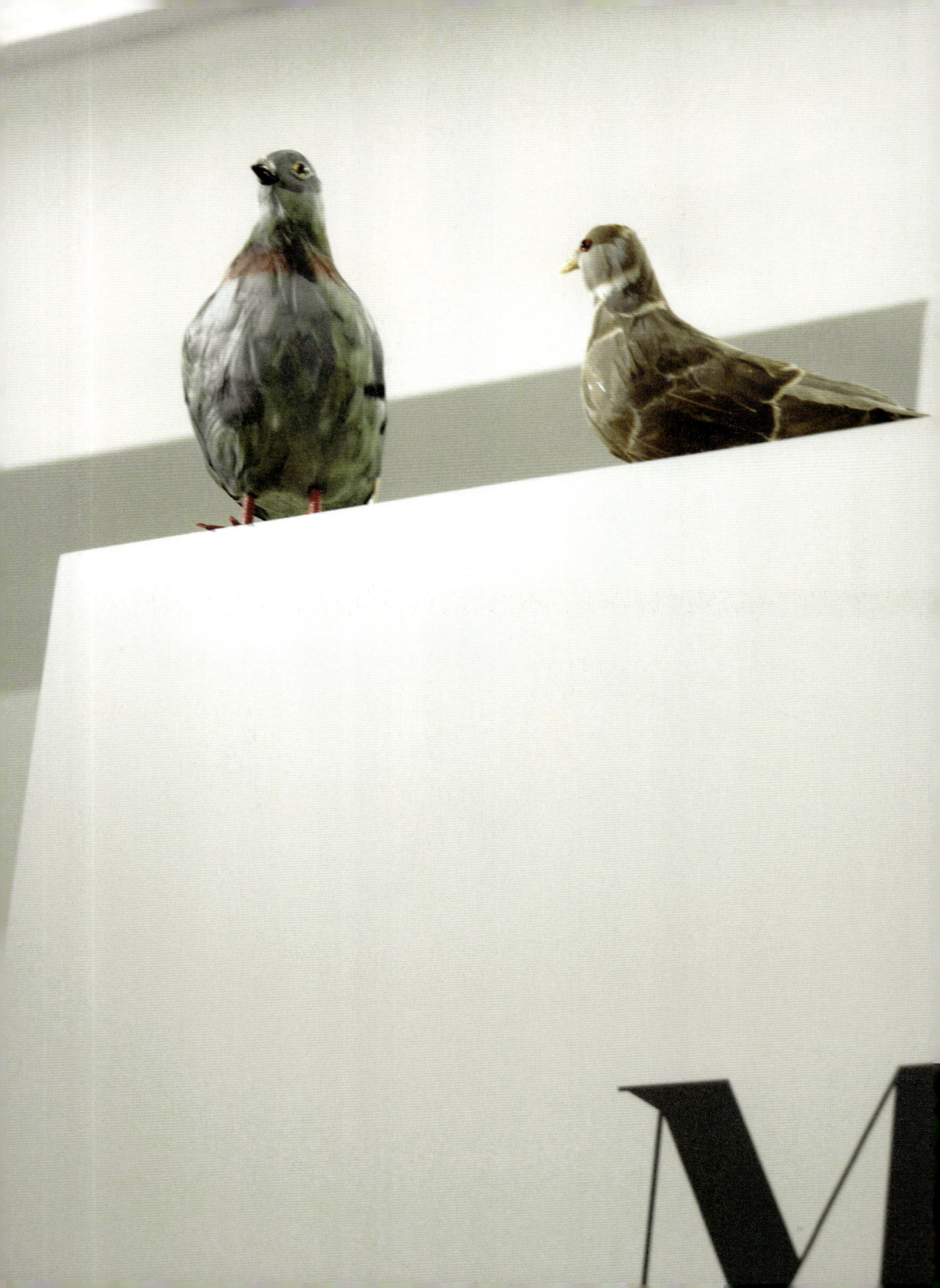
M

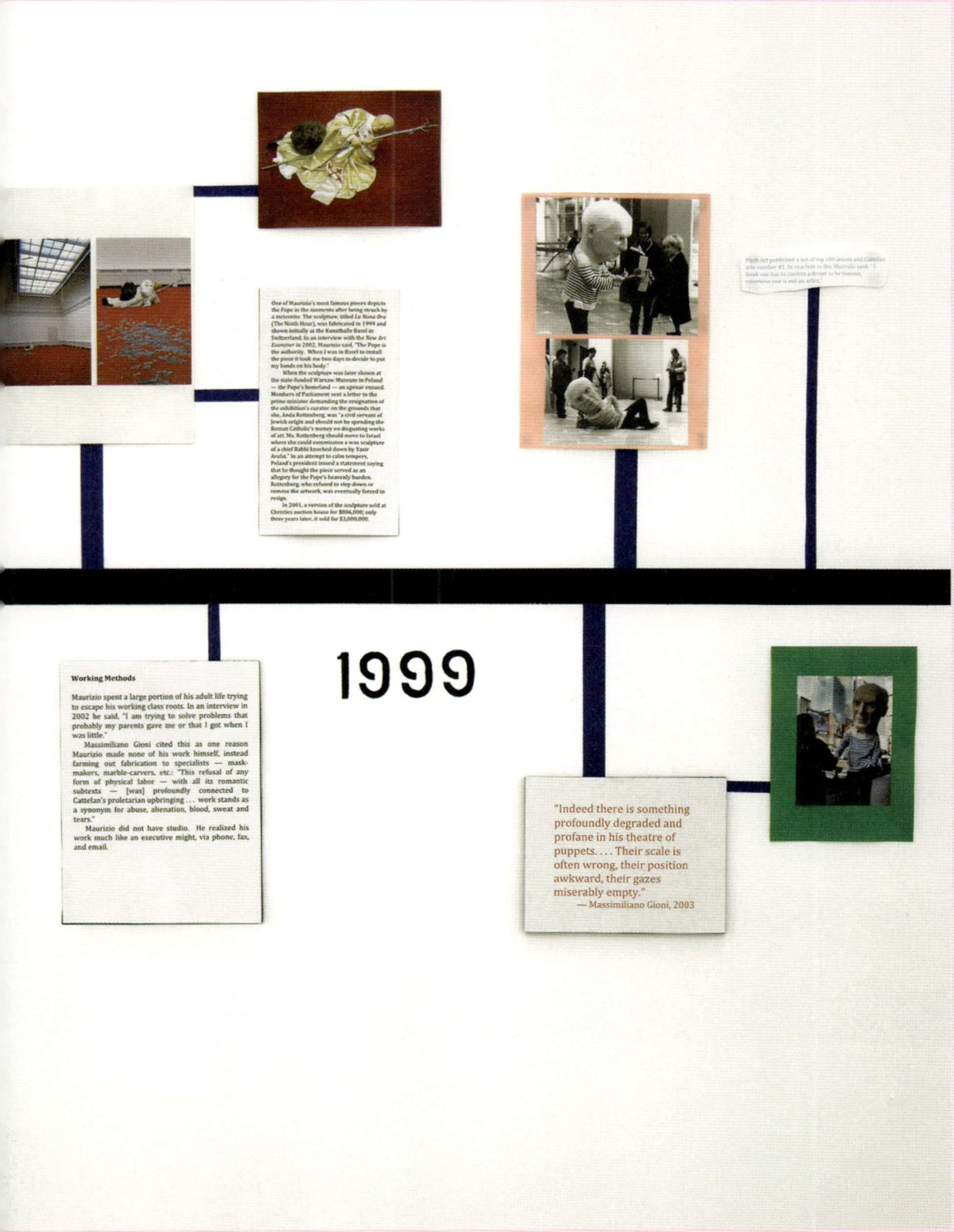
One of Maurizio's most famous pieces depicts the Pope in the moments after being struck by a meteorite. The sculpture, titled La Nona Ora (The Ninth Hour), was fabricated in 1999 and shown initially at the Kunsthalle Basel in Switzerland. In an interview with the New Art Examiner in 2002, Maurizio said, "The Pope is the authority. When I was in Basel to install the piece it took me two days to decide to put my hands on his body."
When the sculpture was later shown at the state-funded Warsaw Museum in Poland — the Pope's homeland — an uproar ensued. Members of Parliament sent a letter to the prime minister demanding the resignation of the exhibition's curator on the grounds that she, Anda Rottenberg, was "a civil servant of Jewish origin and should not be spending the Roman Catholic's money on disgusting works of art. Ms. Rottenberg should move to Israel where she could commission a wax sculpture of a chief Rabbi knocked down by Yasir Arafat." In an attempt to calm tempers, Poland's president issued a statement saying that he thought the piece served as an allegory for the Pope's heavenly burden. Rottenberg, who refused to step down or remove the artwork, was eventually forced to resign.
In 2001, a version of the sculpture sold at Christies auction house for $886,000; only three years later, it sold for $3,000,000.
Flash Art published a list of top 100 artists and Cattelan was number #1. In reaction to this Maurizio said, "I think one has to confess a desire to be famous, otherwise one is not an artist."
1999
Working Methods
Maurizio spent a large portion of his adult life trying to escape his working class roots. In an interview in 2002 he said, "I am trying to solve problems that probably my parents gave me or that I got when I was little."
Massimiliano Gioni cited this as one reason Maurizio made none of his work himself, instead farming out fabrication to specialists — mask-makers, marble-carvers, etc.: "This refusal of any form of physical labor — with all its romantic subtexts — [was] profoundly connected to Cattelan's proletarian upbringing . . . work stands as a synonym for abuse, alienation, blood, sweat and tears."
Maurizio did not have studio. He realized his work much like an executive might, via phone, fax, and email.
"Indeed there is something profoundly degraded and profane in his theatre of puppets. . . . Their scale is often wrong, their position awkward, their gazes miserably empty."
— Massimiliano Gioni, 2003

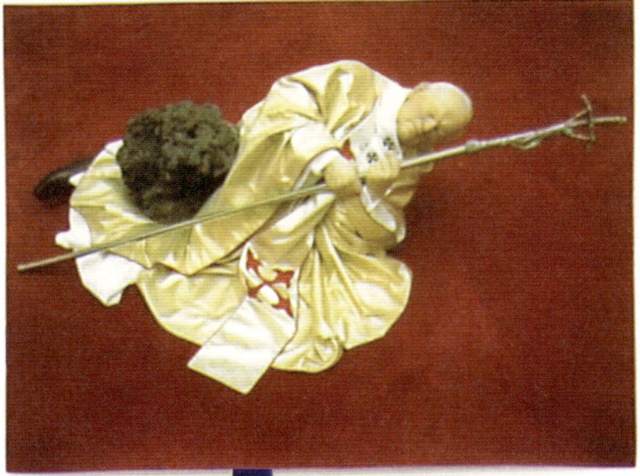

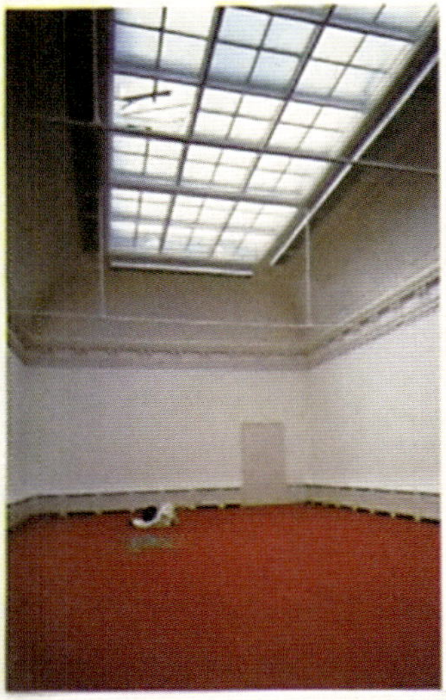

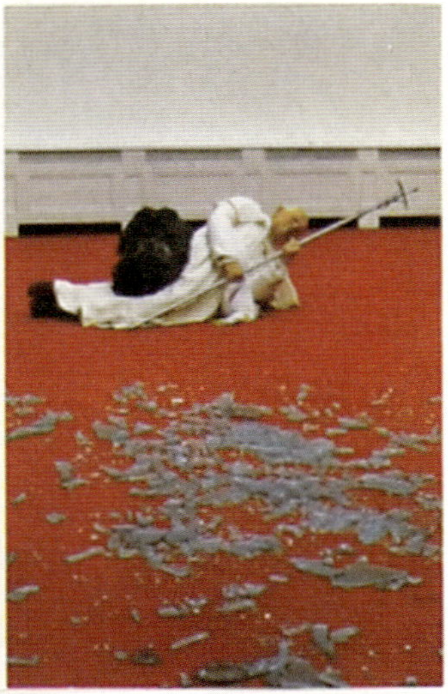

One of Maurizio's most famous pieces depicts the Pope in the moments after being struck by a meteorite. The sculpture, titled *La Nona Ora* (The Ninth Hour), was fabricated in 1999 and shown initially at the Kunsthalle Basel in Switzerland. In an interview with the *New Art Examiner* in 2002, Maurizio said, "The Pope is the authority. When I was in Basel to install the piece it took me two days to decide to put my hands on his body."

When the sculpture was later shown at the state-funded Warsaw Museum in Poland —the Pope's homeland—an uproar ensued. Members of Parliament sent a letter to the prime minister demanding the resignation of the exhibition's curator on the grounds that she, Anda Rottenberg, was "a civil servant of Jewish origin and should not be spending the Roman Catholic's money on disgusting works of art. Ms. Rottenberg should move to Israel where she could commission a wax sculpture of a chief Rabbi knocked down by Yasir Arafat." In an attempt to calm tempers, Poland's president issued a statement saying that he thought the piece served as an allegory for the Pope's heavenly burden. Rottenberg, who refused to step down or remove the artwork, was eventually forced to resign.

In 2001, a version of the sculpture sold at Christie's auction house for $886,000; three years later, it sold for $3,000,000.

Working Methods

Maurizio spent a large portion of his adult life trying to escape his working-class roots. In an interview in 2002 he said, "I am trying to solve problems that probably my parents gave me or that I got when I was little."

Curator Massimiliano Gioni cited this as one reason Maurizio made none of his work himself, instead farming out fabrication to specialists—mask-makers, marble-carvers, etc.: "This refusal of any form of physical labor—with all its romantic subtexts—[was] profoundly connected to Cattelan's proletarian upbringing . . . work stands as a synonym for abuse, alienation, blood, sweat, and tears."

Maurizio did not have a studio. He realized his work much like an executive might, via phone, fax, and email.

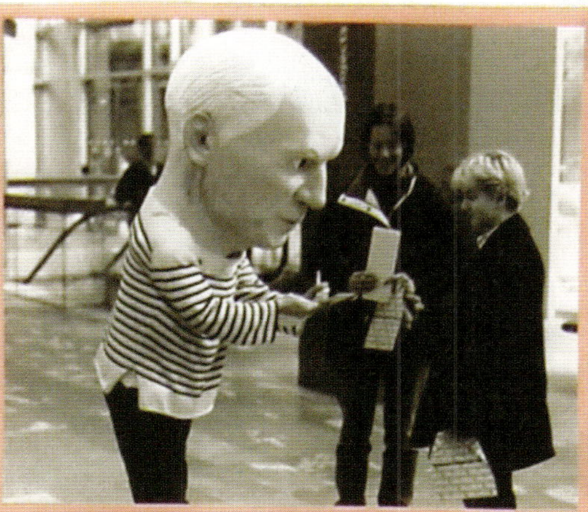

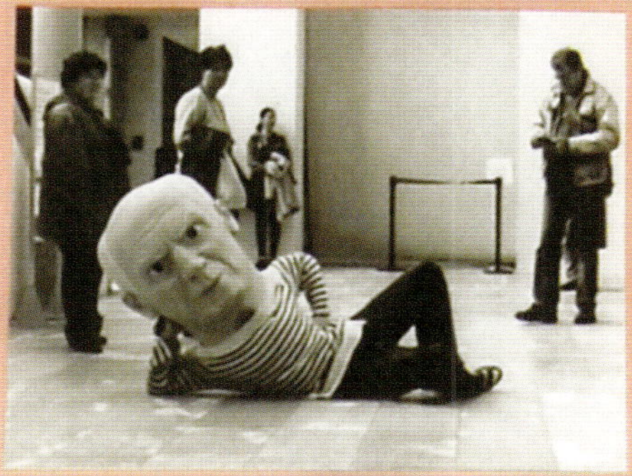

Flash Art magazine published a list of the top 100 artists and Maurizio was #1. In reaction, Maurizio said, "I think one has to confess a desire to be famous, otherwise one is not an artist."

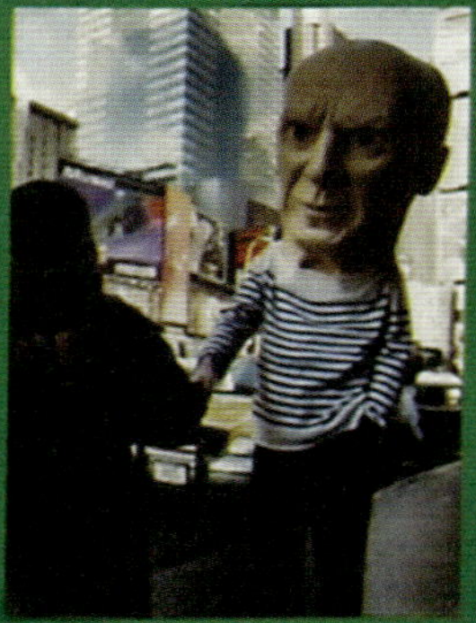

"Indeed there is something profoundly degraded and profane with his theater of puppets. . . . Their scale is often wrong, their position awkward, their gazes miserably empty."
—Massimiliano Gioni, 2003

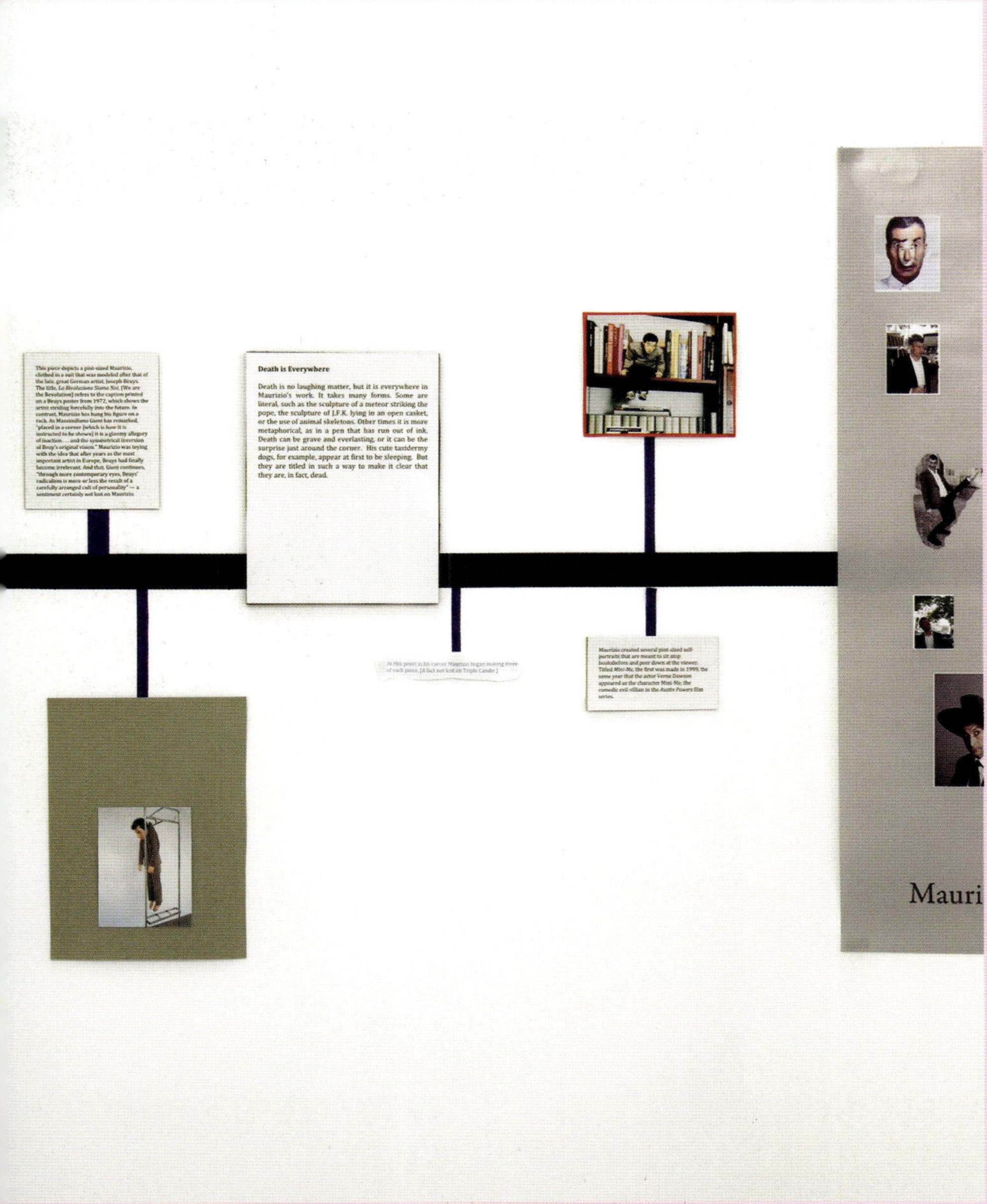
This piece depicts a pint-sized Maurizio, clothed in a suit that was modeled after that of the late, great German artist, Joseph Beuys. The title, La Rivoluzione Siamo Noi, [We are the Revolution] refers to the caption printed on a Beuys poster from 1972, which shows the artist striding forcefully into the future. In contrast, Maurizio has hung his figure on a rack. As Massimiliano Gioni has remarked, "placed in a corner [which is how it is instructed to be shown] it is a gloomy allegory of inaction . . . and the symmetrical inversion of Beuy's original vision." Maurizio was toying with the idea that after years as the most important artist in Europe, Beuys had finally become irrelevant. And that, Gioni continues, "through more contemporary eyes, Beuys' radicalism is more or less the result of a carefully arranged cult of personality" — a sentiment certainly not lost on Maurizio.
Death is Everywhere
Death is no laughing matter, but it is everywhere in Maurizio's work. It takes many forms. Some are literal, such as the sculpture of a meteor striking the pope, the sculpture of J.F.K. lying in an open casket, or the use of animal skeletons. Other times it is more metaphorical, as in a pen that has run out of ink. Death can be grave and everlasting, or it can be the surprise just around the corner. His cute taxidermy dogs, for example, appear at first to be sleeping. But they are titled in such a way to make it clear that they are, in fact, dead.
Maurizio created several pint-sized self-portraits that are meant to sit atop bookshelves and peer down at the viewer. Titled Mini-Me, the first was made in 1999, the same year that the actor Verne Dowson appeared as the character Mini-Me, the comedic evil villain in the Austin Powers film series.
Mauri

This piece depicts a pint-sized Maurizio, clothed in a suit that was modeled after that of the late, great German artist Joseph Beuys. The title, *La Rivoluzione Siamo Noi* (We Are the Revolution) refers to the caption printed on a Beuys poster from 1972, which shows the artist striding forcefully into the future. In contrast, Maurizio has hung his figure on a rack. As Massimiliano Gioni has remarked, "placed in a corner [which is how it is instructed to be shown] it is a gloomy allegory of inaction . . . and the symmetrical inversion of Beuy's original vision." Maurizio was toying with the idea that after years as the most important artist in Europe, Beuys had finally become irrelevant. And that, Gioni continues, "through more contemporary eyes, Beuys' radicalism is more or less the result of a carefully arranged cult of personality"—a sentiment certainly not lost on Maurizio.

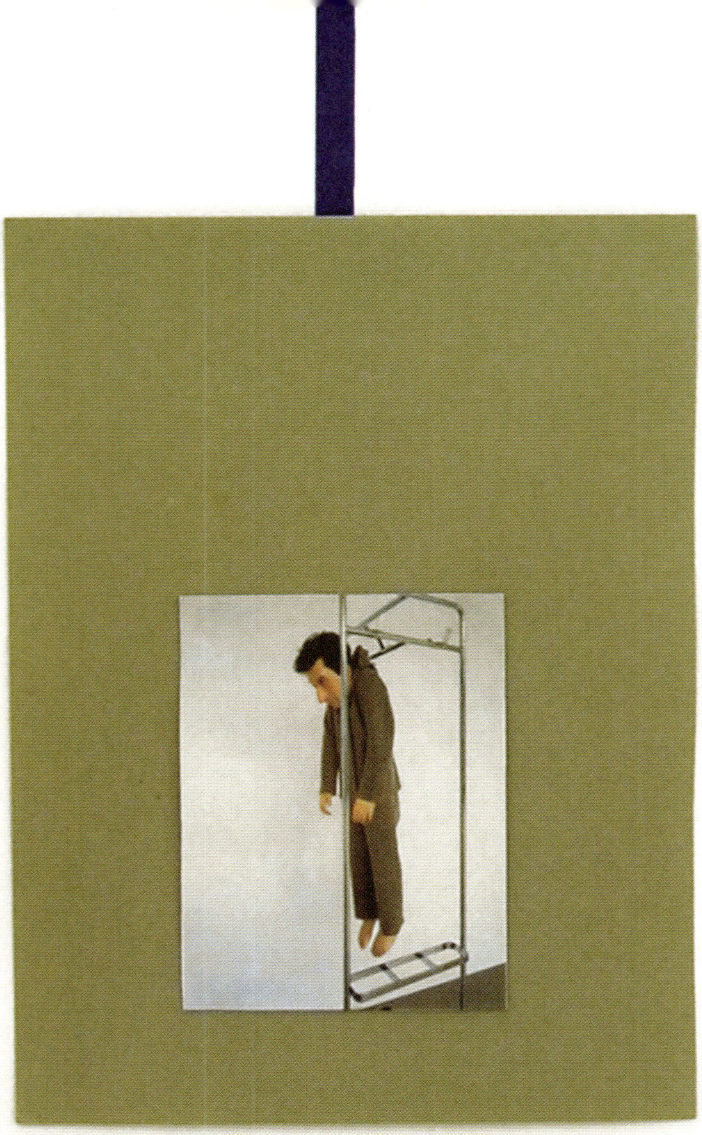

Death is Everywhere

Death is no laughing matter, but it is everywhere in Maurizio's work, and takes many forms. Some are literal, such as the sculpture of the meteor striking the Pope, the sculpture of J.F.K. lying in an open casket (not included here), or the use of animal skeletons. Other times it is more metaphorical, as in a pen that has run out of ink. Death can be grave and everlasting, or it can be the surprise just around the corner. Maurizio's taxidermied dogs, for example, appear at first to be sleeping. But they are titled in such a way to emphasize the fact that they are, indeed, dead, dead, dead.

At this point in his career, Maurizio began making three of each piece.

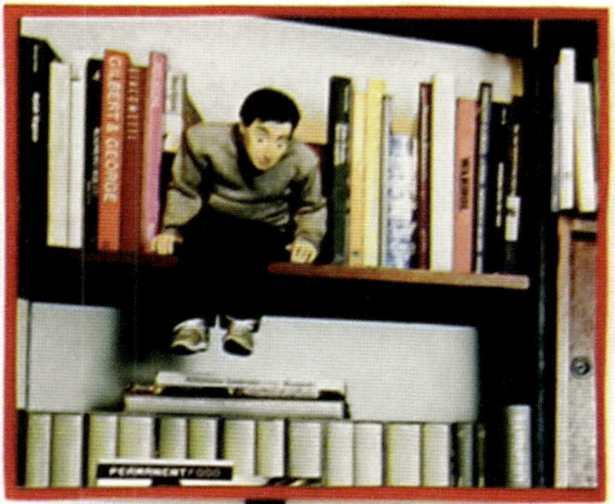

Maurizio created several pint-sized self-portraits that are meant to sit atop bookshelves and peer down at the viewer. Titled *Mini-Me*, the first was made in 1999, the same year that the actor Verne Troyer appeared as the character of Mini-Me, the comedic evil villain in the Austin Powers film series.

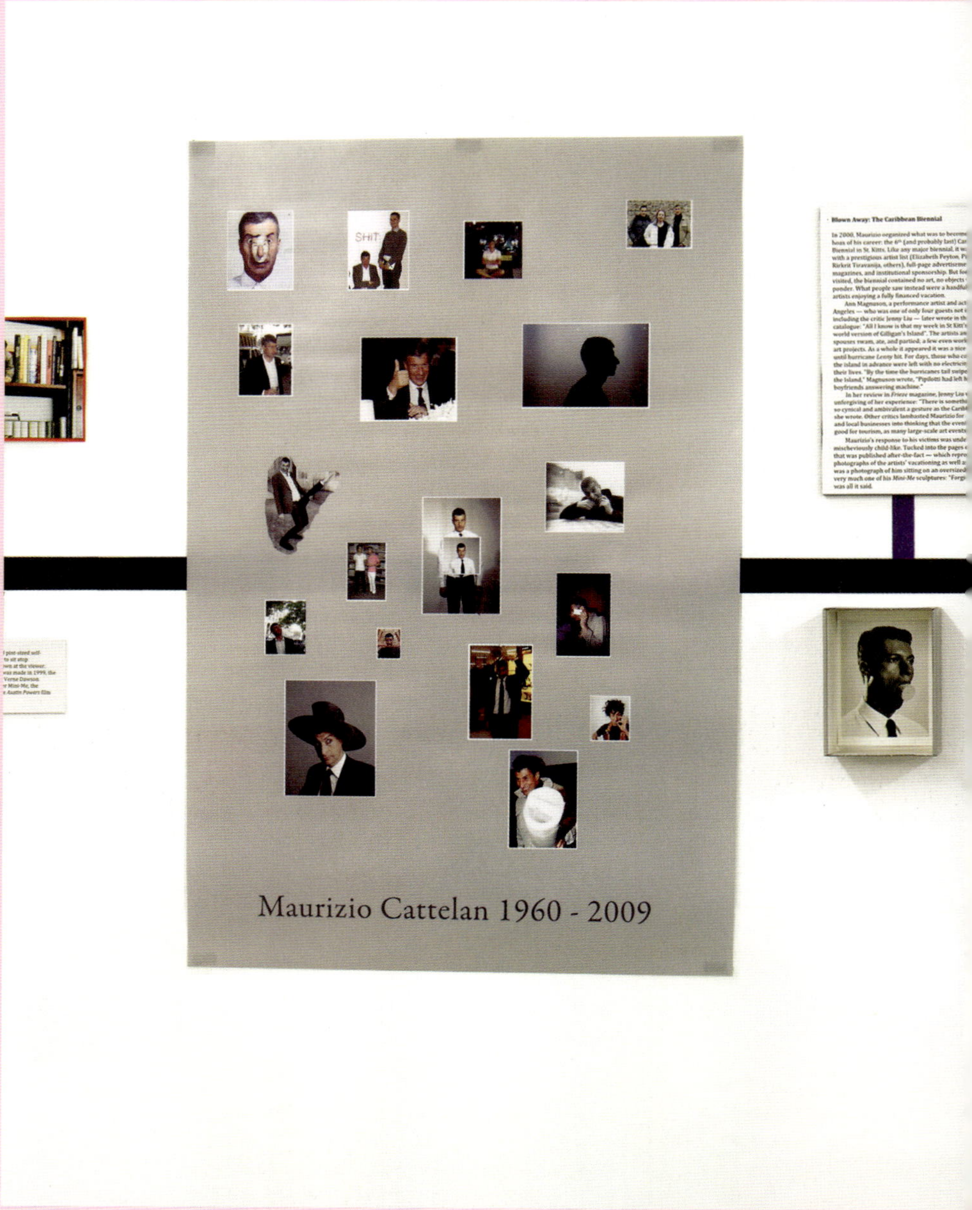
Blown Away: The Caribbean Biennial
SHIT
Maurizio Cattelan 1960 - 2009

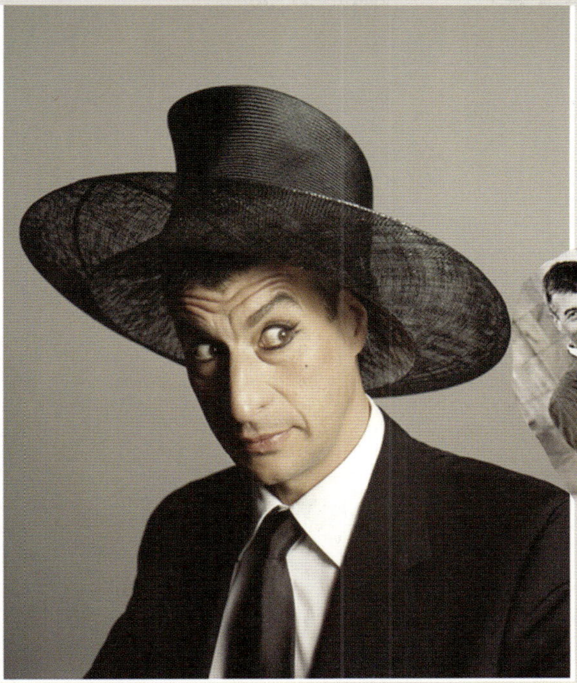

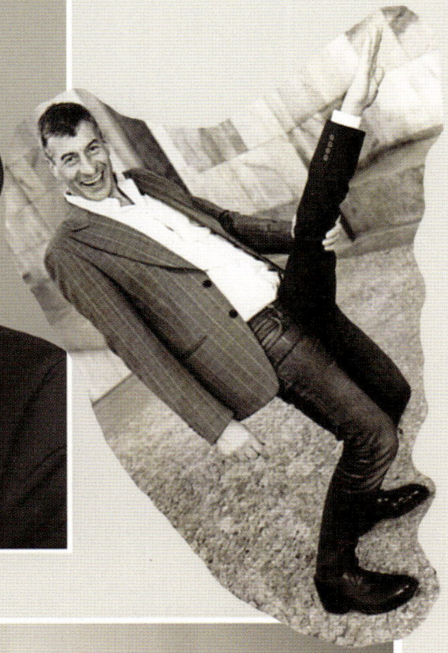

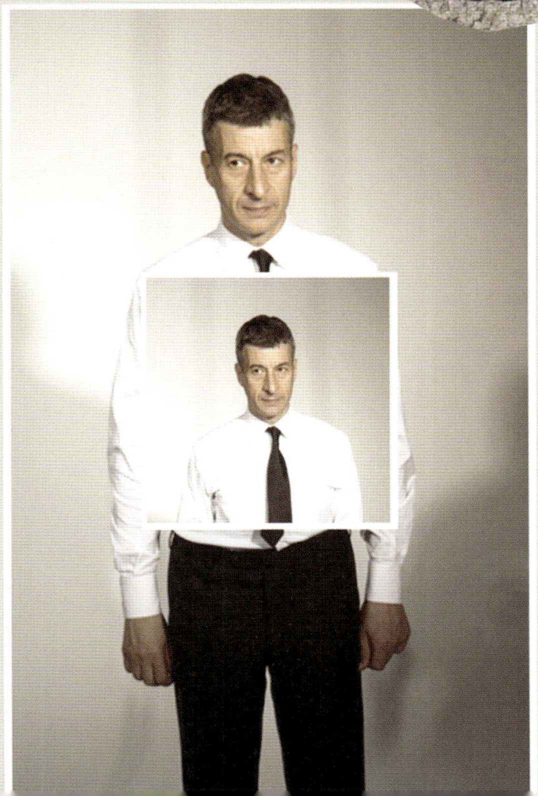

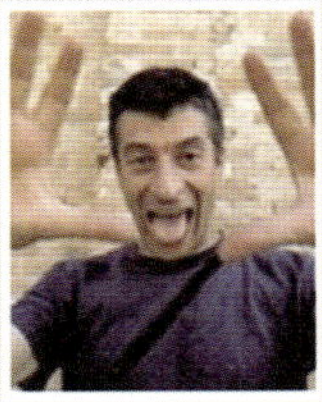

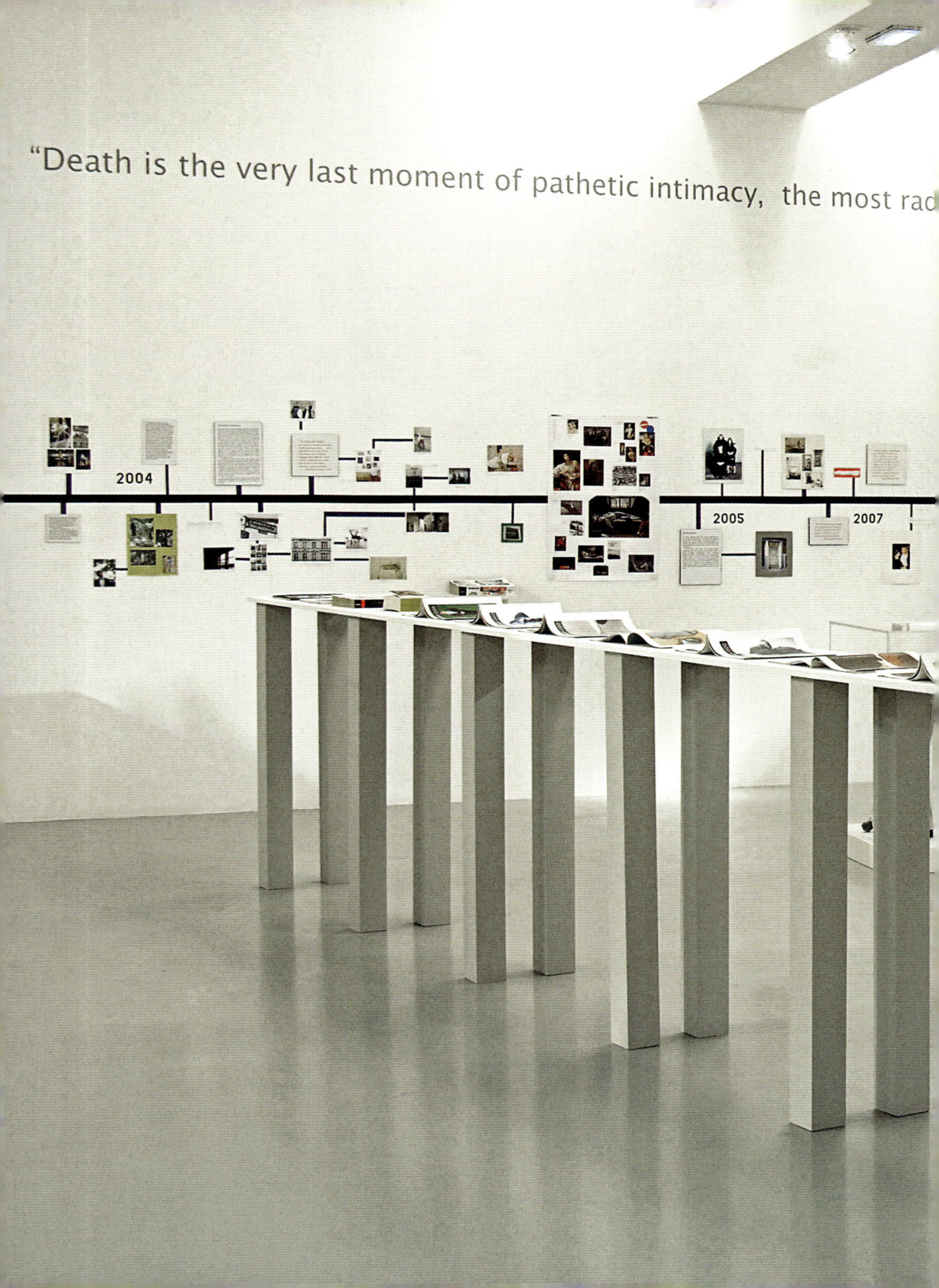
"Death is the very last moment of pathetic intimacy, the most rad
2004
2005
2007

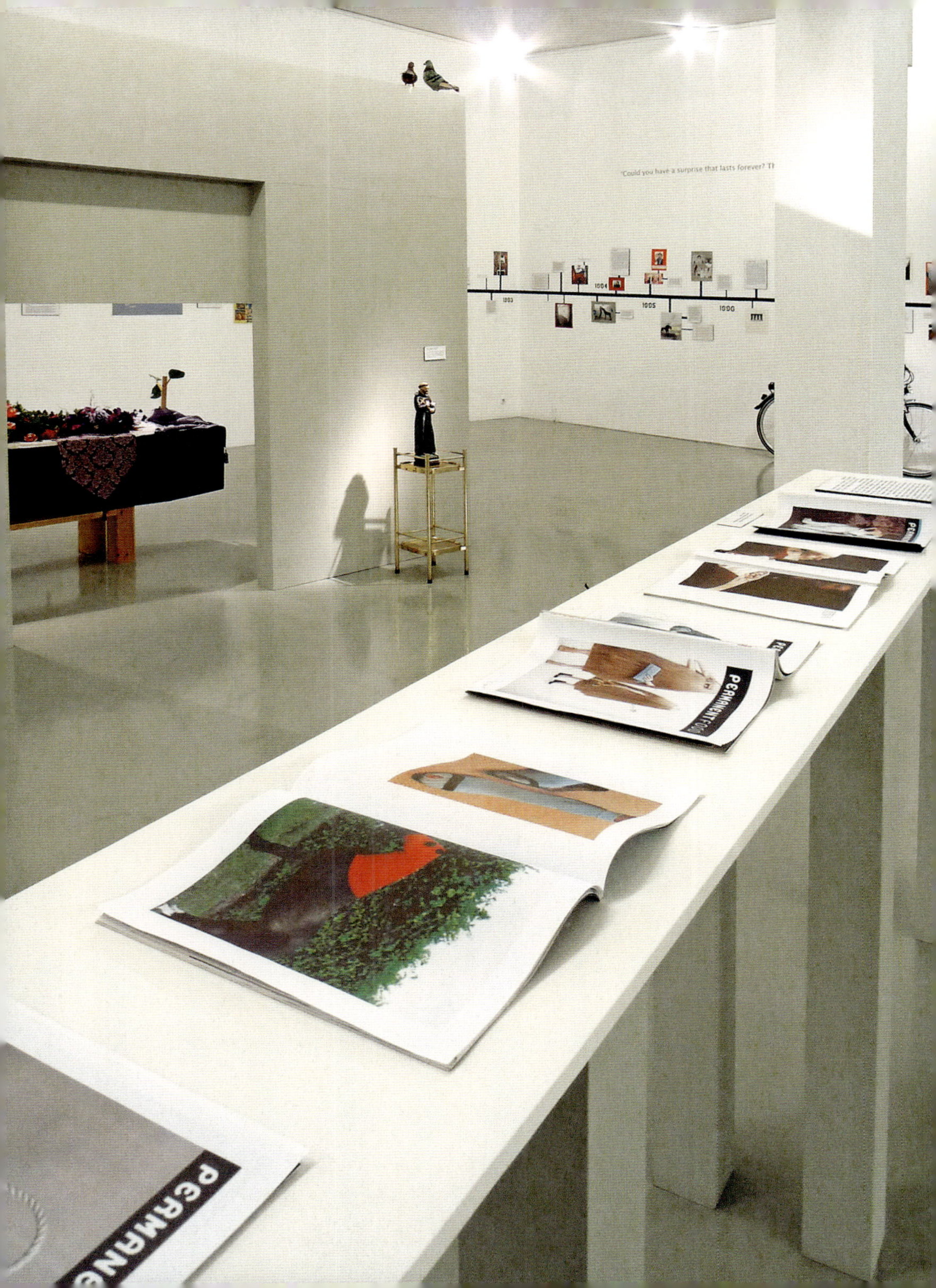
'Could you have a surprise that lasts forever? Th
1993
1994
1995
1996
PERMANENT FOOD
PERMANE

The Magazines

Maurizio was a small-time publisher of decidedly non-commercial magazines. In 1995 with the French artist Dominique Gonzalez-Foerster, he started *Permanent Food*. For the first three issues, the duo asked artist-friends to send them altered images, which they arranged and published. Subsequent issues were realized in collaboration with Paola Manfrin, an art director in Milan. The content consisted soley of images stolen from other magazines. In the spring of 2002, Maurizio started another magazine titled simply *Charley*. Published in collaboration with curators Massimiliano Gioni and Ali Subotnick, his future collaborators on The Wrong Gallery, it presented the work of other artists, but did so by reproducing images culled from preexisting catalogues, brochures, press clips, postcards, and other visuals. In an interview in 2002, Maurizio said, "I am a copier. I am like a Xerox machine. I'm really seduced by images that already belong to everybody."

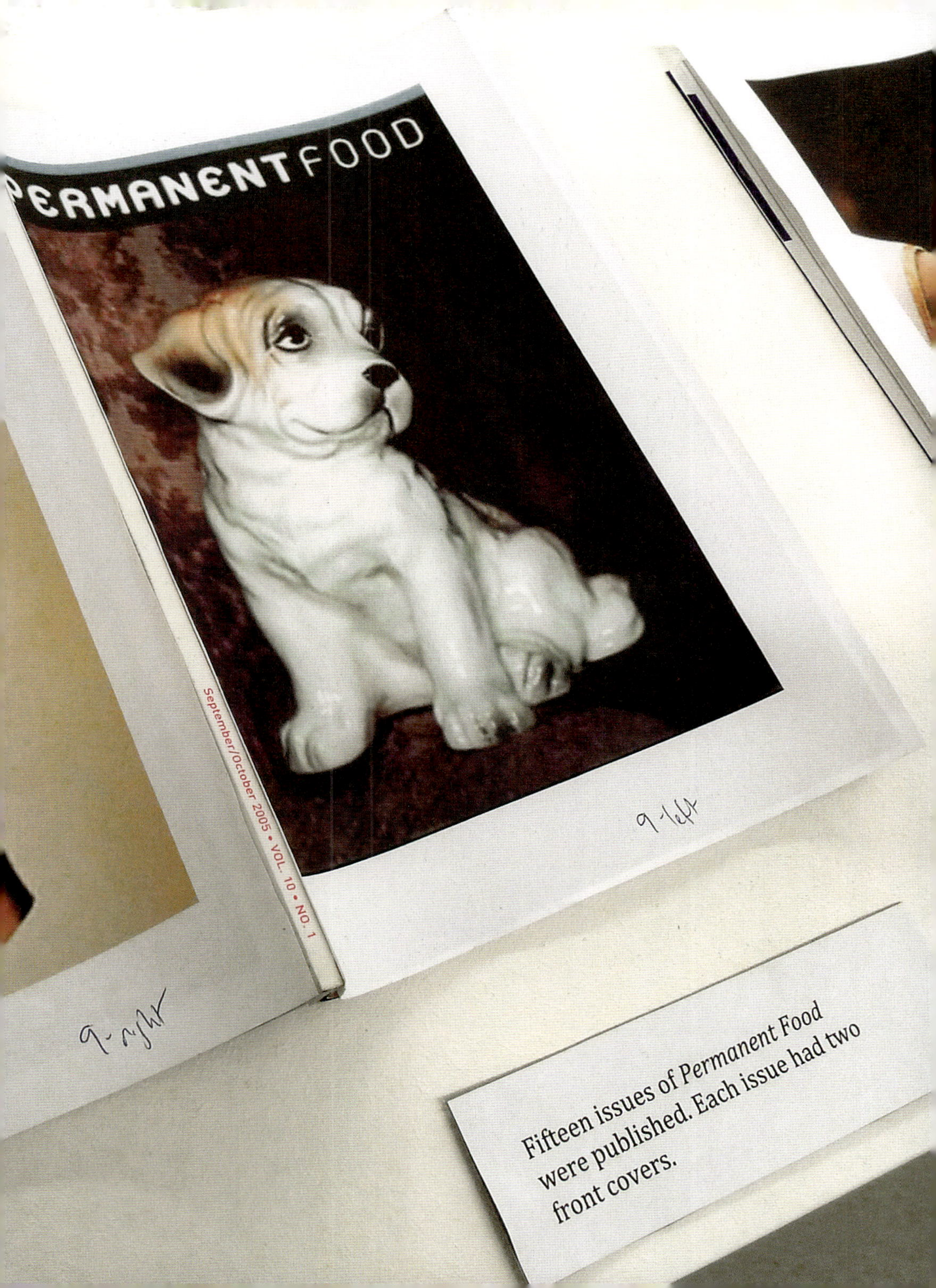
PERMANENT FOOD
September/October 2005 • VOL. 10 • NO. 1
9-left
9-right
Fifteen issues of *Permanent Food* were published. Each issue had two front covers.

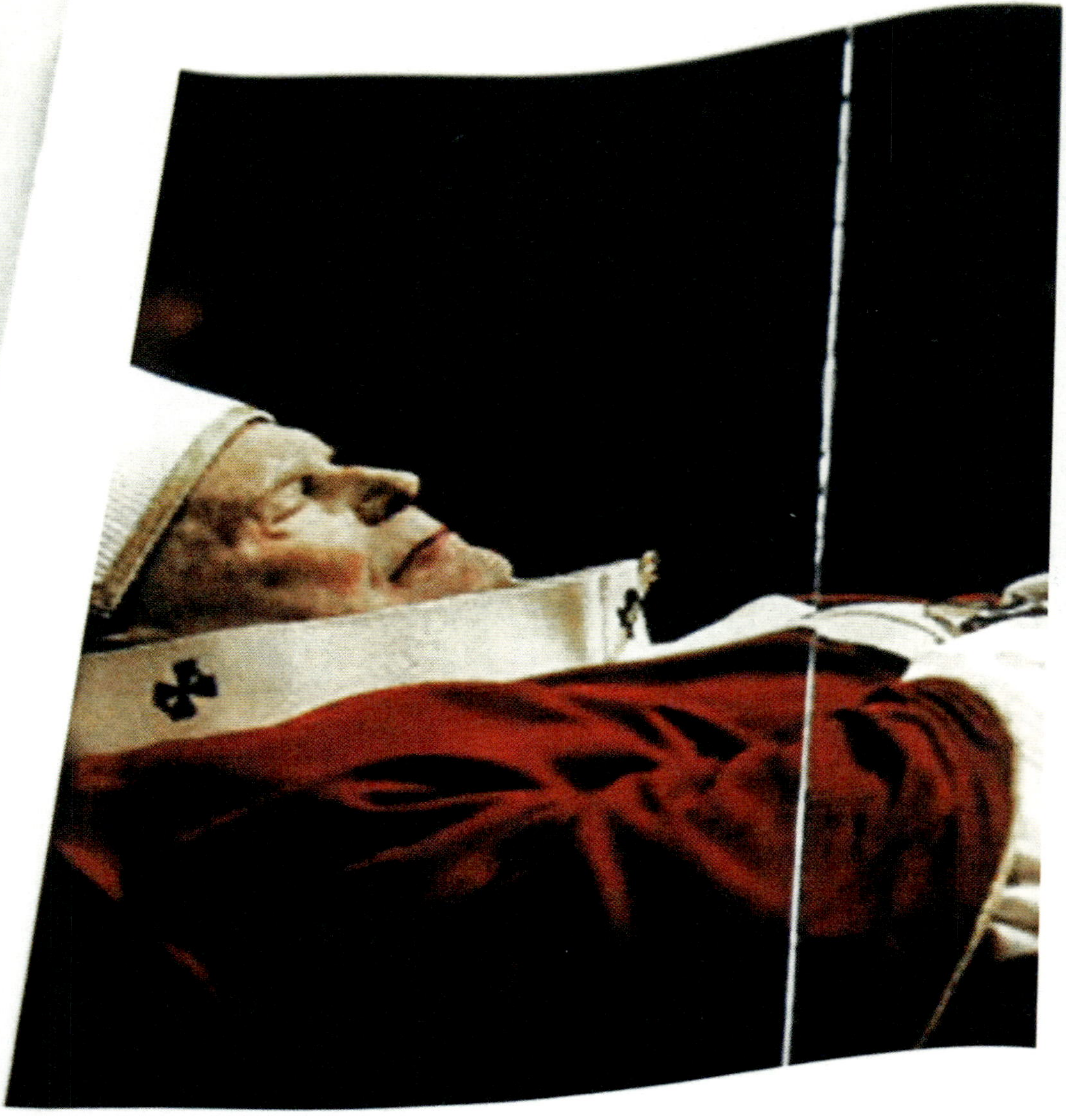

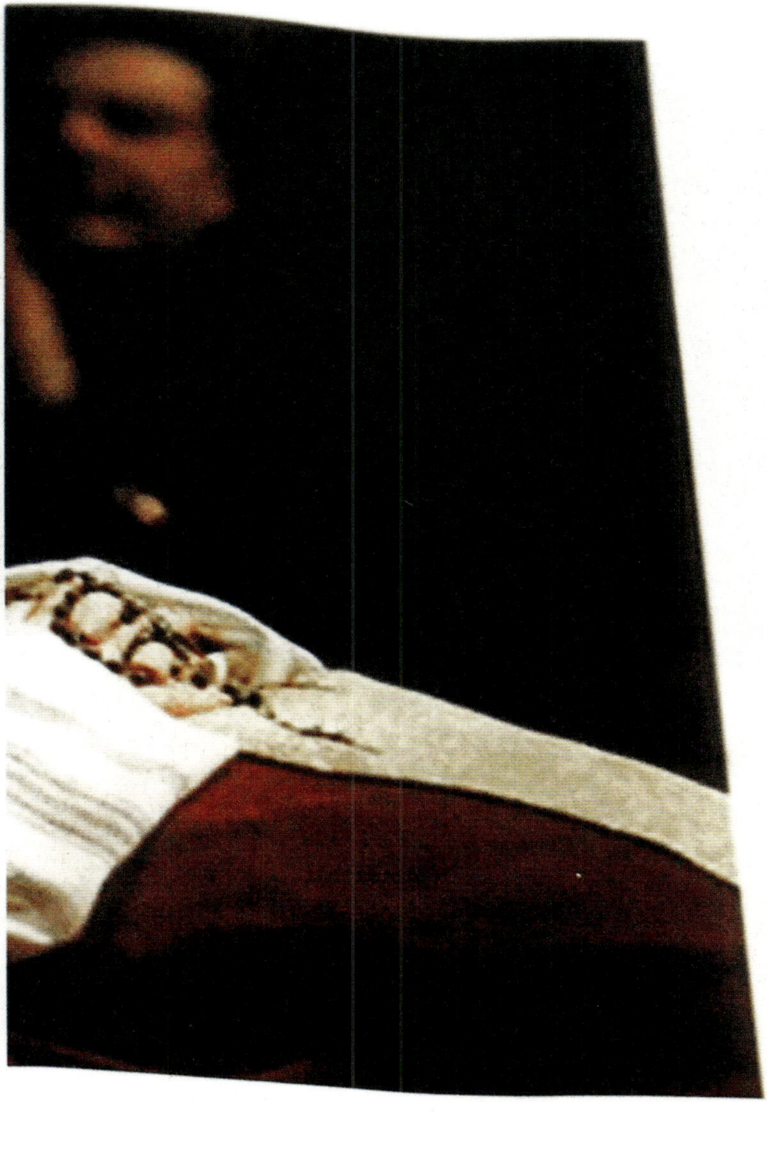

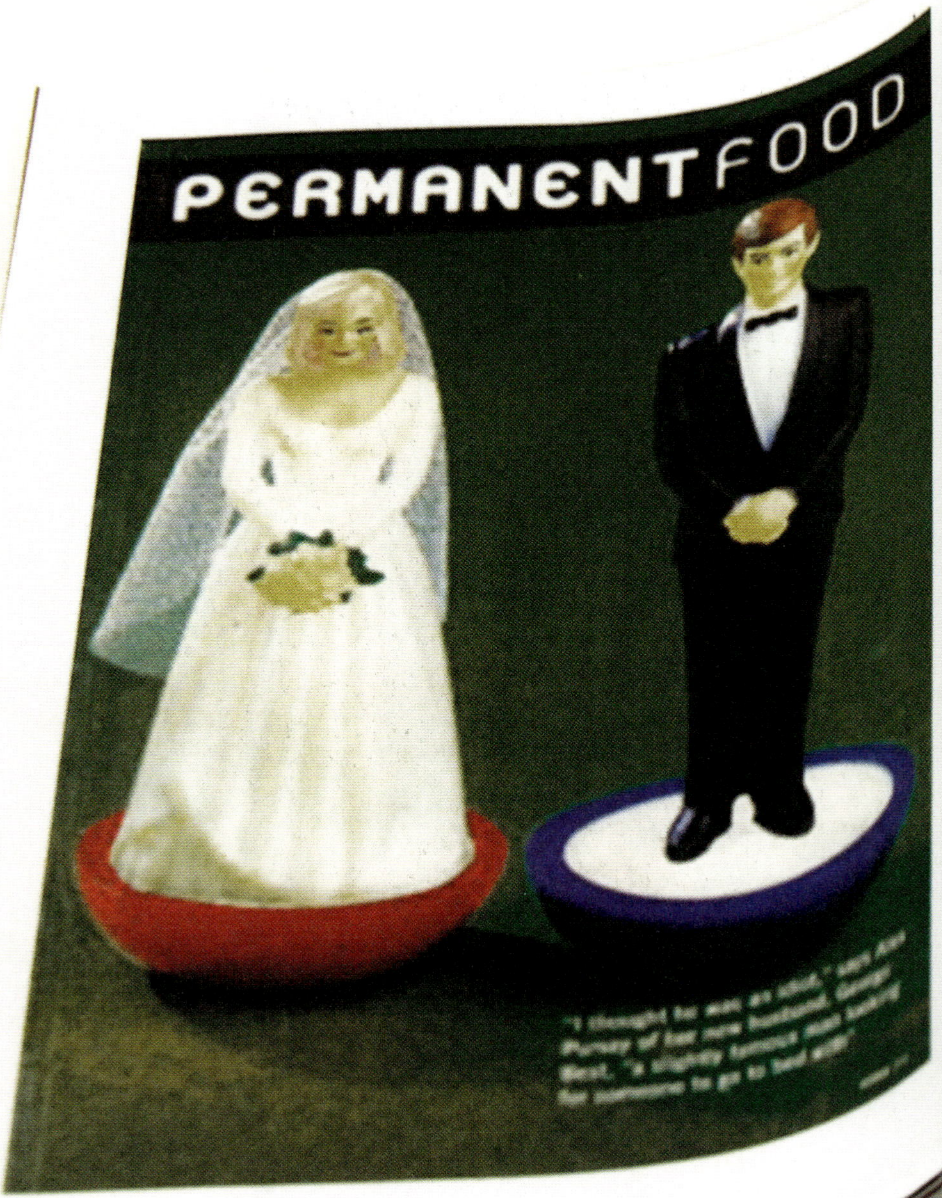

#3 right

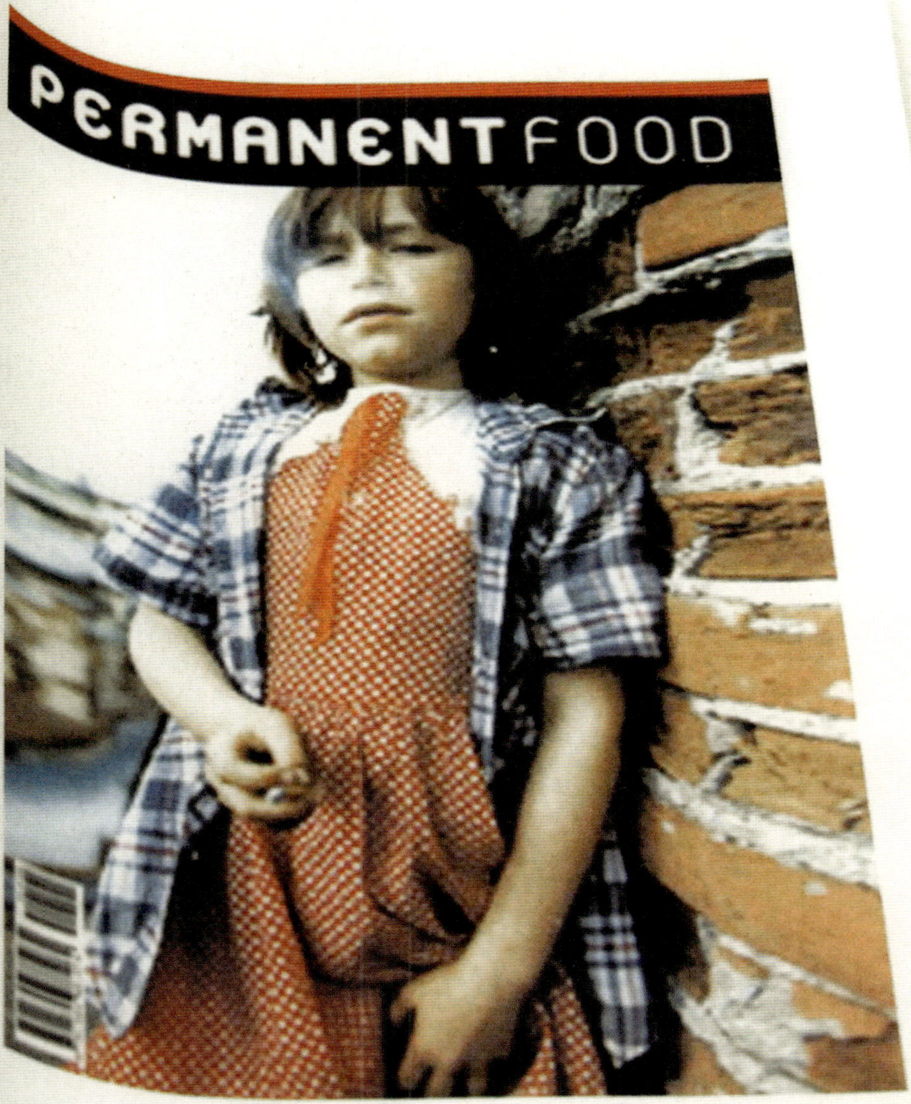

#11 left

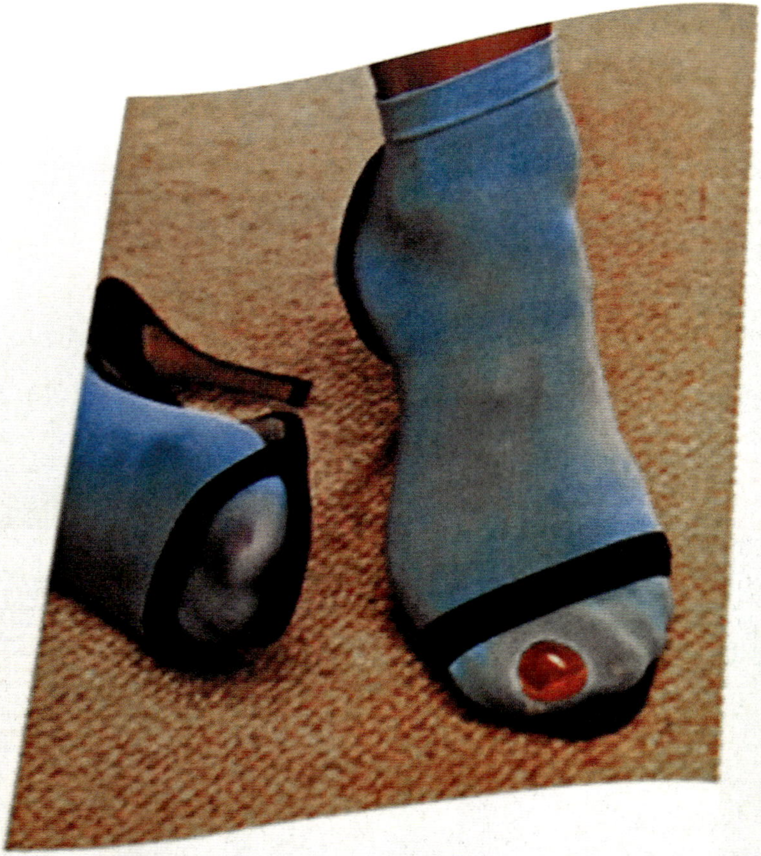

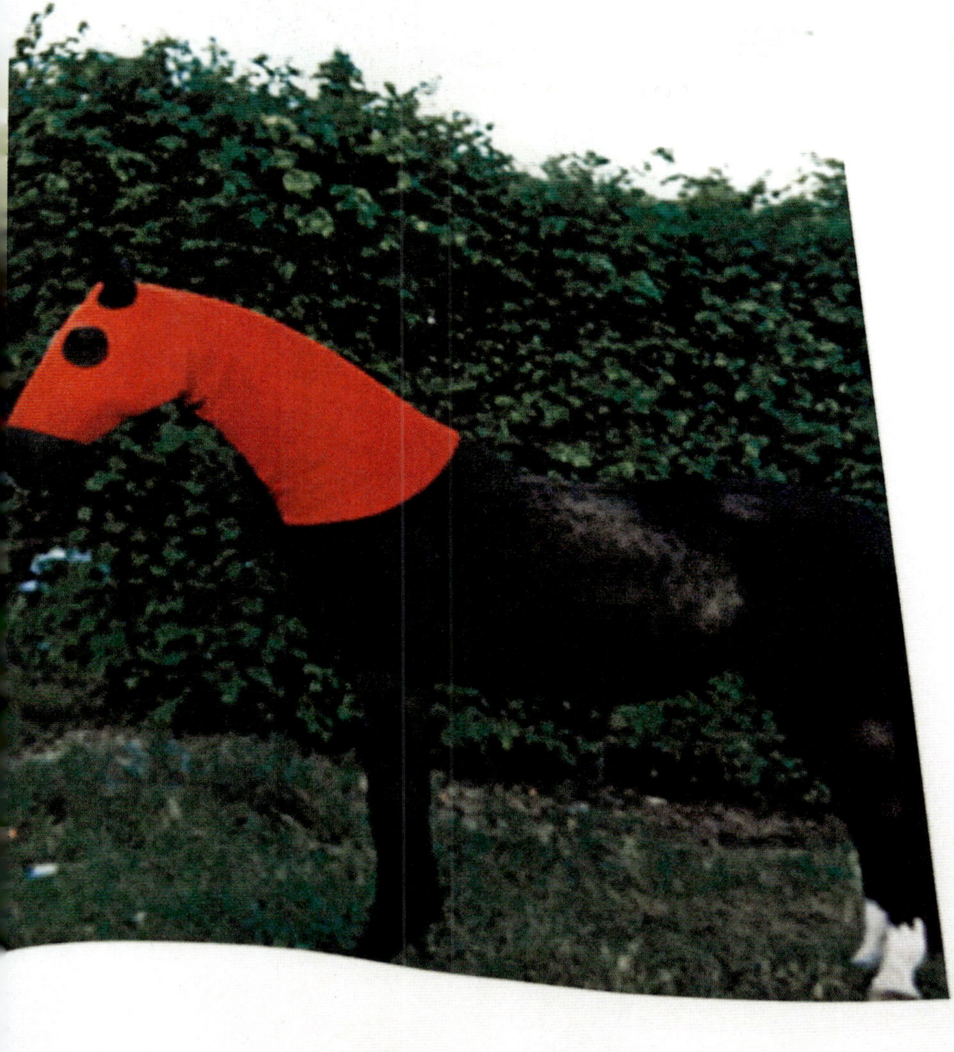

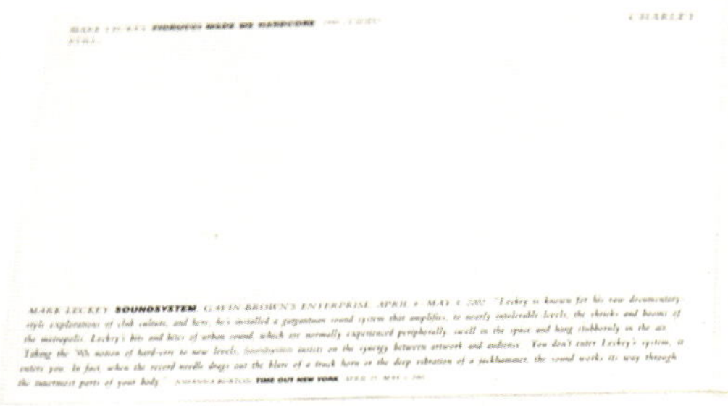

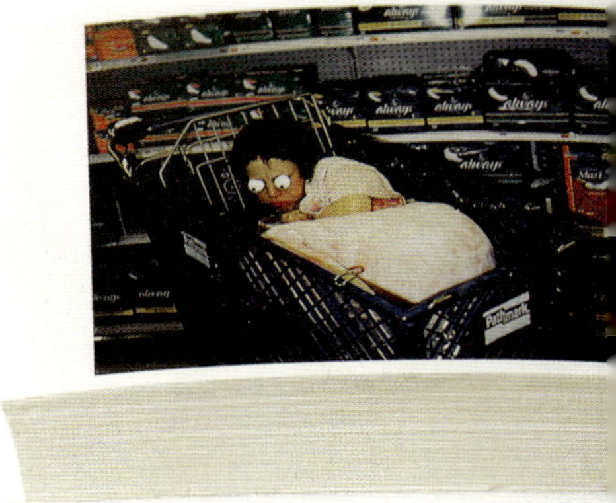

Five issues of *Charley* were published between 2001 and 2007. Issues no. 1, 2, 3, and 5 are on display here. Issue no. 4 was published on the occasion of the Berlin Biennial as *Checkpoint Charley* and is on view on the adjacent wall with material about that exhibition.

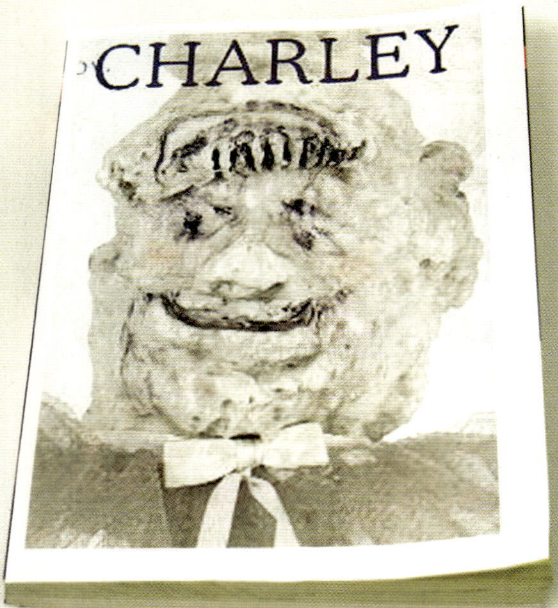

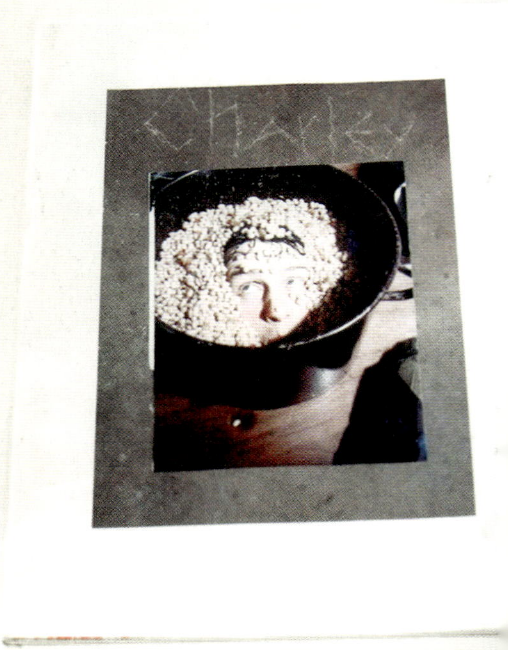

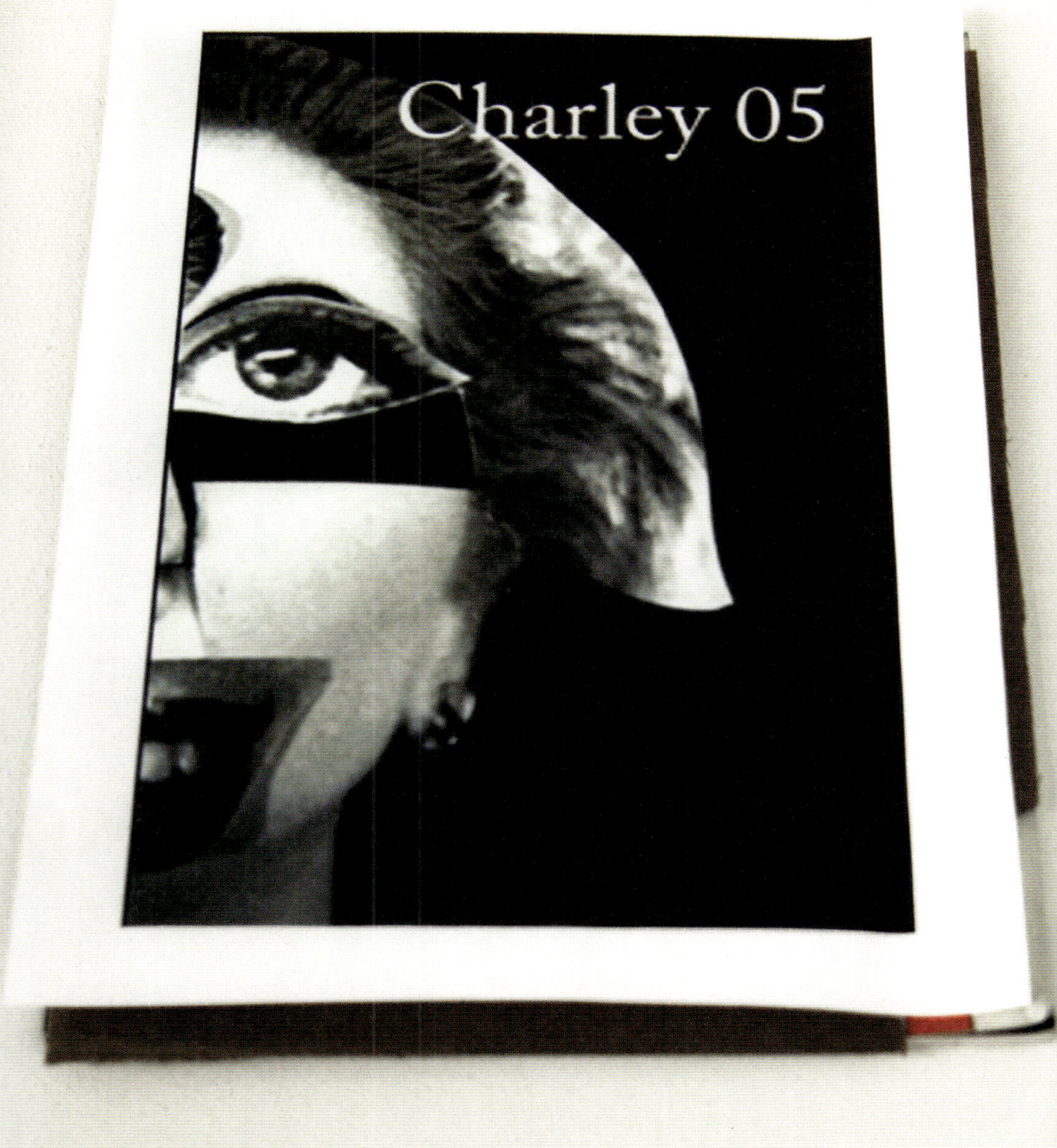
Charley 05

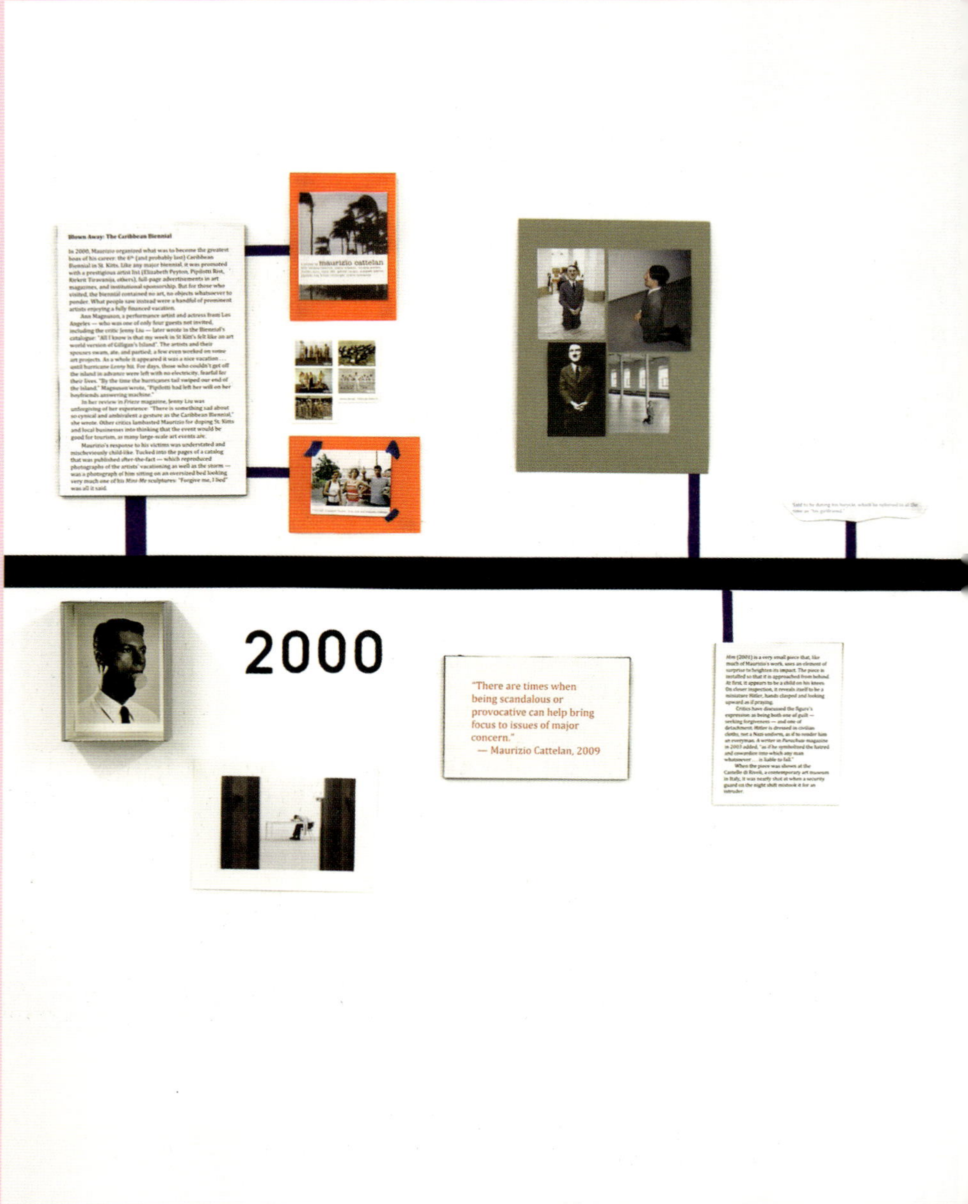
Blown Away: The Caribbean Biennial
In 2000, Maurizio organized what was to become the greatest hoax of his career: the 6th (and probably last) Caribbean Biennial in St. Kitts. Like any major biennial, it was promoted with a prestigious artist list (Elizabeth Peyton, Pipilotti Rist, Rirkrit Tiravanija, others), full-page advertisements in art magazines, and institutional sponsorship. But for those who visited, the biennial contained no art, no objects whatsoever to ponder. What people saw instead were a handful of prominent artists enjoying a fully financed vacation.
Ann Magnuson, a performance artist and actress from Los Angeles — who was one of only four guests not invited, including the critic Jenny Liu — later wrote in the Biennial's catalogue: "All I know is that my week in St Kitt's felt like an art world version of Gilligan's Island". The artists and their spouses swam, ate, and partied; a few even worked on some art projects. As a whole it appeared it was a nice vacation . . . until hurricane Lenny hit. For days, those who couldn't get off the island in advance were left with no electricity, fearful for their lives. "By the time the hurricanes tail swiped our end of the island," Magnuson wrote, "Pipilotti had left her will on her boyfriends answering machine."
In her review in Frieze magazine, Jenny Liu was unforgiving of her experience: "There is something sad about so cynical and ambivalent a gesture as the Caribbean Biennial," she wrote. Other critics lambasted Maurizio for duping St. Kitts and local businesses into thinking that the event would be good for tourism, as many large-scale art events are.
Maurizio's response to his victims was understated and mischeviously child-like. Tucked into the pages of a catalog that was published after-the-fact — which reproduced photographs of the artists' vacationing as well as the storm — was a photograph of him sitting on an oversized bed looking very much one of his Mini-Me sculptures: "Forgive me, I lied" was all it said.
2000
"There are times when being scandalous or provocative can help bring focus to issues of major concern."
— Maurizio Cattelan, 2009
Him (2001) is a very small piece that, like much of Maurizio's work, uses an element of surprise to heighten its impact. The piece is installed so that it is approached from behind. At first, it appears to be a child on his knees. On closer inspection, it reveals itself to be a miniature Hitler, hands clasped and looking upward as if praying.
Critics have discussed the figure's expression as being both one of guilt — seeking forgiveness — and one of detachment. Hitler is dressed in civilian cloths, not a Nazi uniform, as if to render him an everyman. A writer in Parachute magazine in 2003 added, "as if he symbolized the hatred and cowardice into which any man whatsoever . . . is liable to fall."
When the piece was shown at the Castello di Rivoli, a contemporary art museum in Italy, it was nearly shot at when a security guard on the night shift mistook it for an intruder.

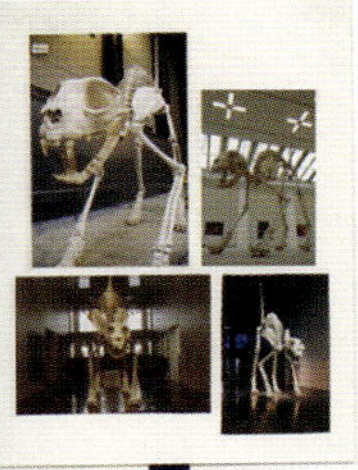

In 2004 Maurizio conceived of a piece specifically for the Piazza XXIV Maggio in Milan; it was commissioned by the Fondazione Nicola Trussardi. The installation consisted of three very life-like figures—made of wax—of children dressed in t-shirts, overalls and jeans, with bare, dirty feet. Their eyes open, hanging with ropes by their necks, from the oldest and largest oak tree in the city: an area that was heavily trafficked. The piece infuriated many people, most of whom thought it would give their children nightmares. One man, Franco De Benedetto, 44, was so incensed that on the morning of May 6, he climbed the tree and cut down two of the mannequins before falling from the tree himself. The two mannequins broke their hands and feet, he also suffered injuries. Later that year, despite the vandalism and the rage the piece evoked, the Contemporary Art Biennial brought the piece to Seville, Spain. However, only the undamaged figure was installed. Harold Szeemann, the curator, said it was a self-portrait of the artist.

Of Mice and Men: The Berlin Biennial

Five years after the Caribbean Biennial, Maurizio again played the role of biennial curator, this time with Ali Subotnick and Massimiliano Gioni in Berlin. The 4th Berlin Biennial was everything that the St. Kits' project was not: organized locally with the involvement of Berlin artists and residents (the curators lived in Berlin for a year to plan the event), and conceived as a means of showcasing artists' work. "We focused on the idea of planting solid roots and establishing connections with the city of Berlin and its region," Maurizio later said.

They kicked off the festival by starting a gallery, which they named The Gagosian Gallery — stealing the name from the powerful New York gallery that also has branches in New York, Los Angeles, and London. They produced six exhibitions, four of them in advance of the official start of the Biennial, before closing it down. In an interview in *Modern Painters* magazine in 2006, the curators commented, "For us, Gagosian is not only as important as the whole biennial. It's *our favorite child*." As for the real Gagosian's reaction, "we knew at the beginning that he was laughing. Then once he realized that we were doing a show every month, or so, he wasn't quite so happy about it."

The bulk of the Biennial opened later "without tricks" and the work of hundreds of artists. The idea was to make an exhibition about life as observed through the simplest elements. They selected a prominent Berlin street and invited artists to install their works in a variety of spaces along it. Curator Nancy Spector wrote that "visiting the exhibition, one [was] taken through a variety of settings and experiences, opening doors into forgotten buildings and hidden sites . . . apartments, offices, abandoned schools, churches . . . . At times it was about entering spaces where people live, seeing how they have chosen to live or how they were forced to by circumstances." The curators added, "We have constructed an exhibition that would unravel as a loose narrative."

When asked what he liked best about organizing the Berlin Biennial, Maurizio responded, "It was about getting to know the limits and potentials of institution and learning how to turn them into strengths."

2004

When invited by the Museum of Contemporary Art, Chicago, in 2004 to make a new sculpture, Maurizio responded with *Felix the Cat*, a 46-foot-long skeleton of the 1940's cartoon character. With its tail extended 26 feet in the air and its arched body position, the cat is clearly in attack mode.

The piece was inspired by *Sue* — the largest and most complete Tyrannosaurus Rex ever found — at the nearby Field Museum. *Sue* draws millions of visitors to the Field Museum every year. One can only assume that Maurizio hoped that *Felix*, which shares *Sue*'s dimensions, would be just as popular.

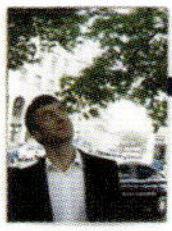

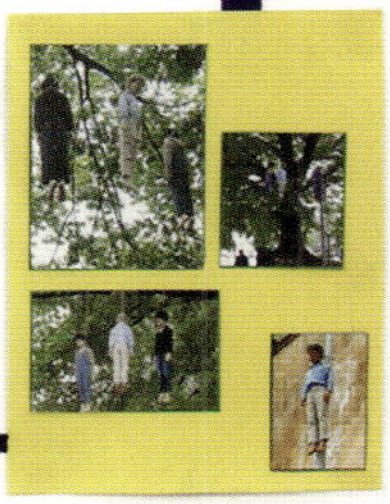

Maurizio was bestowed with an honorary degree in sociology by the university of Trento.

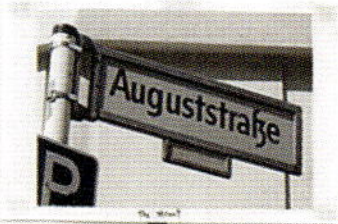

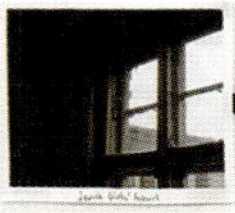

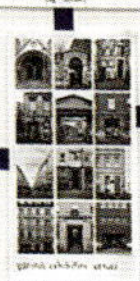

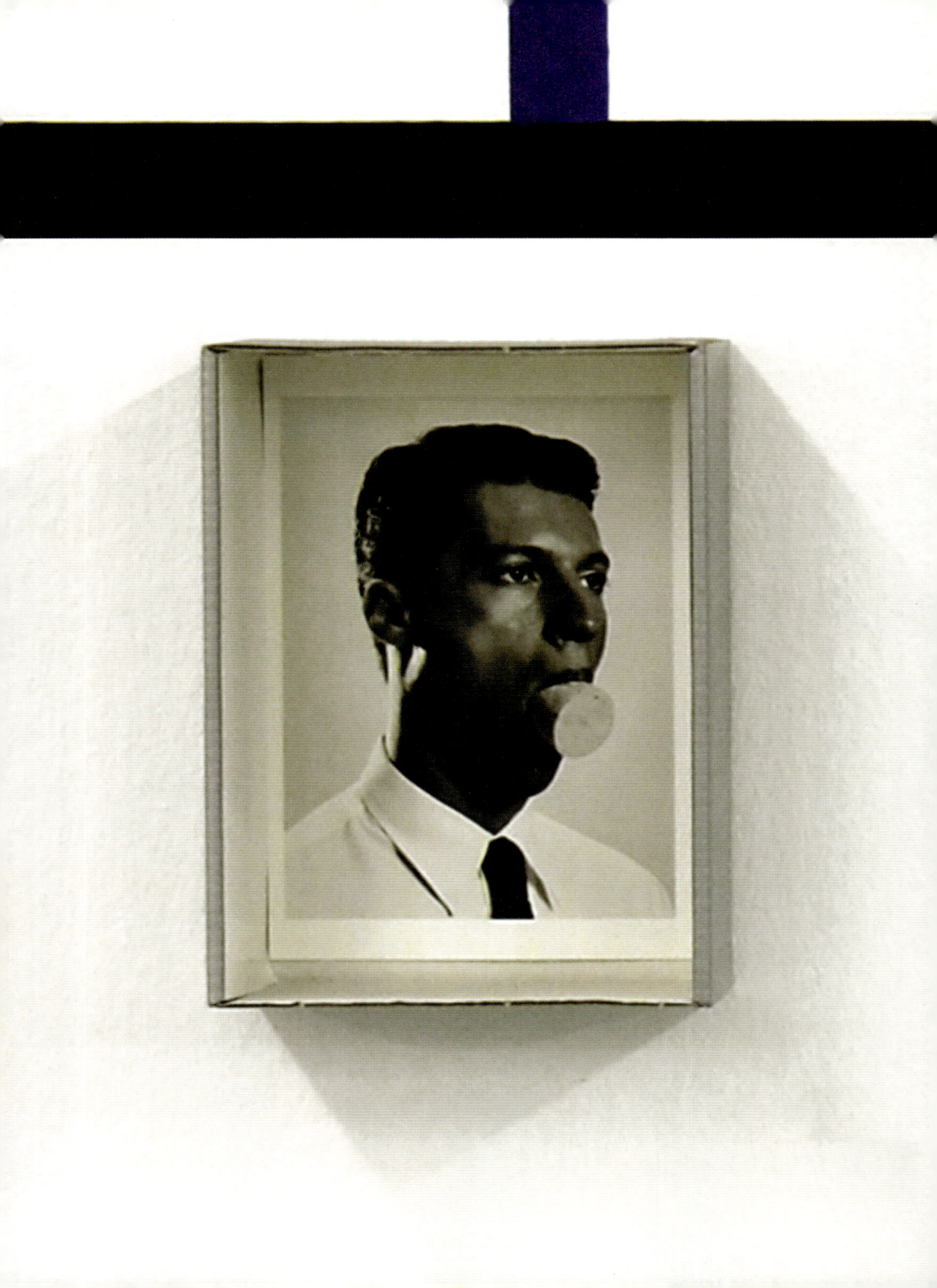

Blown Away: The Caribbean Biennial

In 2000, Maurizio organized, with the assistance of the curator Jens Hoffmann, what was to become the greatest hoax of his career: The 6th (and probably last) Caribbean Biennial in St. Kitts. Like any major biennial, it was promoted with a prestigious artist list (Elizabeth Peyton, Pipilotti Rist, Rirkrit Tiravanija, and others), full-page advertisements in art magazines, and institutional sponsorship. But for those who visited, they witnessed a biennial that contained no art, no objects whatsoever to ponder. What they saw instead, was a handful of prominent artists enjoying a fully financed vacation. Ann Magnuson, a performance artist and actress from Los Angeles—one of only four uninvited guests, including the critic Jenny Liu—later wrote about the experience: "All I know is that my week in St Kitts felt like an art world version of Gilligan's Island." The artists and their spouses swam, ate, and partied; a few worked on art projects. As a whole, it was an extravagant, elitest, nepotistic event. Yet the party continued as planned until Hurricane Lenny hit. For days, those who couldn't get off the island in advance were left with no electricity, fearful for their lives. "By the time the hurricane's tail swiped our end of the island," Magnuson wrote, "Pipilotti had left her will on her boyfriend's answering machine." In her review in *Frieze* magazine, Jenny Liu was unforgiving: "There is something sad about so cynical and ambivalent a gesture as the Caribbean Biennial." Other critics lambasted Maurizio for duping St. Kitts's local businesses into thinking that the event would be good for tourism. Maurizio's response to his "victims" was understated and mischievously child-like. Tucked into the pages of a catalogue that was published after-the-fact—which reproduced photographs of the artists vacationing as well as of the storm—was a photograph of Maurizio sitting on an oversized bed looking very much like one of his Mini-Me sculptures: "Forgive me, I lied," was all it read.

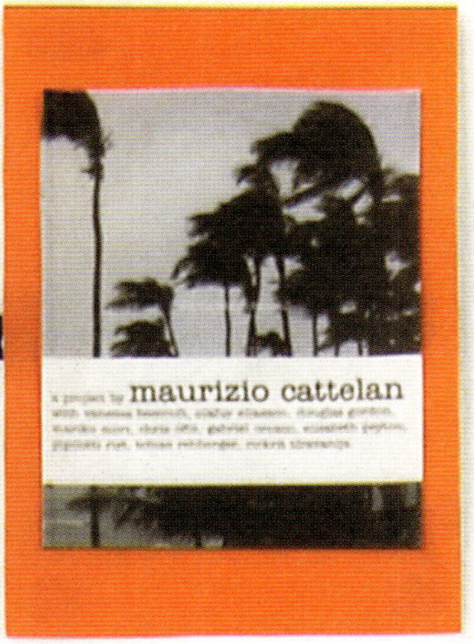

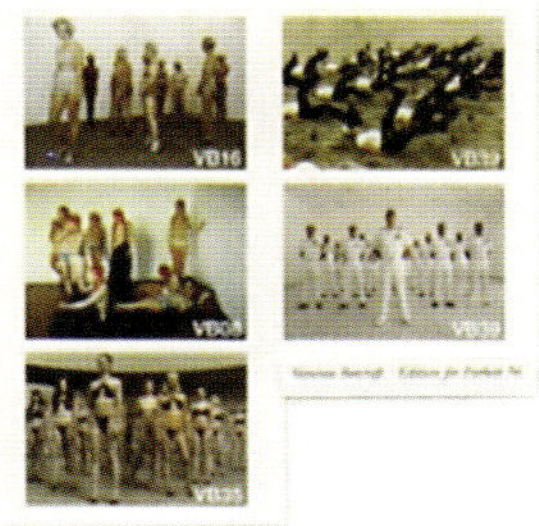

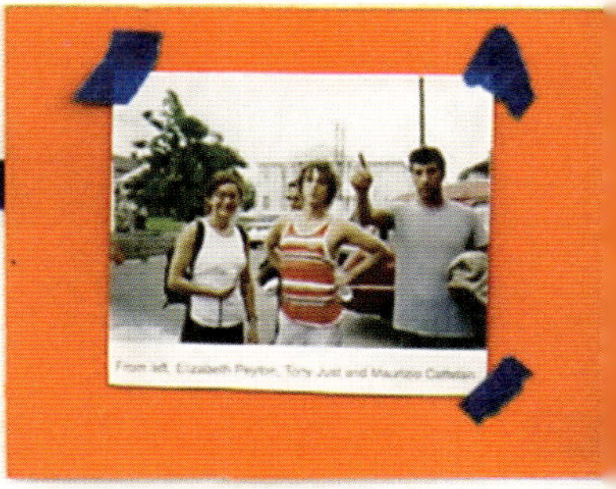

Said to be dating his bicycle, which he referred to as "his girlfriend."

"There are times when being scandalous or provocative can help bring focus to issues of major concern."
—Maurizio Cattlan, 2009

Him (2001) is a very small sculpture that, like much of Maurizio's work, uses an element of surprise to heighten its impact. The piece is installed so that it is approached from behind. At first, it appears to be a child on his knees but soon reveals itself to be a miniature Hitler, hands clasped and looking upward, as if praying.

Critics have discussed the figure's expression as being both one of guilt— seeking forgiveness—and one of detachment. Hitler is dressed in civilian clothes, not a Nazi uniform, "as if he symbolized the hatred and cowardice into which any man whatsoever . . . is liable to fall," a writer for *Parachute* magazine noted in 2003.

When the piece was shown at the Castello di Rivoli, a contemporary art museum in Italy, it was nearly shot at. A security guard, on the night shift, mistook it for an intruder.

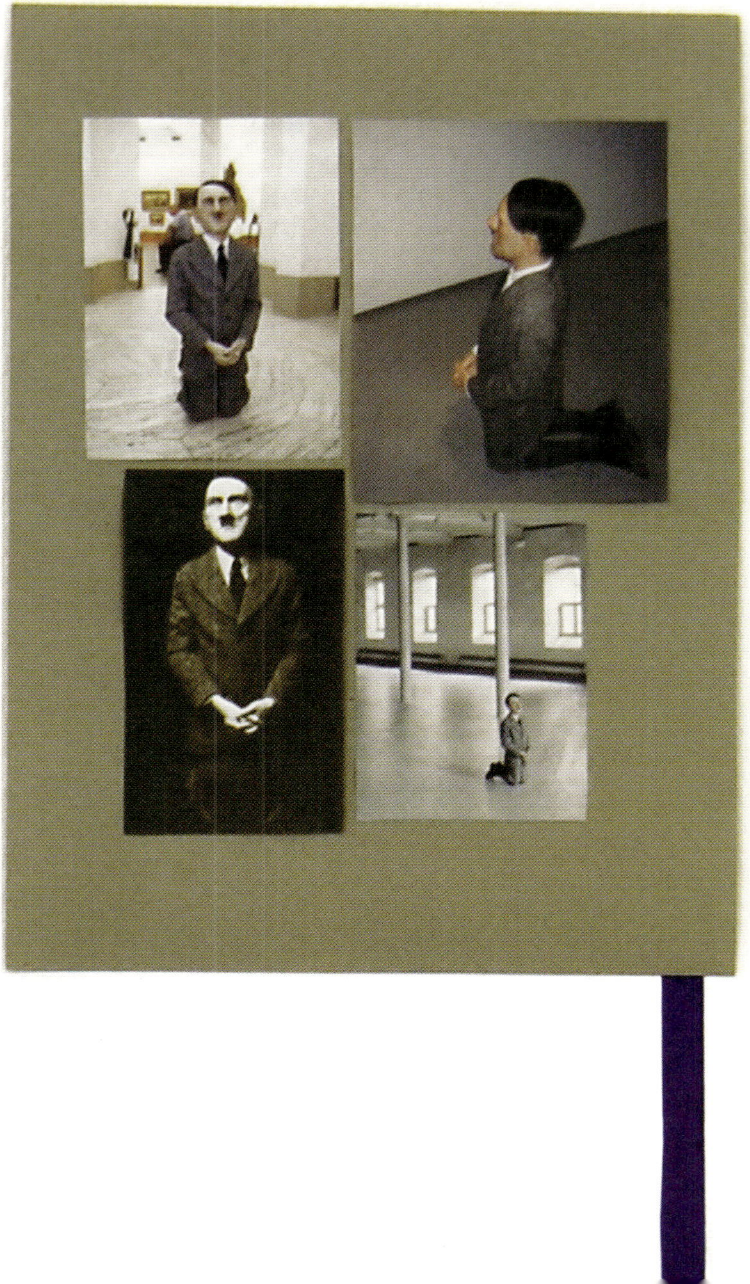

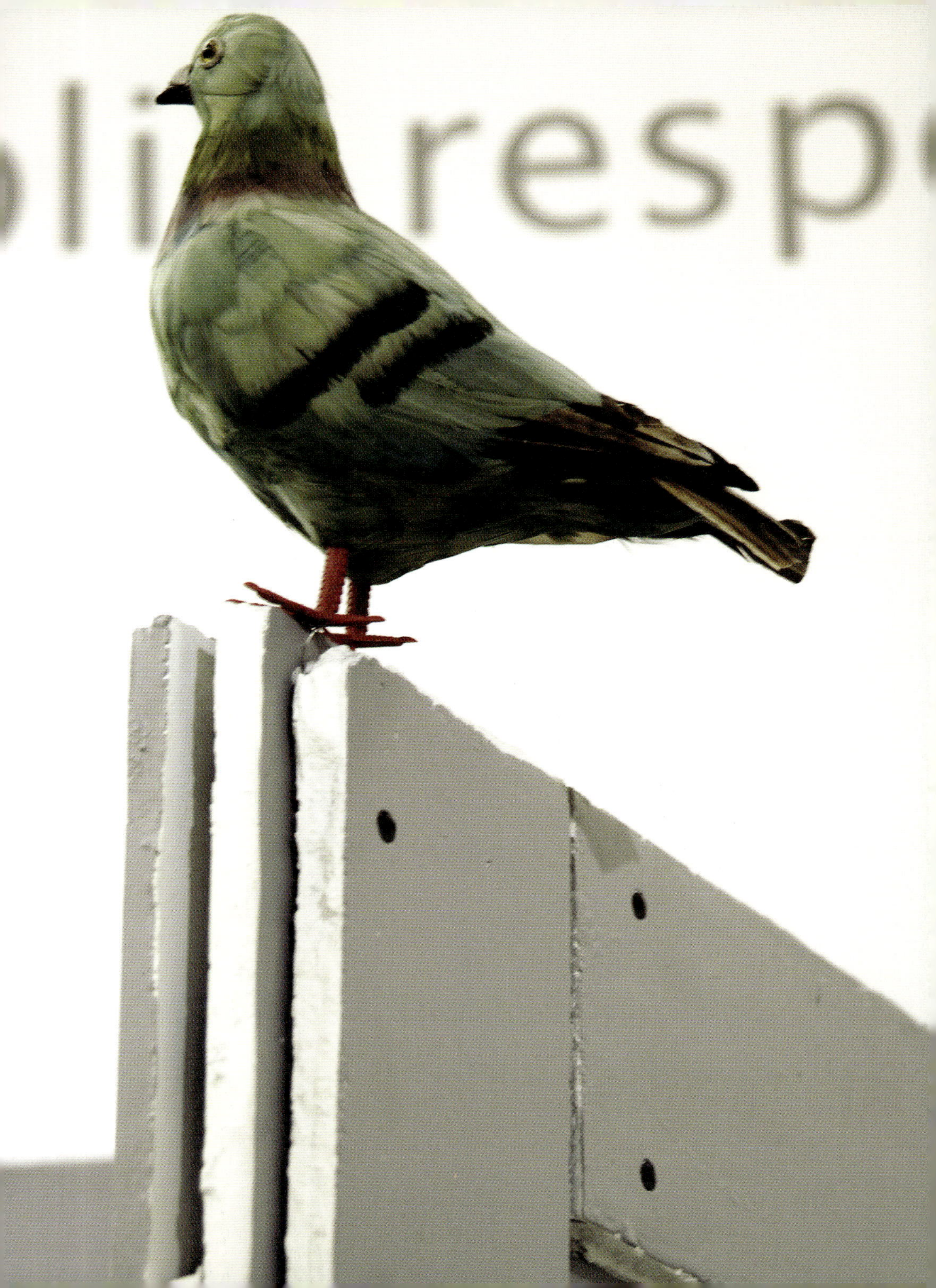

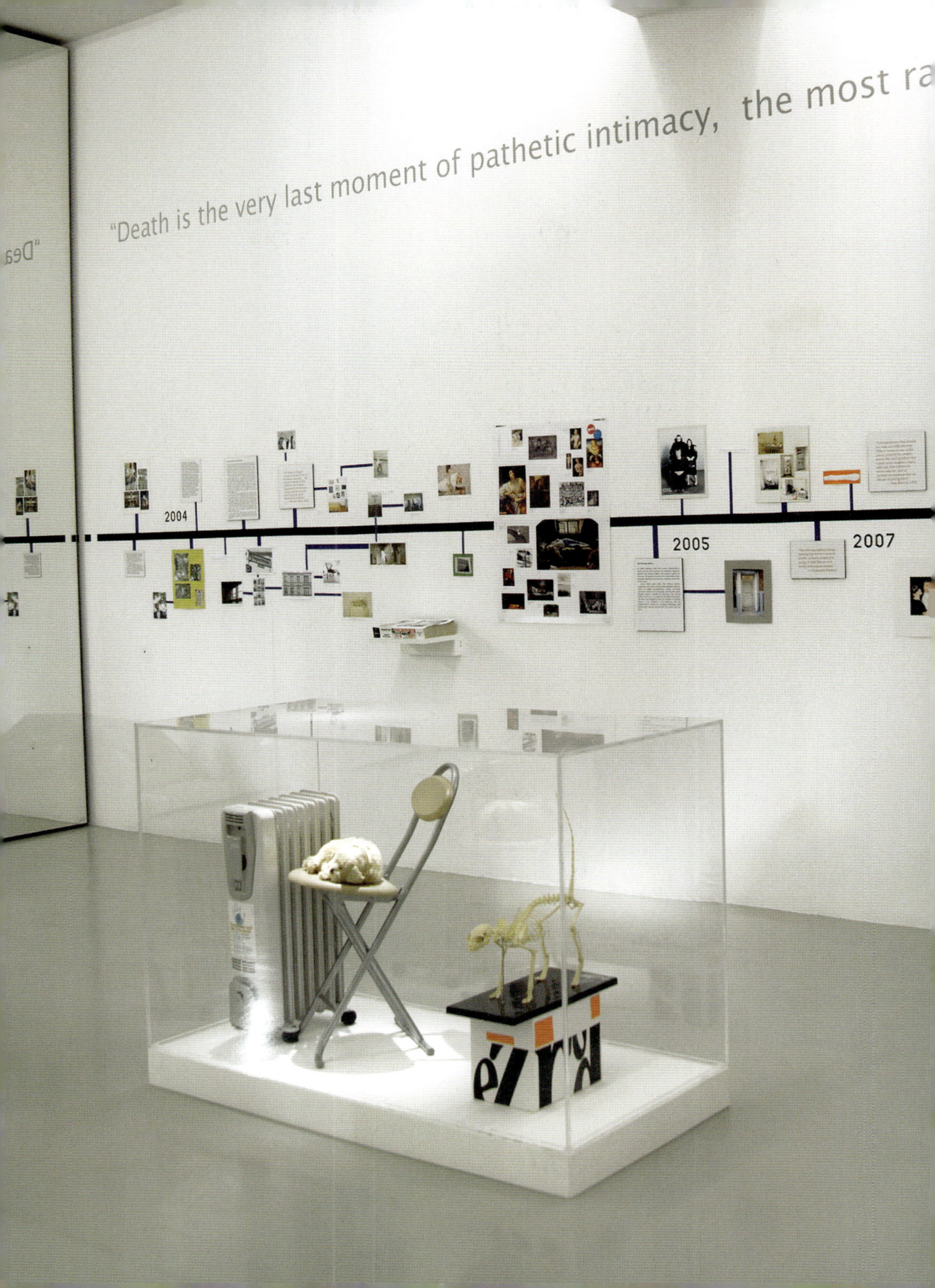
"Death is the very last moment of pathetic intimacy, the most ra
2004
2005
2007

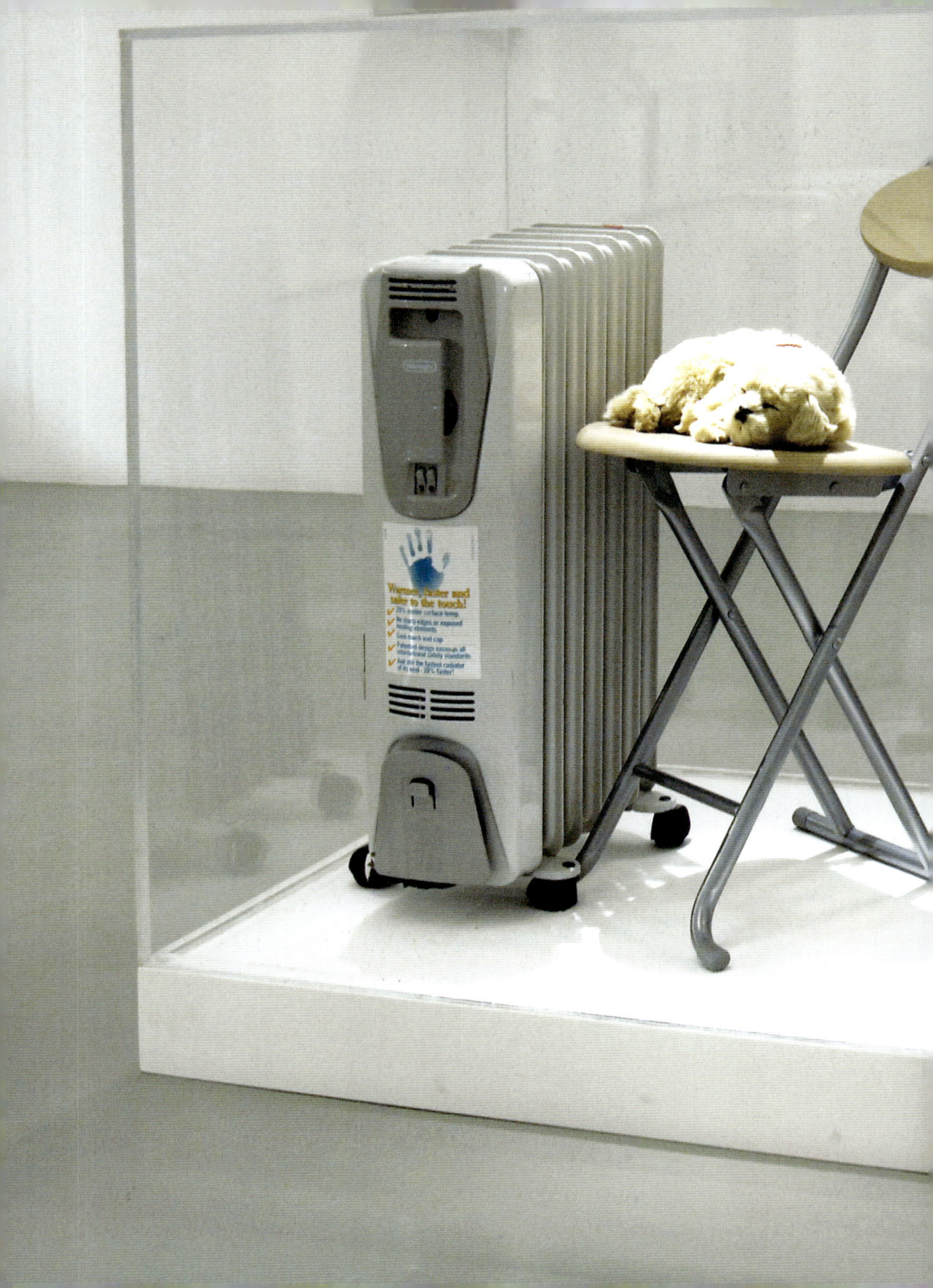

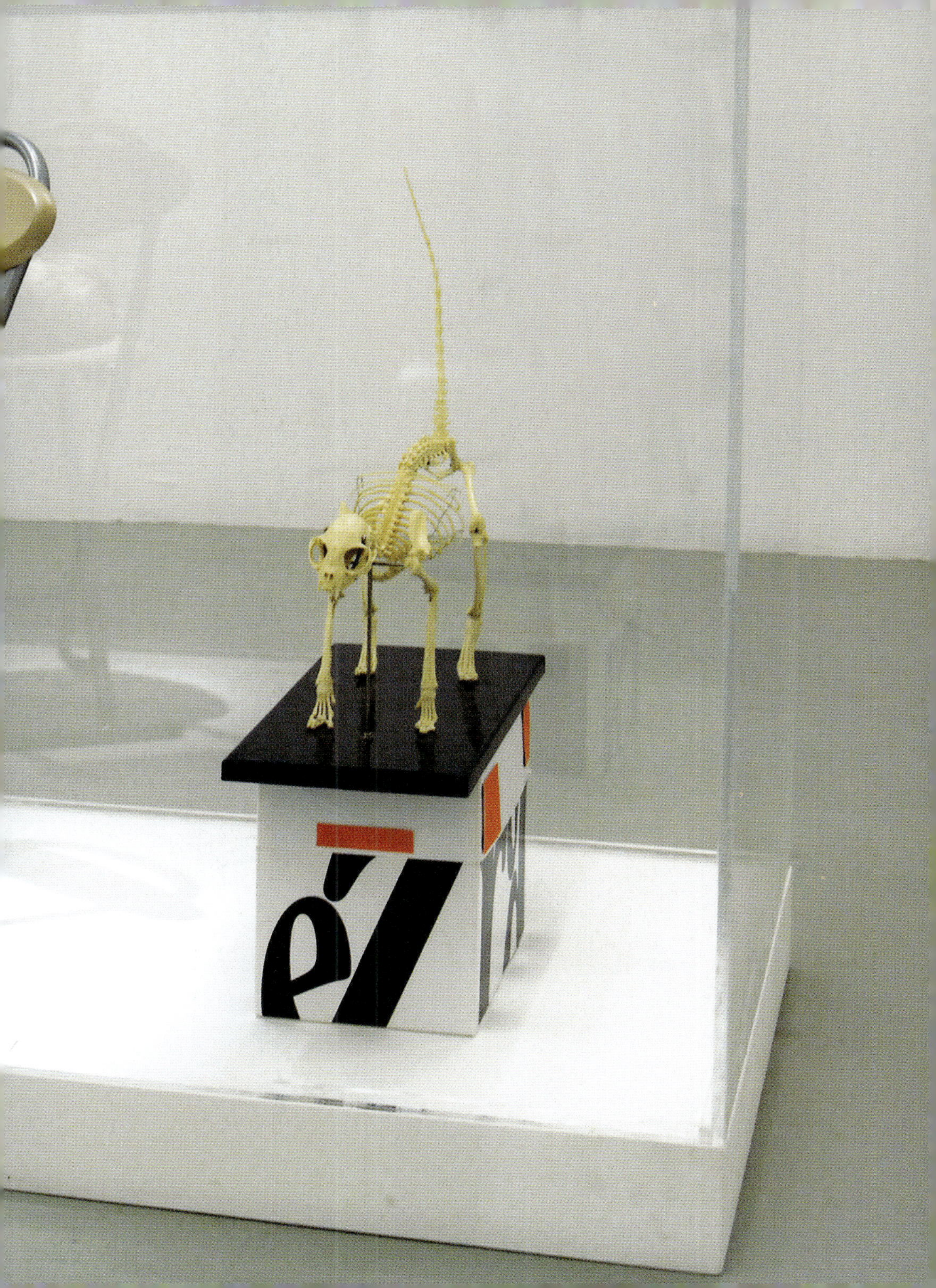

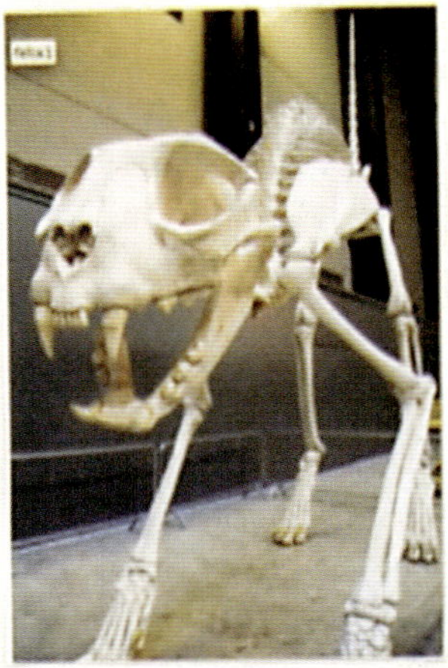

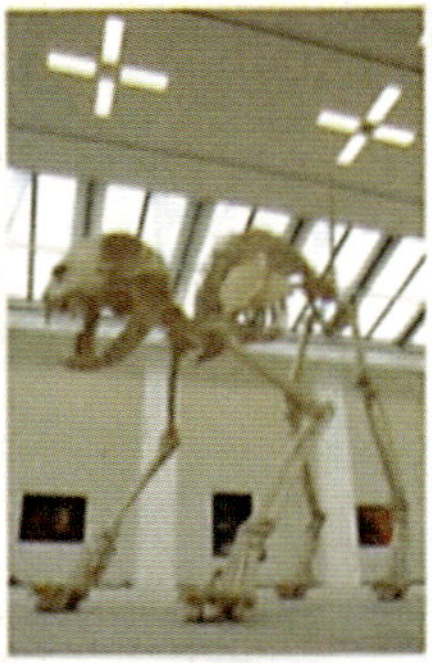

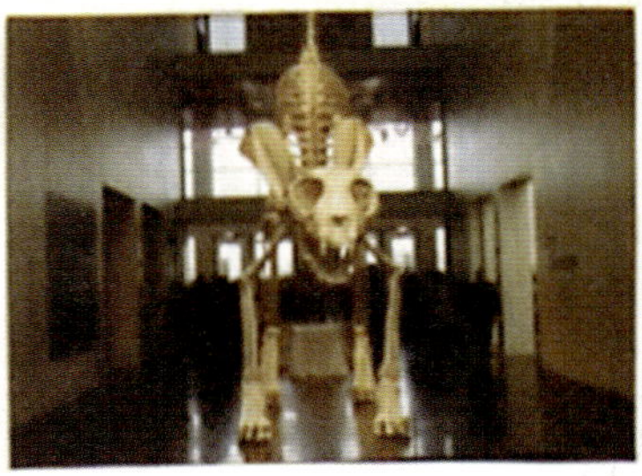

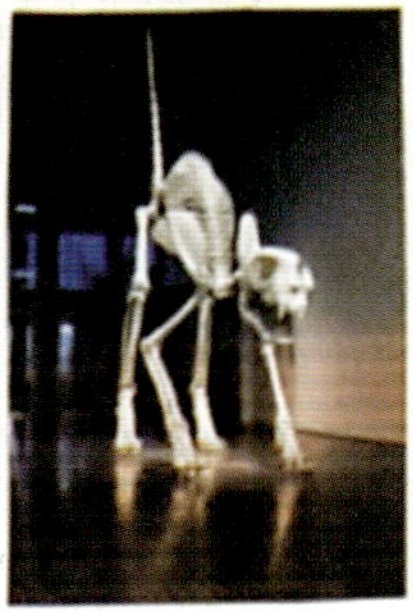

When invited by the Museum of Contemporary Art, Chicago to make a new sculpture, Maurizio responded with *Felix the Cat*, a 46-foot-long skeleton of the 1940s cartoon character. With its tail extended 26 feet in the air and its arched body position, the cat is clearly in attack mode.

The piece was inspired by Sue—the largest and most complete Tyrannosaurus Rex ever found—on view at the nearby Field Museum. Sue draws millions of visitors to the museum every year. One can only assume that Maurizio hoped that Felix, which shares Sue's dimensions, would be just as popular.

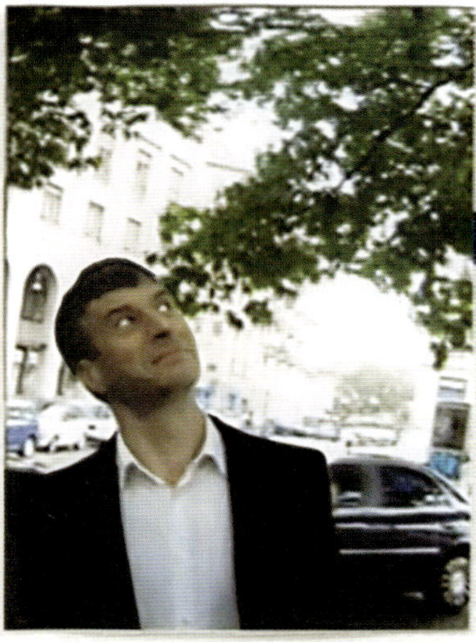

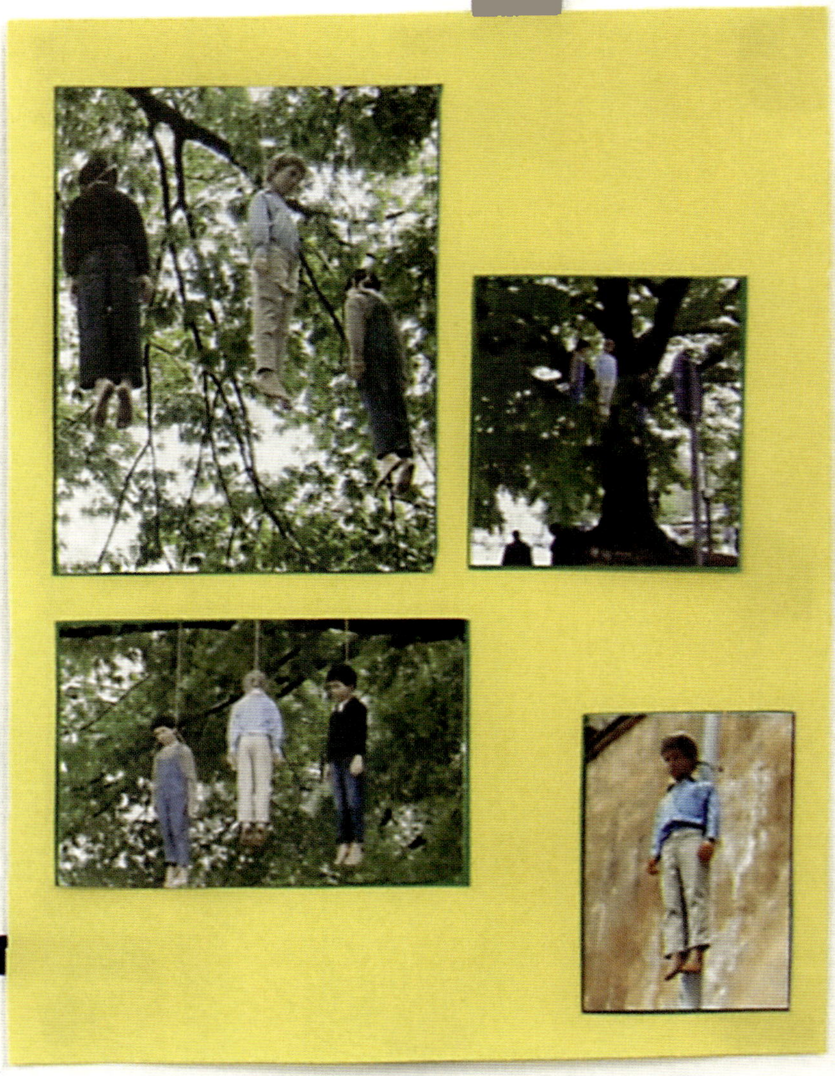

In 2004, Maurizio conceived of a piece for the Piazza XXIV Maggio in Milan that was commissioned by the Fondazione Nicola Trussardi. The installation consisted of three very lifelike figures made of wax—children dressed in t-shirts, overalls, and jeans, with bare, dirty feet. Their eyes were open and they hung by their necks from an old oak tree in a heavily trafficked area. The piece infuriated many people, most of whom thought it would give their children nightmares. One man, Franco De Benedetto, was so incensed that on the morning of May 6, he climbed the tree and cut down two of the mannequins before falling from the tree himself. The two mannequins broke their hands and feet; De Benedetto also suffered injuries. Later that year, despite the vandalism and the rage the piece evoked, the Contemporary Art Biennial in Seville, Spain, exhibited the undamaged figure. Harald Szeemann, the curator, said it was a self-portrait.

2004

Of Mice and Men: The Berlin Biennial

Five years after the Caribbean Biennial, Maurizio again played the role of biennial curator, this time with Ali Subotnick and Massimiliano Gioni in Berlin. The 4th Berlin Biennial was everything that the St. Kits' project was not: organized locally with the involvement of Berlin artists and residents (the curators lived in Berlin for a year to plan the event), and conceived as a means of showcasing artists' work. "We focused on the idea of planting solid roots and establishing connections with the city of Berlin and its region," Maurizio later said.

They kicked off the festival by starting a gallery, which they named The Gagosian Gallery — stealing the name from the powerful New York gallery that also has branches in New York, Los Angeles, and London. They produced six exhibitions, four of them in advance of the official start of the Biennial, before closing it down. In an interview in *Modern Painters* magazine in 2006, the curators commented, "For us, Gagosian is not only as important as the whole biennial, it's our favorite child." As for the real Gagosian's reaction, "we knew at the beginning that he was laughing. Then once he realized that we were doing a show every month, or so, he wasn't quite so happy about it."

The bulk of the Biennial opened later "without tricks" and the work of hundreds of artists. The idea was to make an exhibition about life as observed through the simplest elements. They selected a prominent Berlin street and invited artists to install their works in a variety of spaces along it. Curator Nancy Spector wrote that "visiting the exhibition, one [was] taken through a variety of settings and experiences, opening doors into forgotten buildings and hidden sites . . . apartments, offices, abandoned schools, churches . . . . At times it was about entering spaces where people live, seeing how they have chosen to live or how they were forced to by circumstances." The curators added, "We have constructed an exhibition that would unravel as a loose narrative."

When asked what he liked best about organizing the Berlin Biennial, Maurizio responded, "It was about getting to know the limits and potentials of institution and learning how to turn them into strengths."

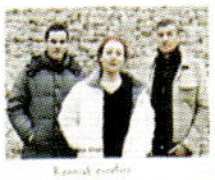

"The Biennial's biggest successes stemmed from its traditional approach. . . . the narrative structure of the exhibition, the in-depth engagement with the local context, and the care with which the works were selected and presented."
— Michael Conner, 2006

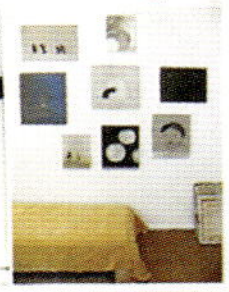

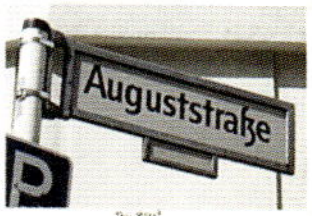

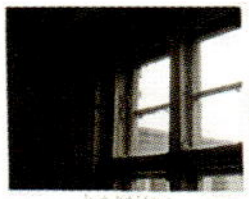

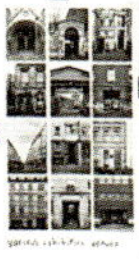

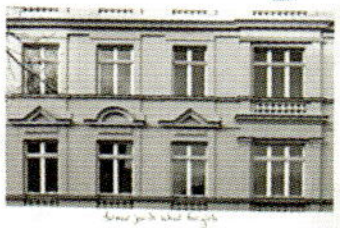

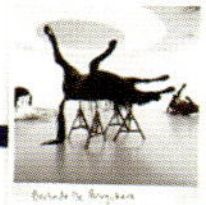

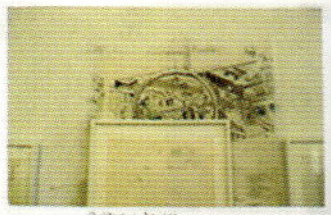

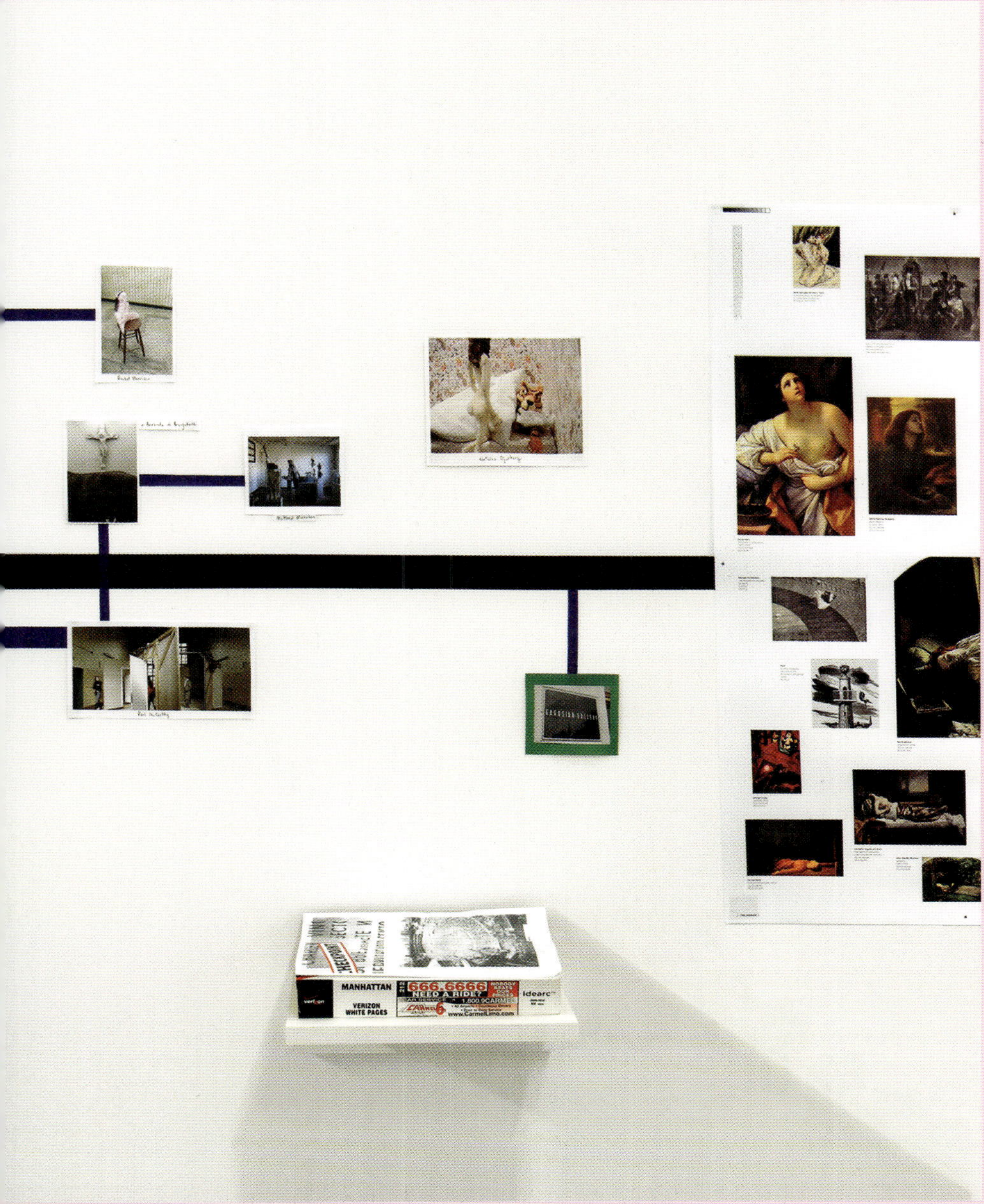
MANHATTAN
VERIZON
WHITE PAGES
666-6666
NEED A RIDE?
1.800.9CARMEL
www.CarmelLimo.com
idearc

Of Mice and Men: The Berlin Biennial

Five years after the Caribbean Biennial, Maurizio again played the role of biennial curator, this time with Ali Subotnick and Massimiliano Gioni in Berlin. The 4th Berlin Biennial was everything that the St. Kitts project was not. "We focused on the idea of planting solid roots and establishing connections with the city of Berlin and its region," Maurizio later said. The curators lived in Berlin for a year, and conceived of the event as a means of showcasing local artists' work.

They kicked off the festival by starting a gallery, which they named the Gagosian Gallery—stealing the moniker from the powerful New York gallery with branches in Los Angeles, London, and elsewhere. They produced six exhibitions, four of them in advance of the official start of the biennial, before closing the gallery down. In an interview for *Modern Painters* magazine in 2006, the curators commented, "For us, Gagosian is not only as important as the whole biennial, it is our favorite child." As for the real [Larry] Gagosian's reaction, the trio stated, "We knew at the beginning he was laughing, but once he realized that we were doing a show every month or so, he wasn't quite so happy."

The bulk of the biennial opened later "without tricks" and with the work of hundreds of artists. The idea was to make an exhibition about life as observed through the simplest elements. The curators selected a prominent Berlin street and invited the artists to install their works in selected spaces along it. Curator Nancy Spector wrote that, "visiting the exhibition, one [was] taken through a variety of settings and experiences, opening doors into forgotten buildings and hidden sites . . . apartments, offices, abandoned schools, churches. . . . At the time, it was about entering spaces where people live, seeing how they have chosen to live or how they were forced to by circumstances." Maurizio and his gang added, "We have constructed an exhibition that would unravel as a loose narrative."

When asked what he liked best about organizing the Berlin Biennial, Maurizio said, "It was about getting to know the limits and potentials of institutions and learning how to turn them into strengths."

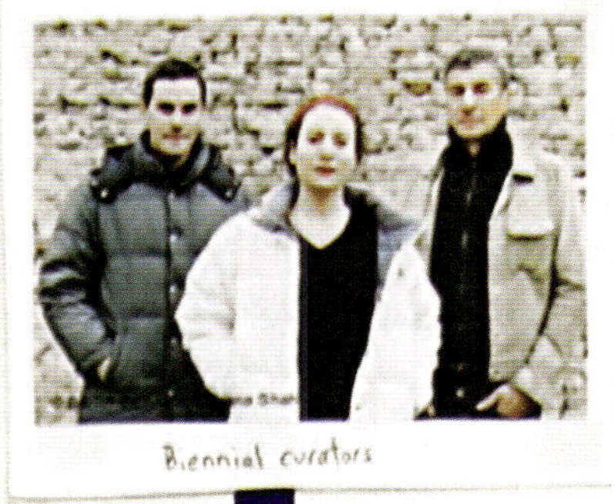

"The Biennial's biggest successes stemmed from its traditional approach . . . the narrative structure of the exhibition, the in-depth engagement with the local context, and the care with which the works were selected and presented."

—Michael Conner, 2006

Maurizio was bestowed with an honorary degree in sociology by the University of Trento.

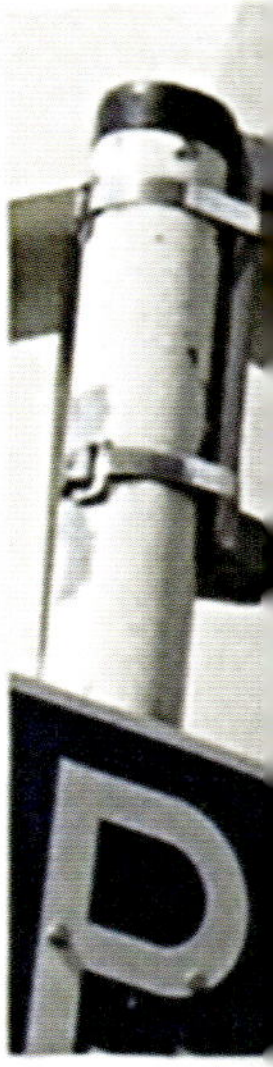

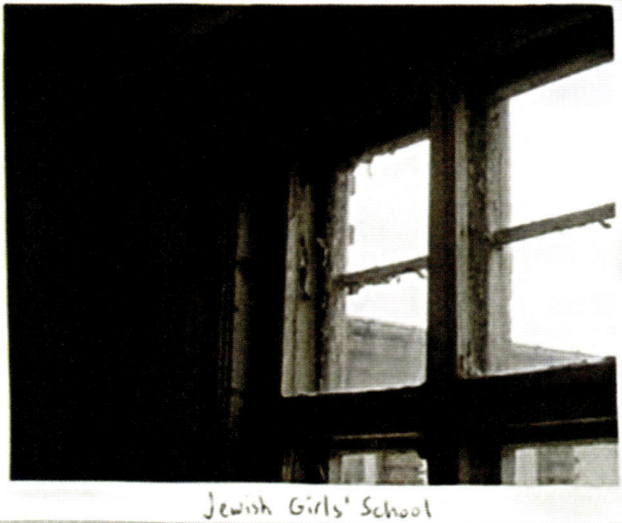

Jewish Girls' School

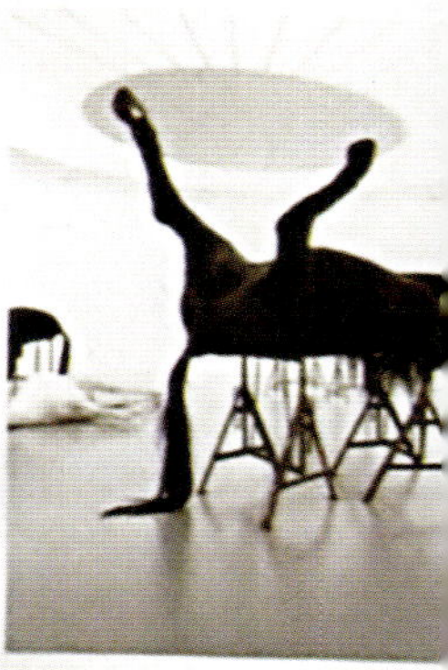

Berlinde De Bruyckere

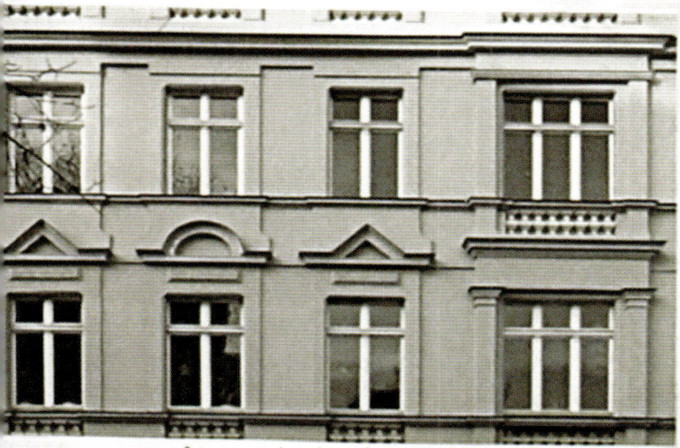

former Jewish school for girls

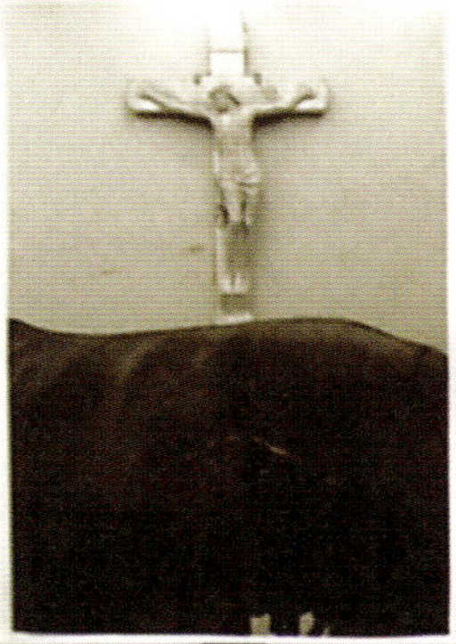

← Berlinde de Bruyckere

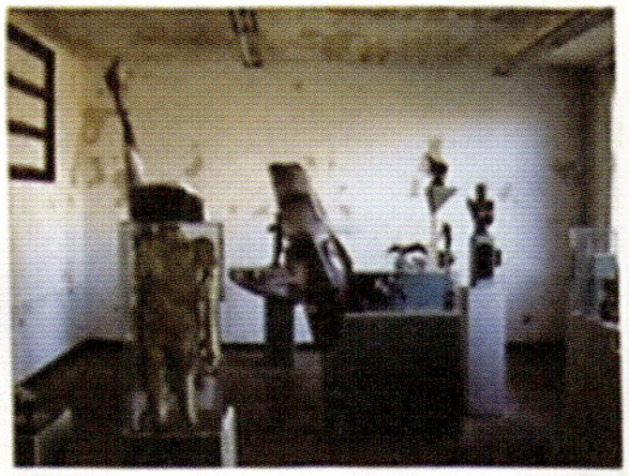

Matthew Monahan

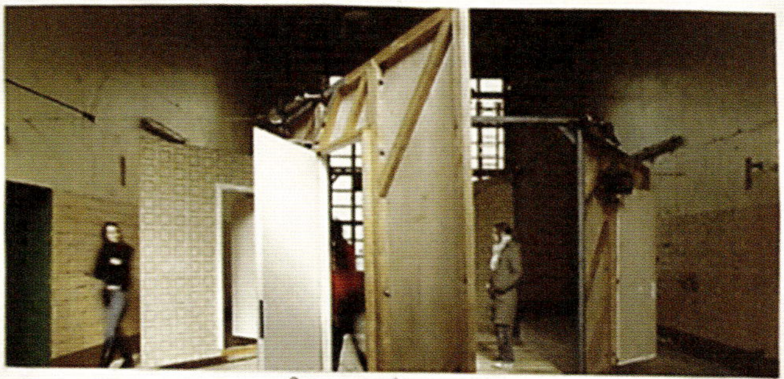

Paul McCarthy

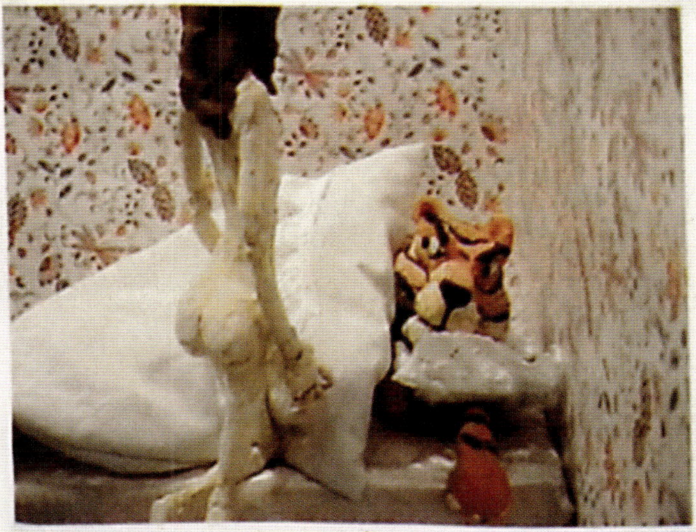

Natalie Djurberg

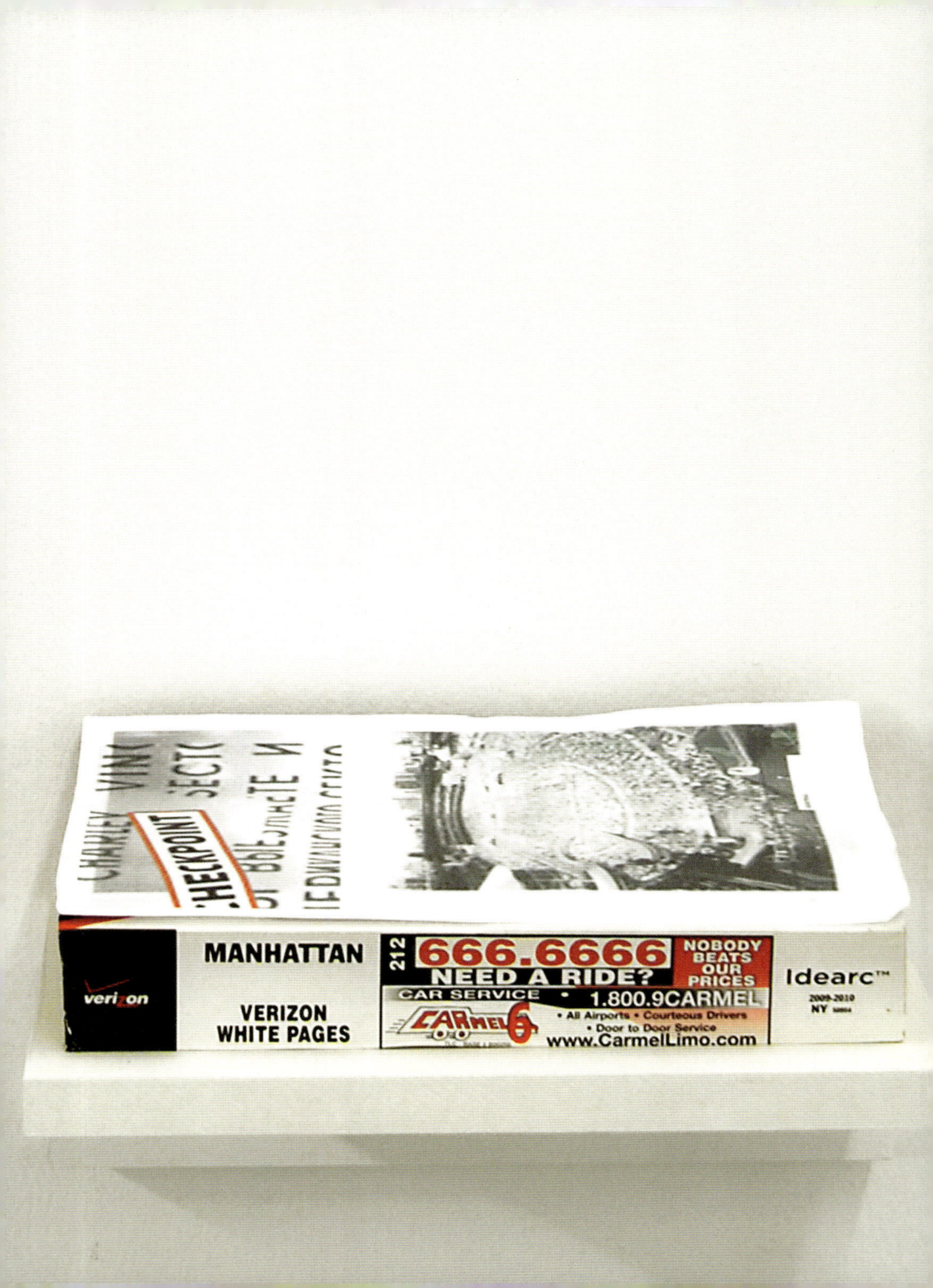
verizon
MANHATTAN
VERIZON
WHITE PAGES
212
666.6666
NEED A RIDE?
NOBODY
BEATS
OUR
PRICES
CAR SERVICE
1.800.9CARMEL
• All Airports • Courteous Drivers
• Door to Door Service
www.CarmelLimo.com
Idearc™
2009-2010
NY

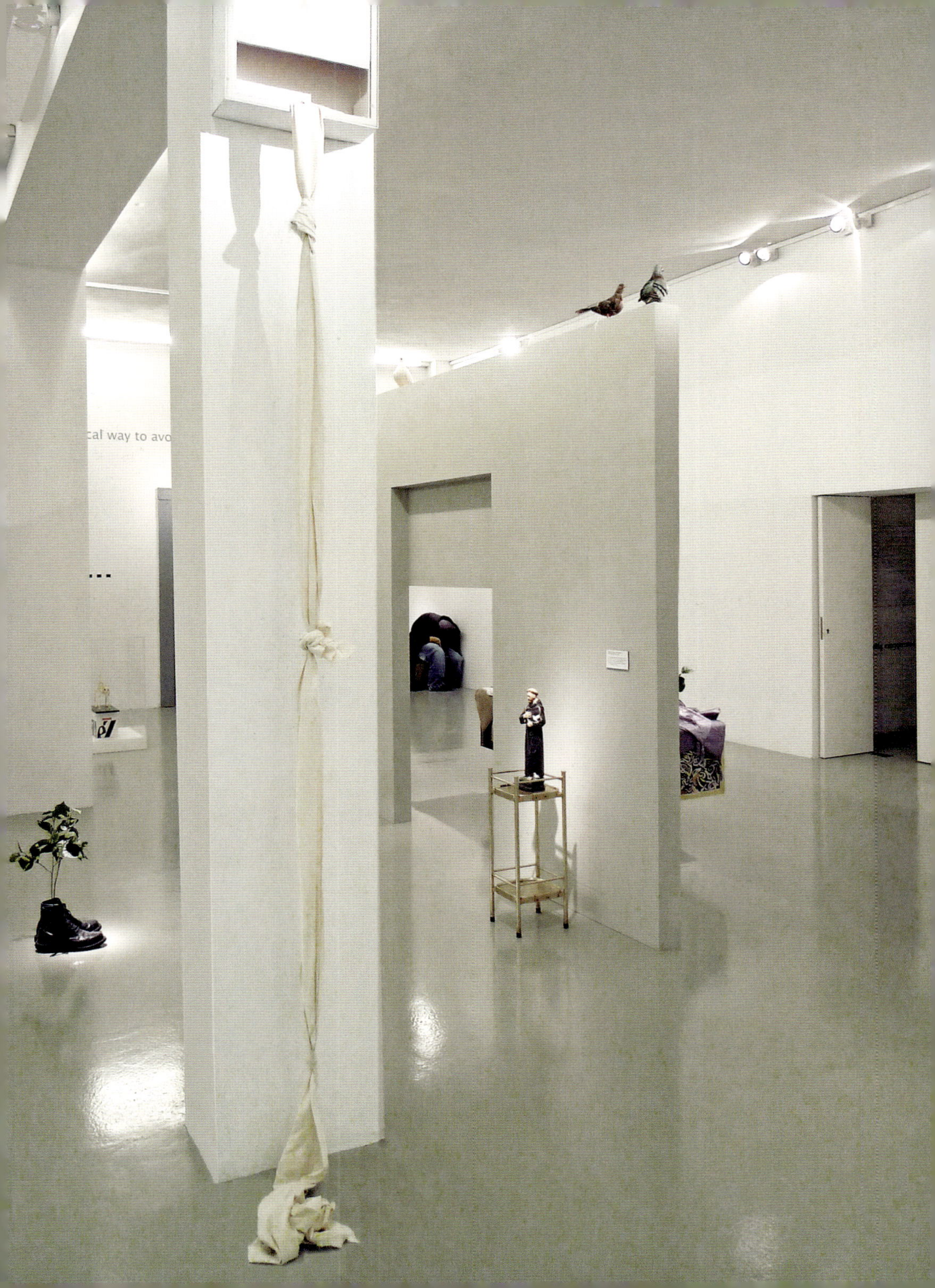

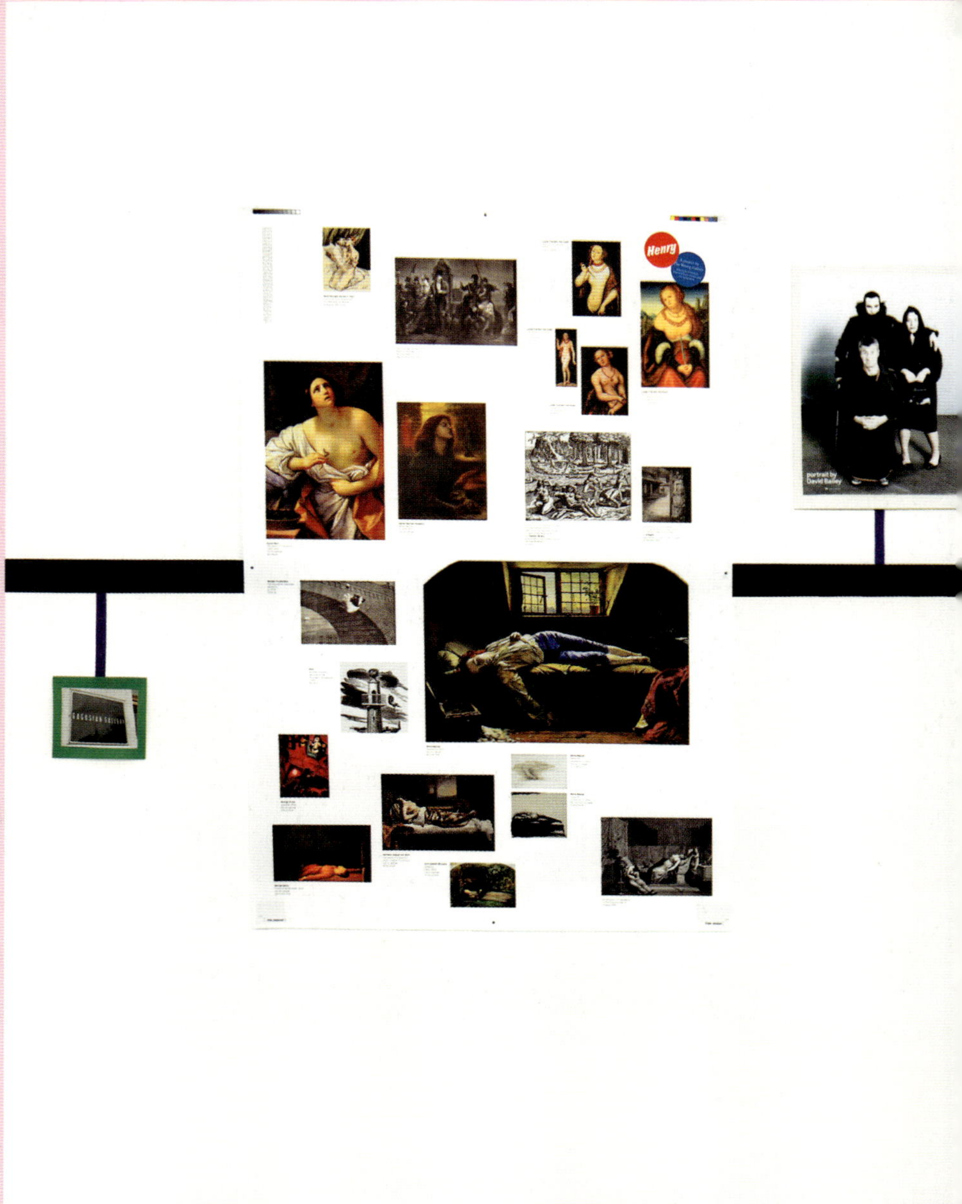
Henry
portrait by
David Bailey

2005

The Wrong Gallery

In 2002, together with the curators Massimiliano Gioni and Ali Subotnick, Maurizio started The Wrong Gallery, the smallest gallery in Chelsea (New York City). It consisted of a locked glass door through which one peered into a shallow, closet-like, white space, most assuredly reflecting back on "Peep Show."

From 2002 until 2005, The Wrong Gallery organized over forty unimpressive projects with an array of highly accomplished artists, including Elizabeth Peyton, Paul McCarthy, and the late Jason Rhoades. After vacating its original location, the gallery lived on as an itinerant project: The door was shipped to the Tate Modern in London where it was installed, with the collaborators curating exhibitions in it and doing other special projects like the poster you see here.

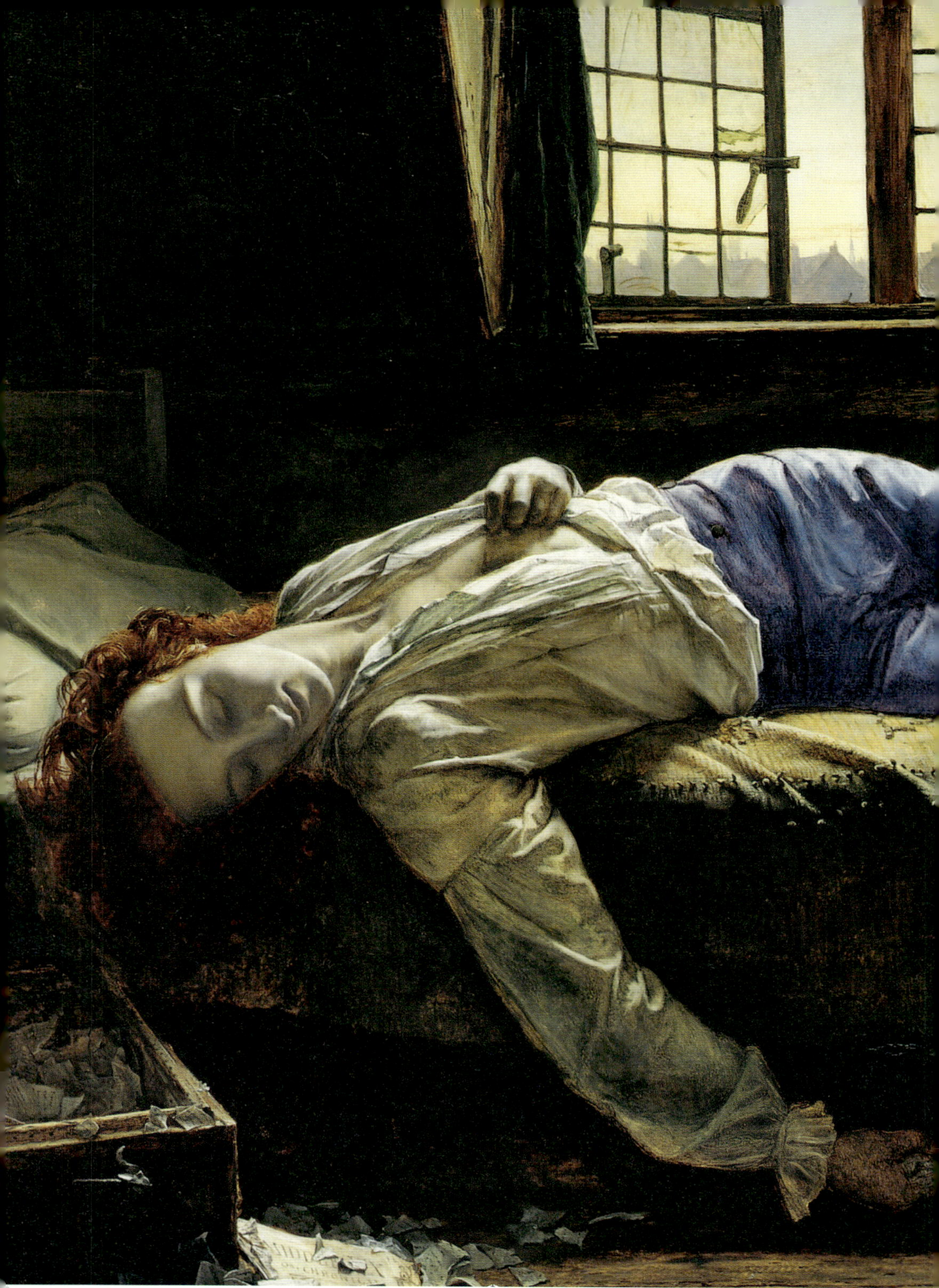

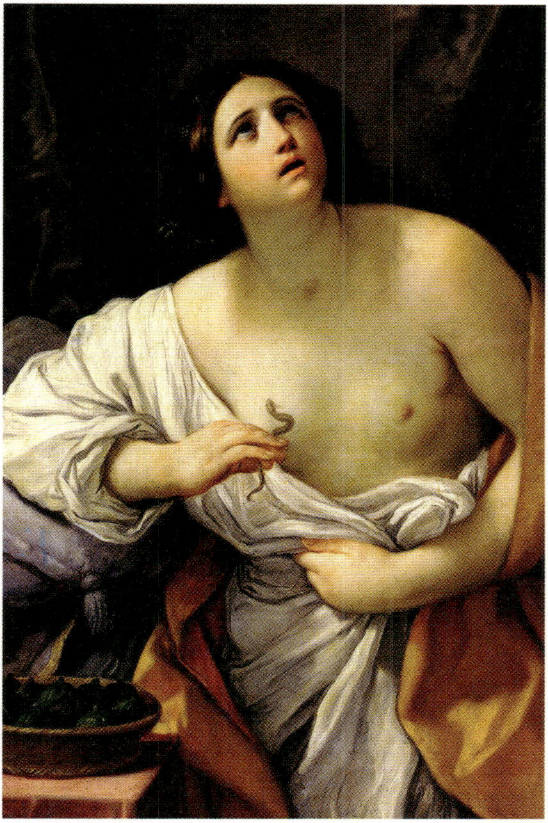

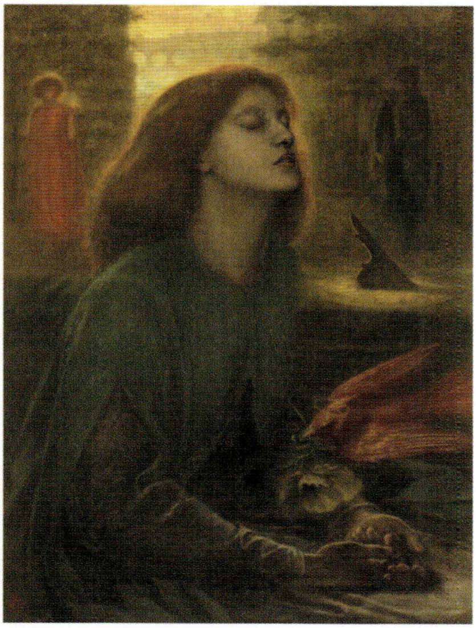

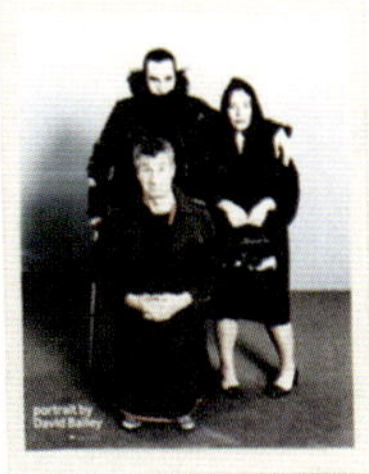

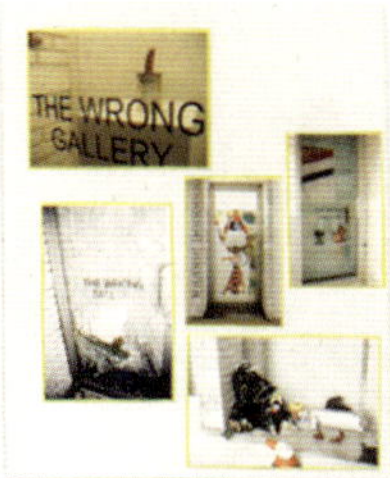

2005

The Wrong Gallery

In 2002, together with the curator Massimiliano Gioni and the editor/writer Ali Subotnick, Maurizio started The Wrong Gallery, the smallest gallery in Chelsea. The gallery consisted of a locked glass door through which one peered into a shallow, closet-like white space.

From 2002 until 2005, The Wrong Gallery organized over forty unimpressive projects, with an array of highly accomplished artists, including Elizabeth Peyton, Paul McCarthy, and the late Jason Rhodes. After it vacated its doorway, The Wrong Gallery lived on as a scattered and ethereal project: the door was shipped to the Tate Modern in London where it was installed in the galleries, and the collaborators worked on curating exhibitions, and doing other special projects like the poster you see here.

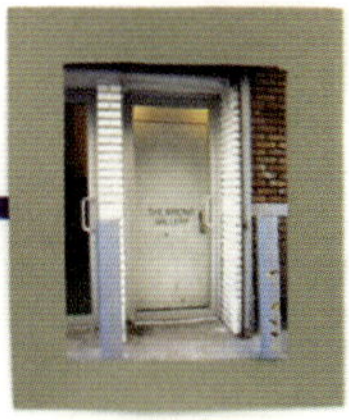

"The [Wrong Gallery] keeps moving but doesn't seem to evolve or know where it is going. It feels like an endlessly delayed ejaculation."
— Francesco Bonami

"Cattelan knows that people are vain and risk adverse. This, it seems to me, is the comic pivot of the artist's work. We can't produce the comic-scale laughter, tears, and rage that Cattelan's work asks for, and so instead we applaud him for the act of asking itself."
— Tom Morton, 1995

2007

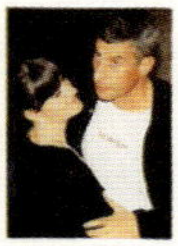

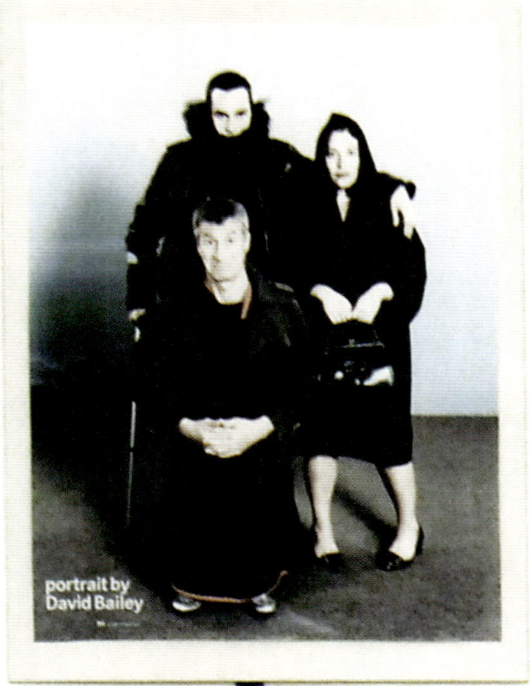

Ballad of Trotsky sold for $2 million.

2005

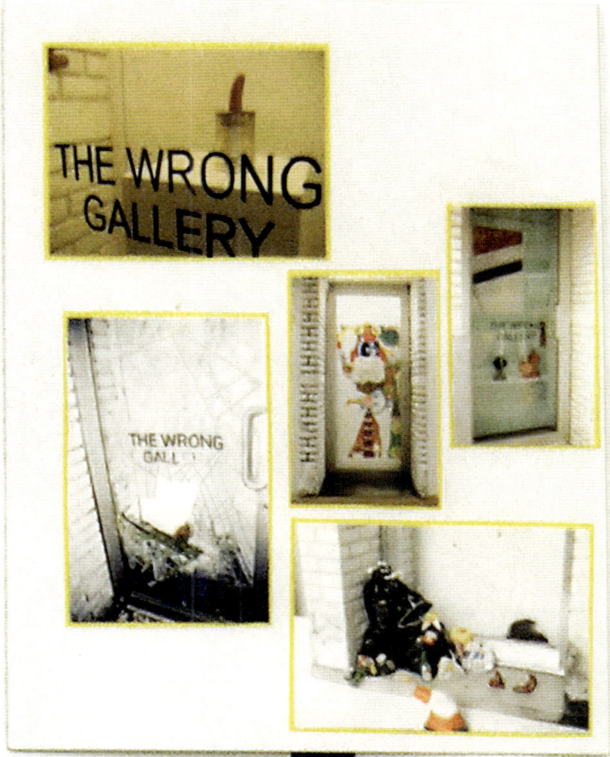
THE WRONG
GALLERY
THE WRONG

Maurizio took two years off from making work.

"The [Wrong Gallery] keeps moving but doesn't seem to evolve or know where it is going. It feels like an endlessly delayed ejaculation."

—Francesco Bonami

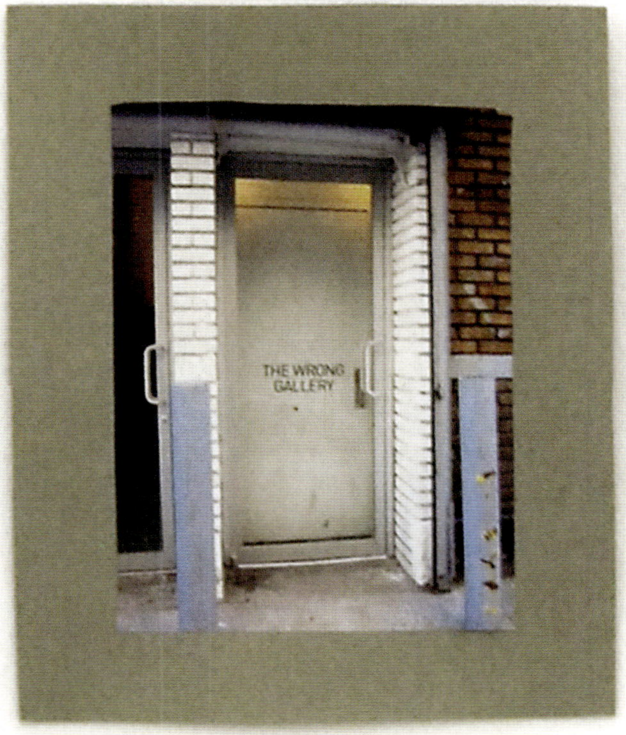
THE WRONG
GALLERY

“Cattelan knows that people are vain and risk adverse. This, it seems to me, is the comic pivot of the artist’s work. We can’t produce the comic-scale laughter, tears, and rage that Cattelan’s work asks for, and so instead we applaud him for the act of asking itself.”

—Tom Morton, 1995

Maurizio was said to be dating Victoria Cabello,
a former VJ with MTV.

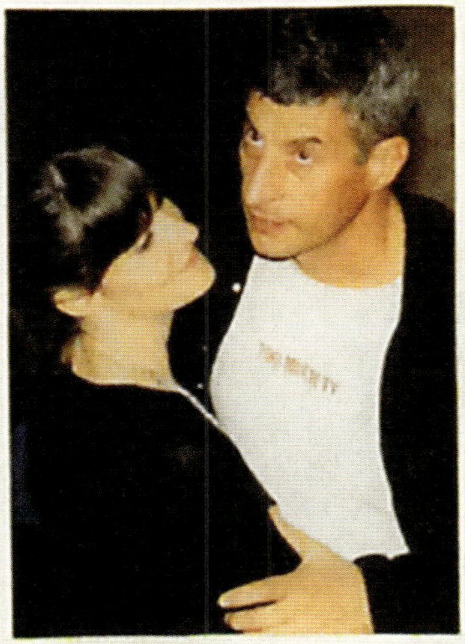

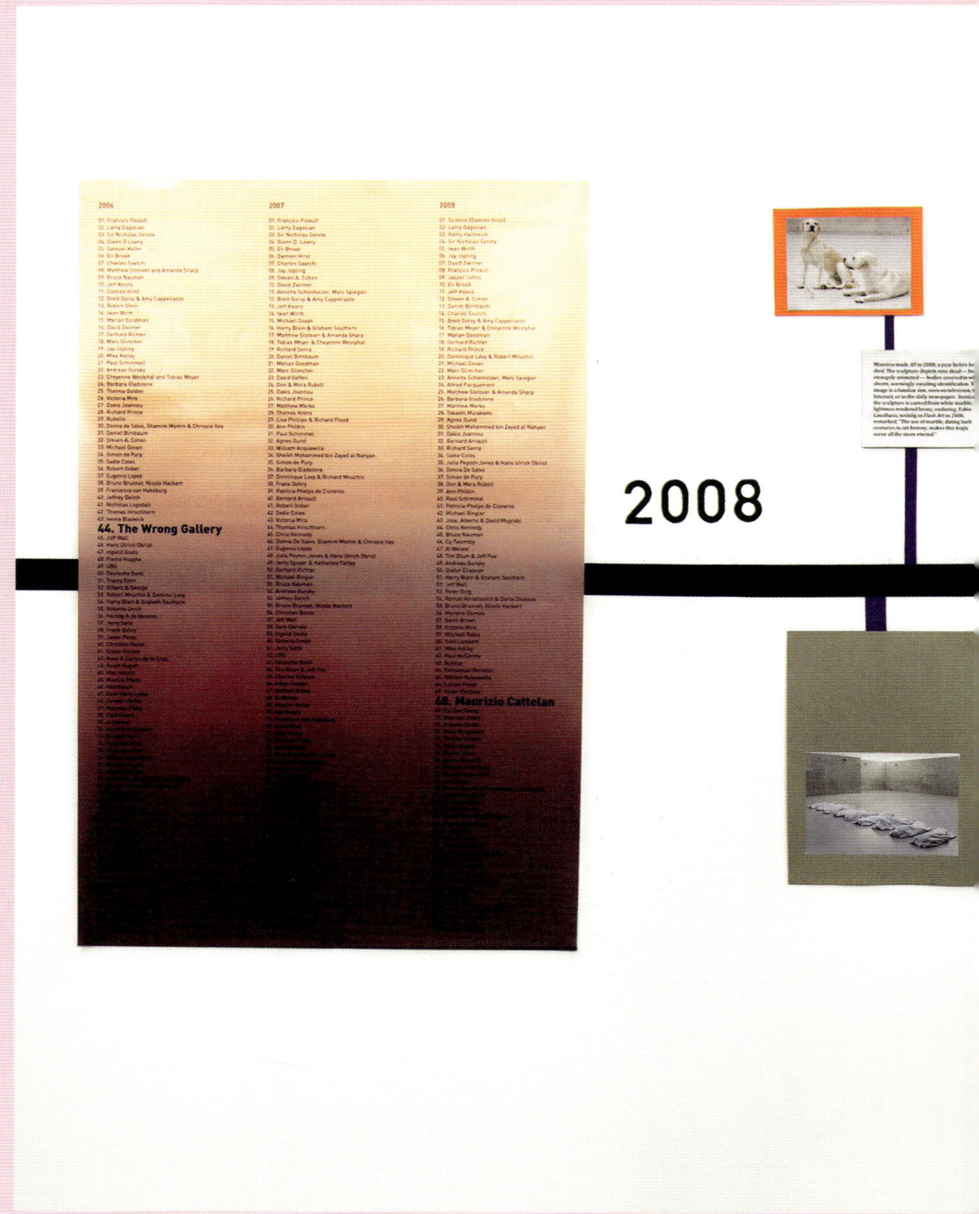
2006
2007
2008
44. The Wrong Gallery
68. Maurizio Cattelan
2008

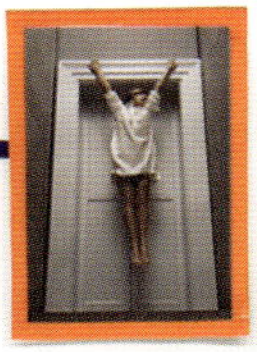

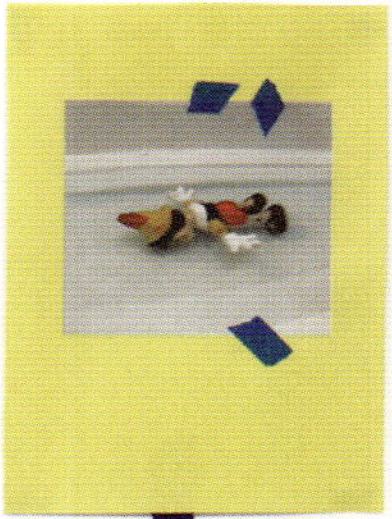

"The raised arm is for me an extraordinary symbol of power, an erection in potential, but also the absolute suspension of judgement."
— Maurizio Cattelan, 2007

The Image of a Sculpture

Maurizio's art occupies a paradoxical position in relationship to its public. Nearly everything he made took the form of sculpture — often in rarefied editions of only 3 copies — thus ensuring its marketability within the upper echelons of the art world. But each of his sculptures was also carefully conceived for photographic reproduction to provide, he hoped, widespread public impact. In 2002, he claimed "I [think] in terms of 'Will this piece be reproduced in magazines?'"

When asked about his sculpture he once admitted to being uncomfortable with the term. Since he didn't make them himself, he said, he thought of them more as "images".

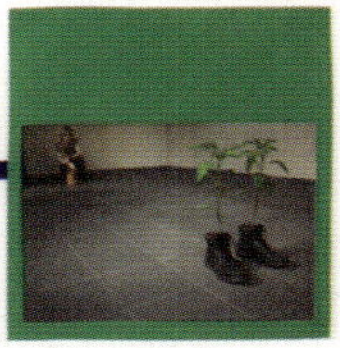

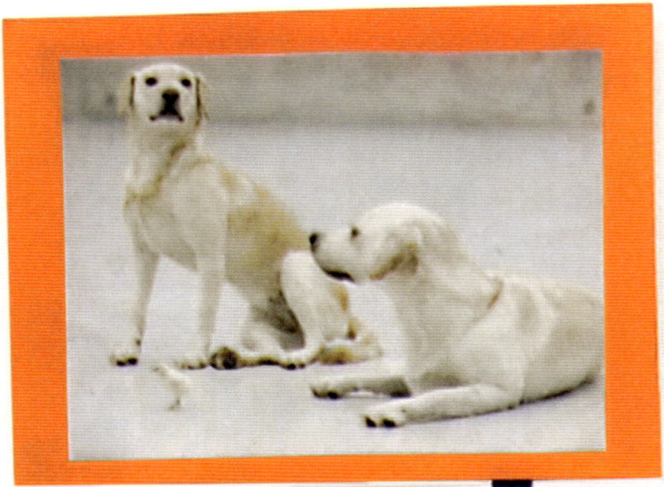

Maurizio made *All* in 2008, a year before he died. The sculpture depicts nine dead—but strangely animated—bodies covered in white sheets, seemingly awaiting identification. The image is a familiar one often seen on television, the Internet, or in the daily newspaper. Ironically, the sculpture is carved from white marble; the lightness rendered heavy, enduring. Fabio Cavallucci, writing in *Flash Art* magazine in 2008, remarked, "The use of marble, dating back centuries in art history, makes this tragic scene all the more eternal."

08

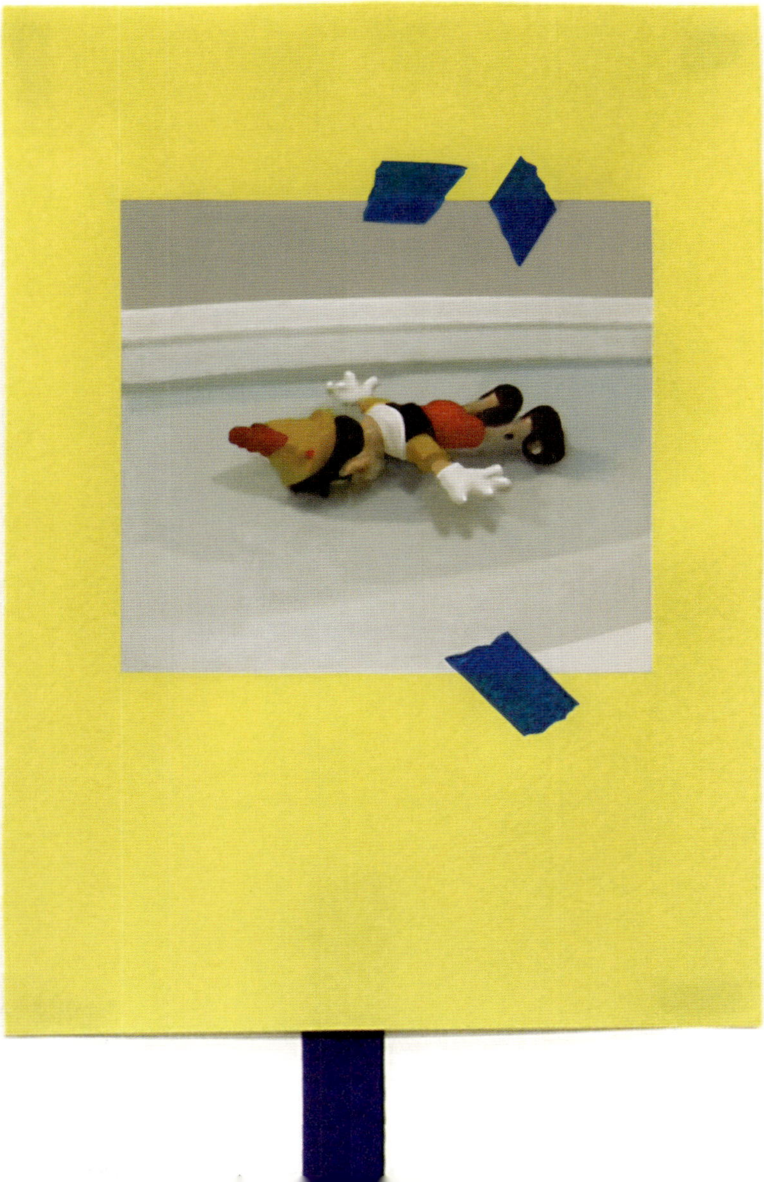

The Image of Sculpture

Maurizio's art occupies a paradoxical position in relationship to its public. Nearly everything he made took the form of sculpture, often in rarefied editions of only three copies—thus ensuring its marketability within the upper echelons of the art world. But each of his sculptures has also been carefully conceived for photographic reproduction to provide, Maurizio hoped, widespread public impact. In 2002, he claimed, "I [think] in terms of 'Will this piece be reproduced in magazines?'"

When asked about his sculpture, Maurizio once admitted to being uncomfortable with the term. Since he didn't make them himself, he said, he thought of them more as images.

"The raised arm is for me an extraordinary symbol of power, an erection in potential, but also the absolute suspension of judgement."
— Maurizio Cattelan, 2007

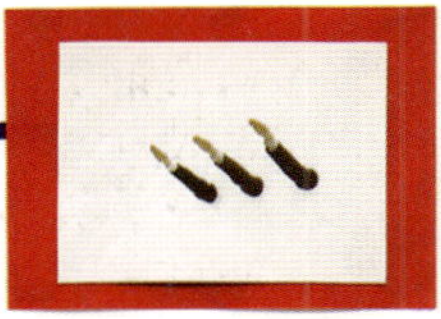

"Back in school days in Italy they used to put a hat on your head — this kind of hat with two big ears — and they'd say 'Bronca'. So I would think 'my God I'm like an ass. . . .'"
— Maurizio Cattelan

[illegible]

[illegible]

[illegible]

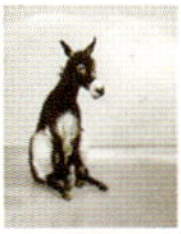

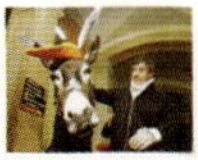

"Gaining recognition and being collected by museums is nice but it can also spell the end of you. Being accepted can be more dangerous than being refused."
— Maurizio Cattelan, 2002

"The raised arm is for me an extraordinary symbol of power, an erection in potential, but also the absolute suspension of judgement."
—Maurizio Cattelan, 2007

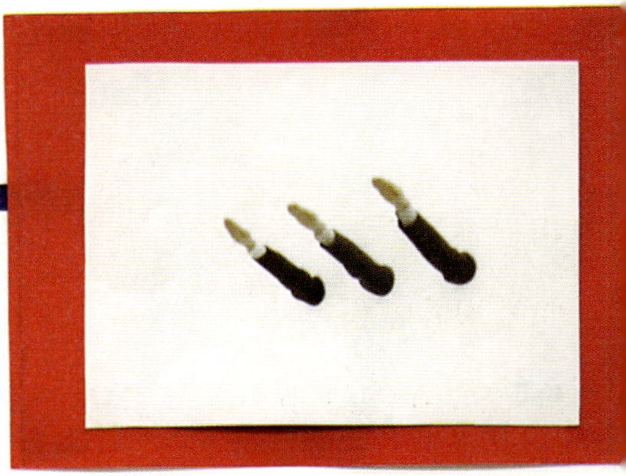

"Back in school days in Italy they used to put a hat on your head—this kind of hat with two big ears—and they'd say 'Branca.' So I would think 'my God I'm like an ass.'"
—Maurizio Cattelan

Kunstkompass listed Maurizio as one of the Top 10 Contemporary Artists.

In March, a gold medal was awarded to Maurizio by the MAXXI Museum of Rome.

One of the Mini-Me sculptures sold for $815,000.

"Gaining recognition and being collected by museums is nice but it can also spell the end of you. Being accepted can be more dangerous than being refused."
—Maurizio Cattelan, 2002

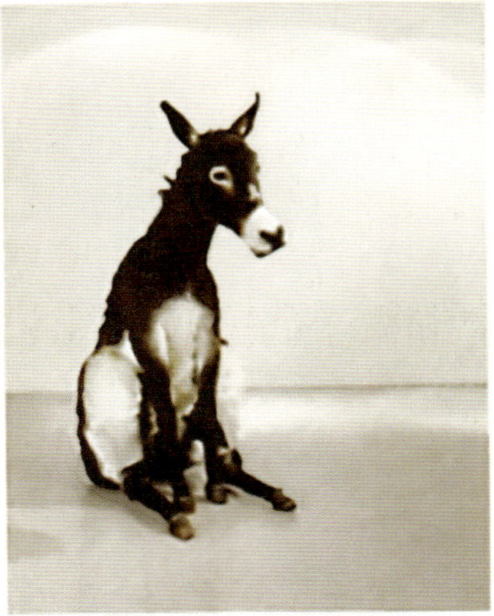

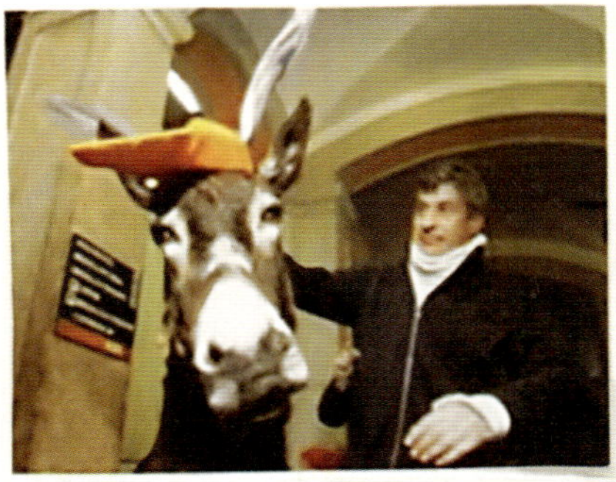

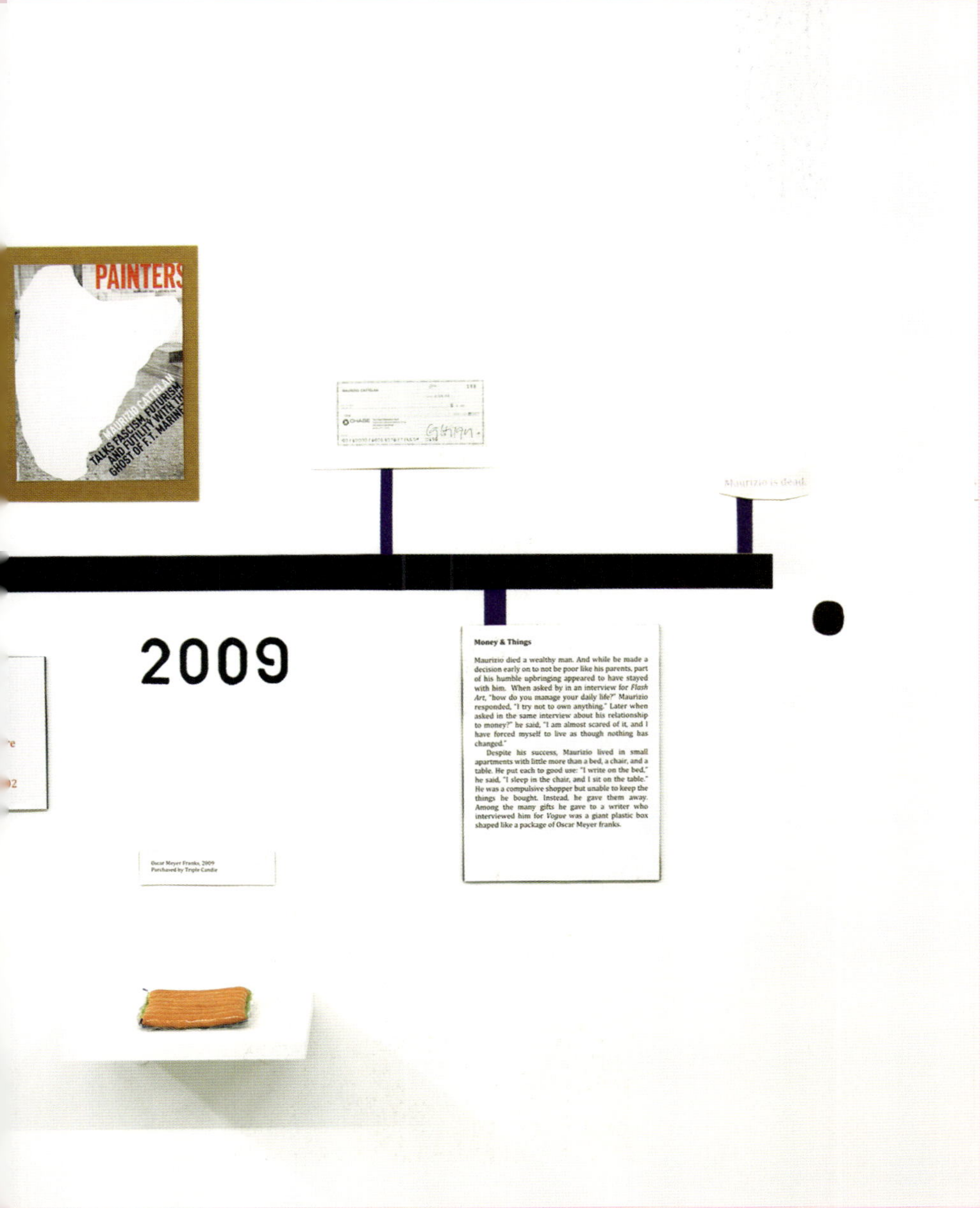
PAINTERS
MAURIZIO CATTELAN
TALKS FASCISM, FUTURISM
AND FUTILITY WITH THE
GHOST OF F.T. MARINE
Maurizio is dead.
2009
Money & Things
Maurizio died a wealthy man. And while be made a decision early on to not be poor like his parents, part of his humble upbringing appeared to have stayed with him. When asked by in an interview for *Flash Art*, "how do you manage your daily life?" Maurizio responded, "I try not to own anything." Later when asked in the same interview about his relationship to money?" he said, "I am almost scared of it, and I have forced myself to live as though nothing has changed."
Despite his success, Maurizio lived in small apartments with little more than a bed, a chair, and a table. He put each to good use: "I write on the bed," he said, "I sleep in the chair, and I sit on the table." He was a compulsive shopper but unable to keep the things he bought. Instead, he gave them away. Among the many gifts he gave to a writer who interviewed him for *Vogue* was a giant plastic box shaped like a package of Oscar Meyer franks.
Oscar Meyer Franks, 2009
Purchased by Triple Candie

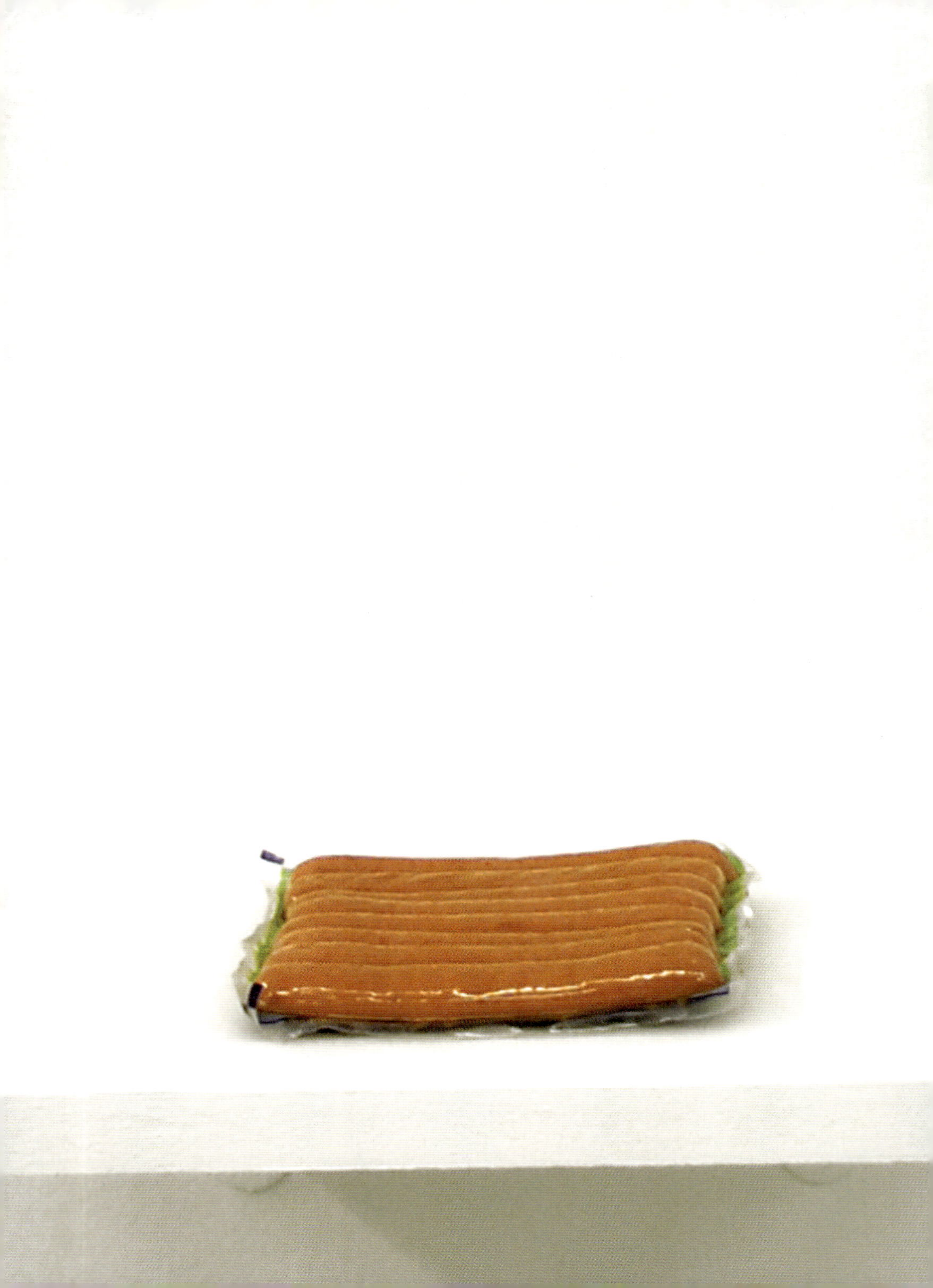

Money & Things

Maurizio died a wealthy man. And while he made a decision early on to not be poor like his parents, part of his humble upbringing appeared to have stayed with him. When asked by a critic in *Flash Art* magazine, "How do you manage your daily life?" Maurizio responded, "I try not to own anything." Later when asked in the same interview about his relationship to money, he said, "I am almost scared of it, and I have forced myself to live as though nothing has changed."

Despite his success, Maurizio lived in a small apartment with little more than a bed, a chair, and a table. He put each to good use: "I write on the bed," he said, "I sleep in the chair, and I sit on the table." He was a compulsive shopper but unable to keep the things he bought. Instead, he gave them away. Among the many gifts he gave to writer Dodie Kazanjian, who interviewed him for *Vogue* magazine, was a giant plastic box shaped like a package of Oscar Meyer franks.

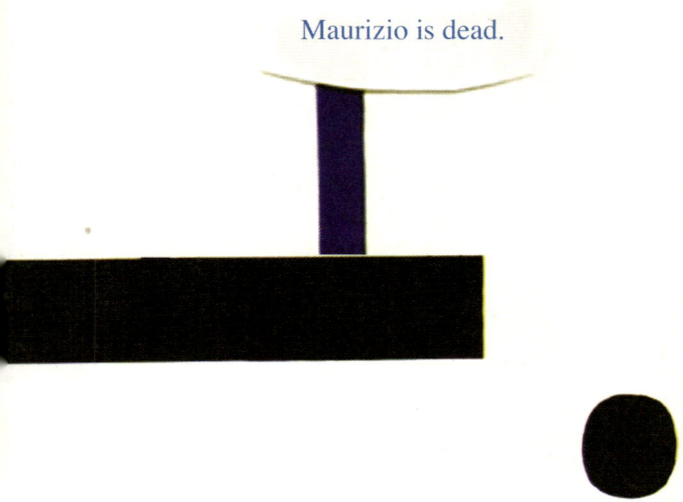
Maurizio is dead.

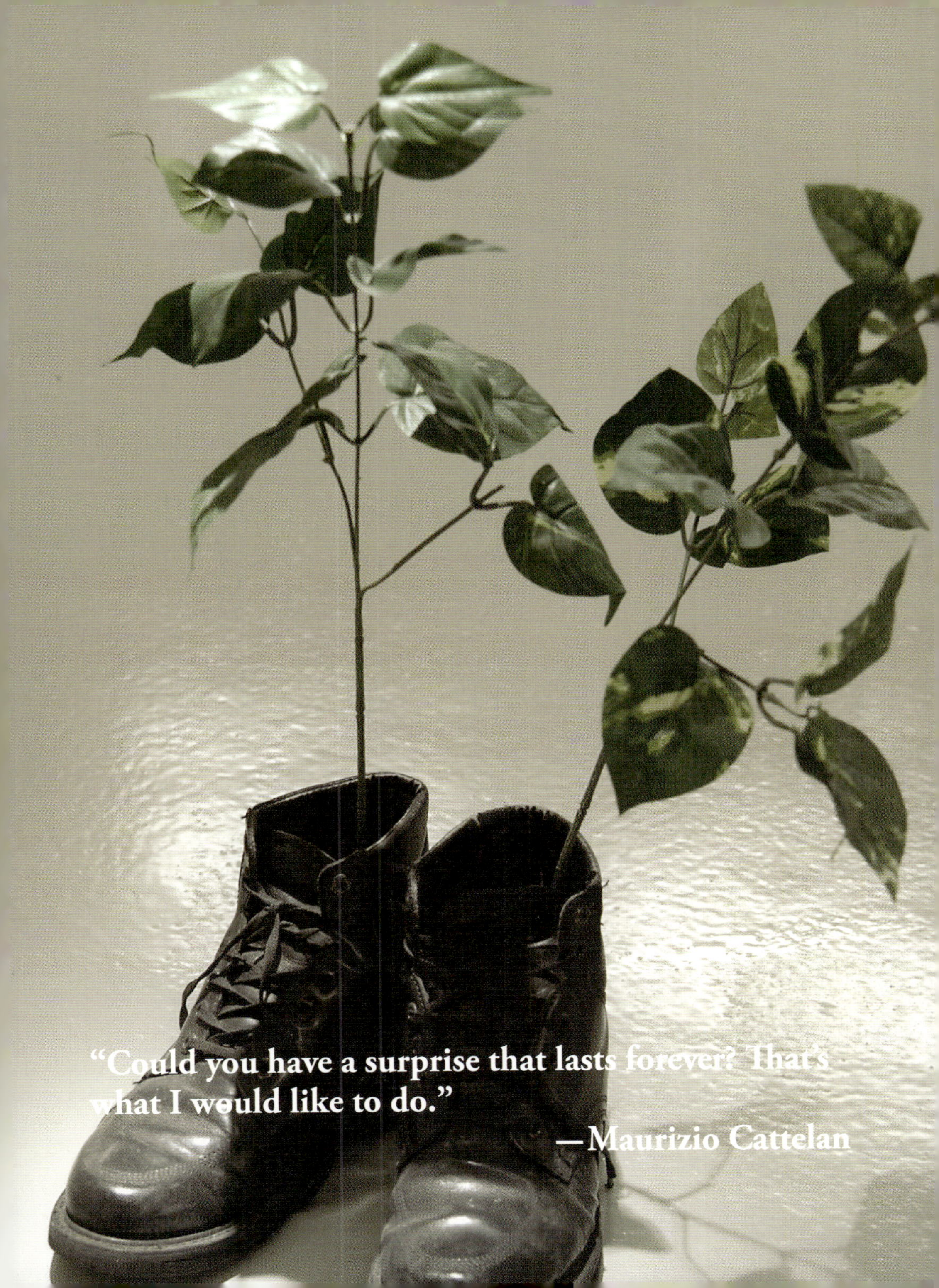
"Could you have a surprise that lasts forever? That's what I would like to do."
—Maurizio Cattelan

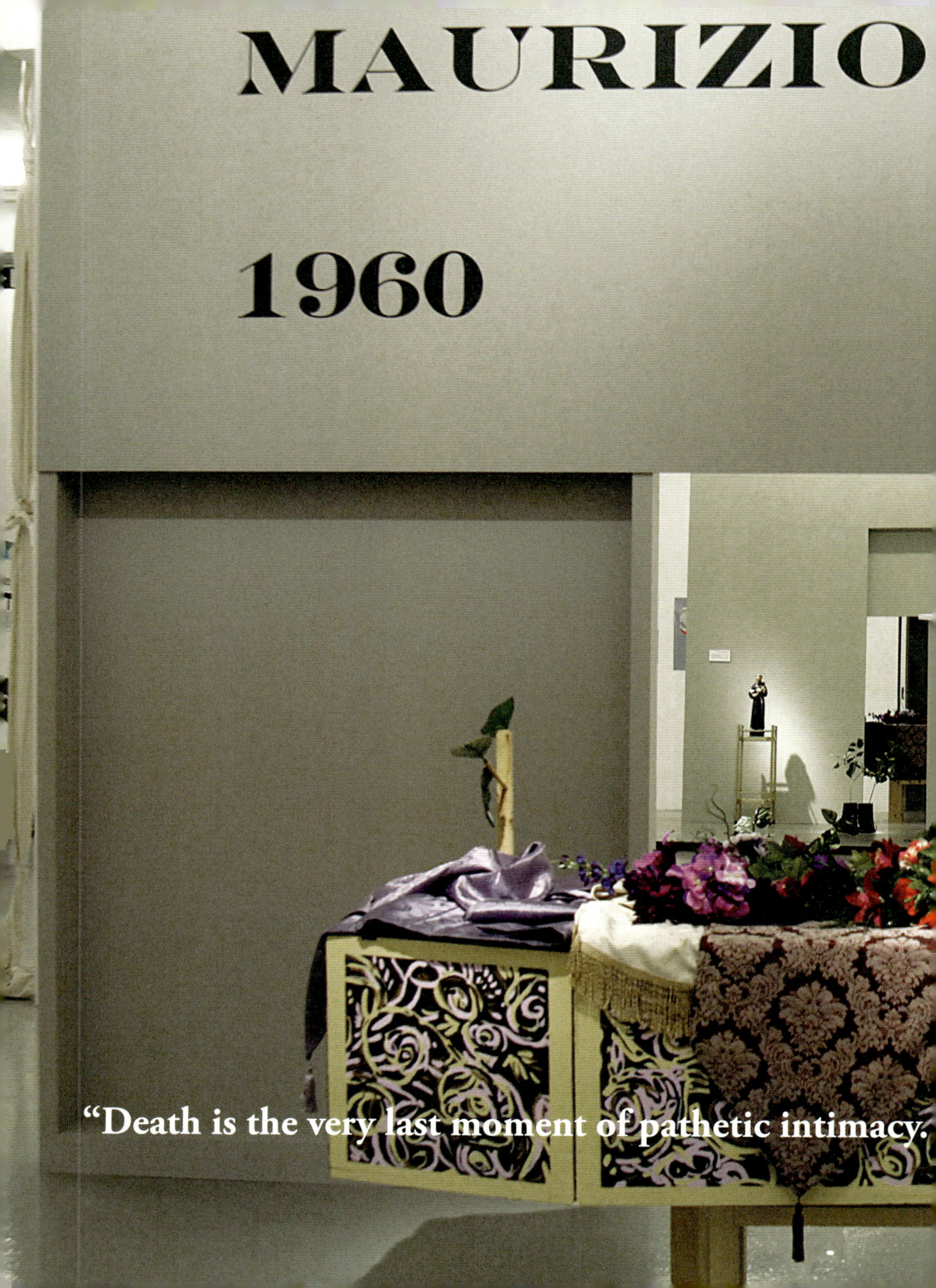

"Death is the very last moment of pathetic intimacy.

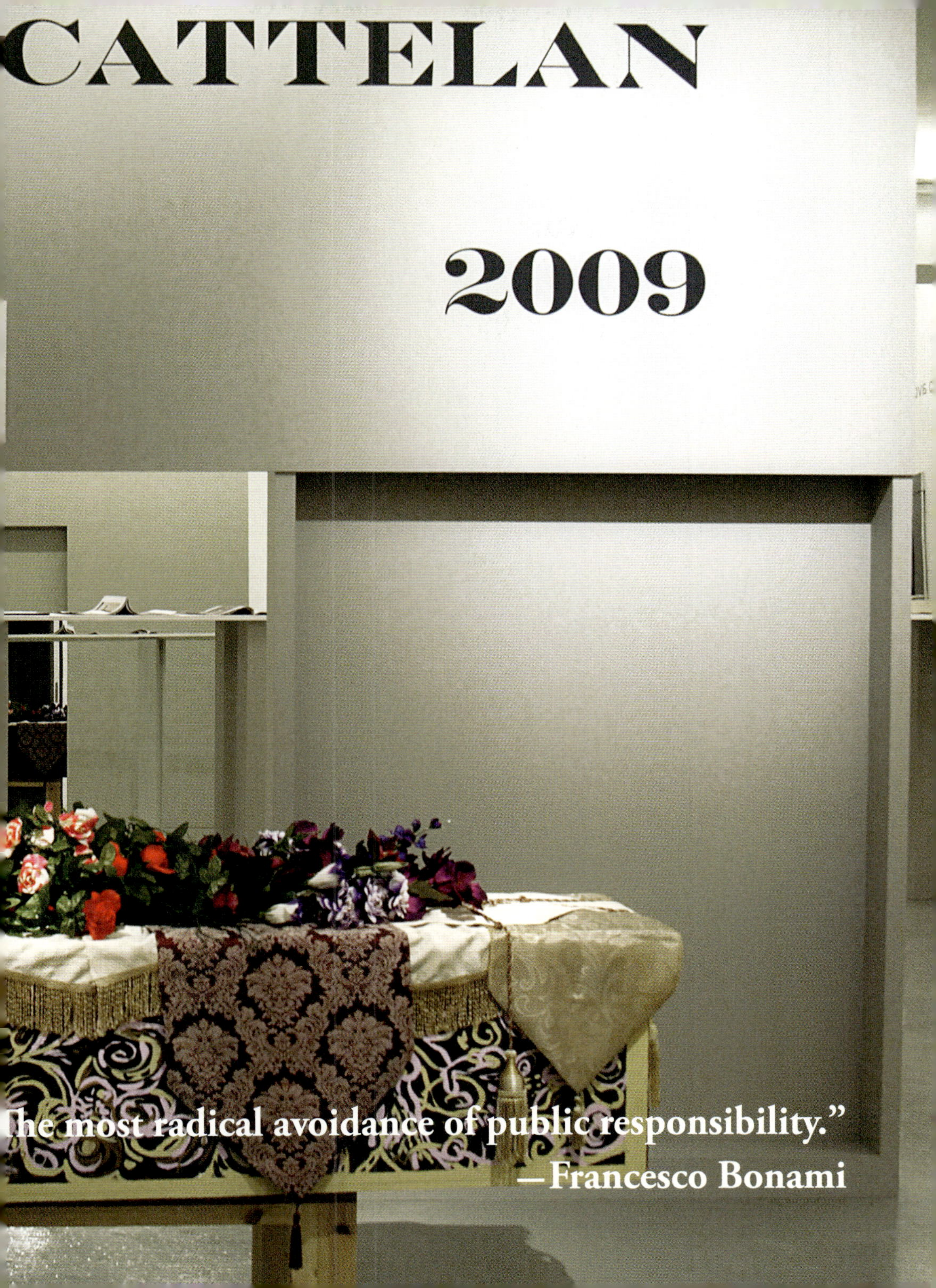

"he most radical avoidance of public responsibility."
—Francesco Bonami

A Note About Context

In the summer of 2009, we presented "Maurizio Cattelan is Dead: Life & Work, 1960–2009," the first retrospective of the artist's work, at our gallery in Harlem. A year later, we installed it, with minor alterations, during the "Alpha Omega" exhibition at the DESTE Foundation for Contemporary Art in Athens. This book documents the latter exhibition, with several amendments and corrections.

At the time of both shows, the artist was still very much alive. The title and the coffin—with a Pinocchio-like nose extruding from its lid—begged, then as now, questions of narrative reliability. Truth be told, the wall texts are based on information gleaned by us in our research. We intentionally re-reported errors from original sources, uncorrected.

Seeing this survey in Athens in 2010 was different from seeing it in Harlem. For one, Dakis Joannou has a long-standing relationship with Maurizio. At DESTE, the material was viewed familiarly, even if the installation's deliberately amateurish styling was incongruous with the Foundation's museum-like polish and artistic sophistication. One could say that the project's provisional curatorial approach, viewed in the context of the protracted tailspin of the Greek economy, foreshadowed a future in which a diminished public sector—not simply in Greece but elsewhere too—coupled with the astronomical expense of acquiring, presenting, and maintaining art, has led to radical changes in the way museums and other cultural organizations operate.

By contrast, in Harlem the exhibition was the latest in a four-year string of shows that we conceived and produced without the involvement of artists. We wanted these exhibitions to be of interest to an audience with limited knowledge of contemporary art and we chose subjects with a direct relationship to our own curatorial work and philosophy. Although Maurizio had no connection to the neighborhood, we surmised that the humor and pathos in his work would resonate locally. It did. As for our own interests, it was Maurizio's unathorized use of other people's work—in some of his shows from the mid-1990s and the magazine projects—to which we were drawn.

Back in 2009, if only briefly, it seemed that the mind-boggling expansion of the contemporary art market that had made careers like Maurizio's possible had come to an end. This, of course, proved not to be true, but at the time it seemed like a glorious possibility.

Triple Candie, Philadelphia, 2012

Maurizio Cattelan is Dead: Life and Work, 1960–2009

Design & Editorial: Triple Candie
Production Coordinator: Regina Alivisatos
Copy Editor: Casey Ruble

Published by:
Triple Candie Inc.
2248 St. Albans Street
Philadelphia, PA 19146
www.triplecandie.org

Distributed in the Americas by:
ARTBOOK | D.A.P.
155 6th Avenue, 2nd Floor
New York, NY 10013 U.S.A.
www.artbook.com

Distributed in Europe by:
Buchhandlung Walther König
Ehrenstrasse 4
D-50672 Köln, Germany
www.buchhandlung-walther-koenig.de

Printed by Amvrosiou Printing & Graphics; Printed in Greece
ISBN: 978-960-99314-4-1

Triple Candie (Shelly Bancroft and Peter Nesbett) would like to express its deep appreciation to Dakis Joannou, whose generosity, trust, and support have been extraordinary. We would also like to thank the entire staff at the DESTE Foundation for Contemporary Art, particularly Regina Alivisatos, Eugenia Stamatopoulou, and Kleio Silvestrou. Thanks also to Karen Marta, Dustin Cosentino, Elizabeth Karp-Evans, and Gregory R. Miller, as well as Todd Bradway, Alexander Galan, and Elisa Leshowitz from ARTBOOK | D.A.P., and Walther König, Franz König, and Eva Möller from Buchhandlung Walther König. We are grateful to Jeffrey Deitch, who encouraged Maurizio to visit the show in Harlem and who introduced us to Dakis Joannou. Thank you to Steve Dettman for being the third candy, and finally to Maurizio Cattelan, who showed up at his own funeral and laughed his way through the service.

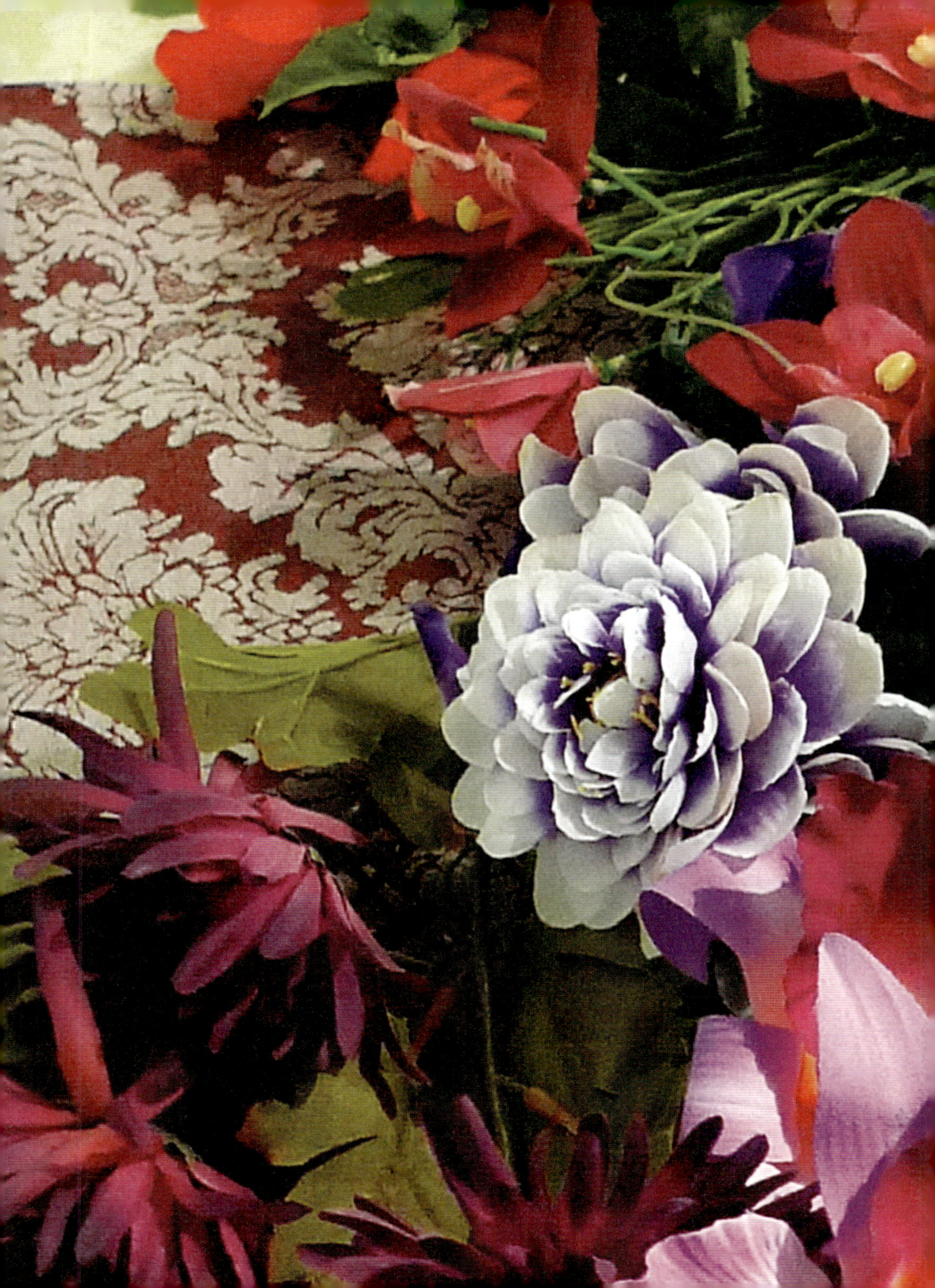

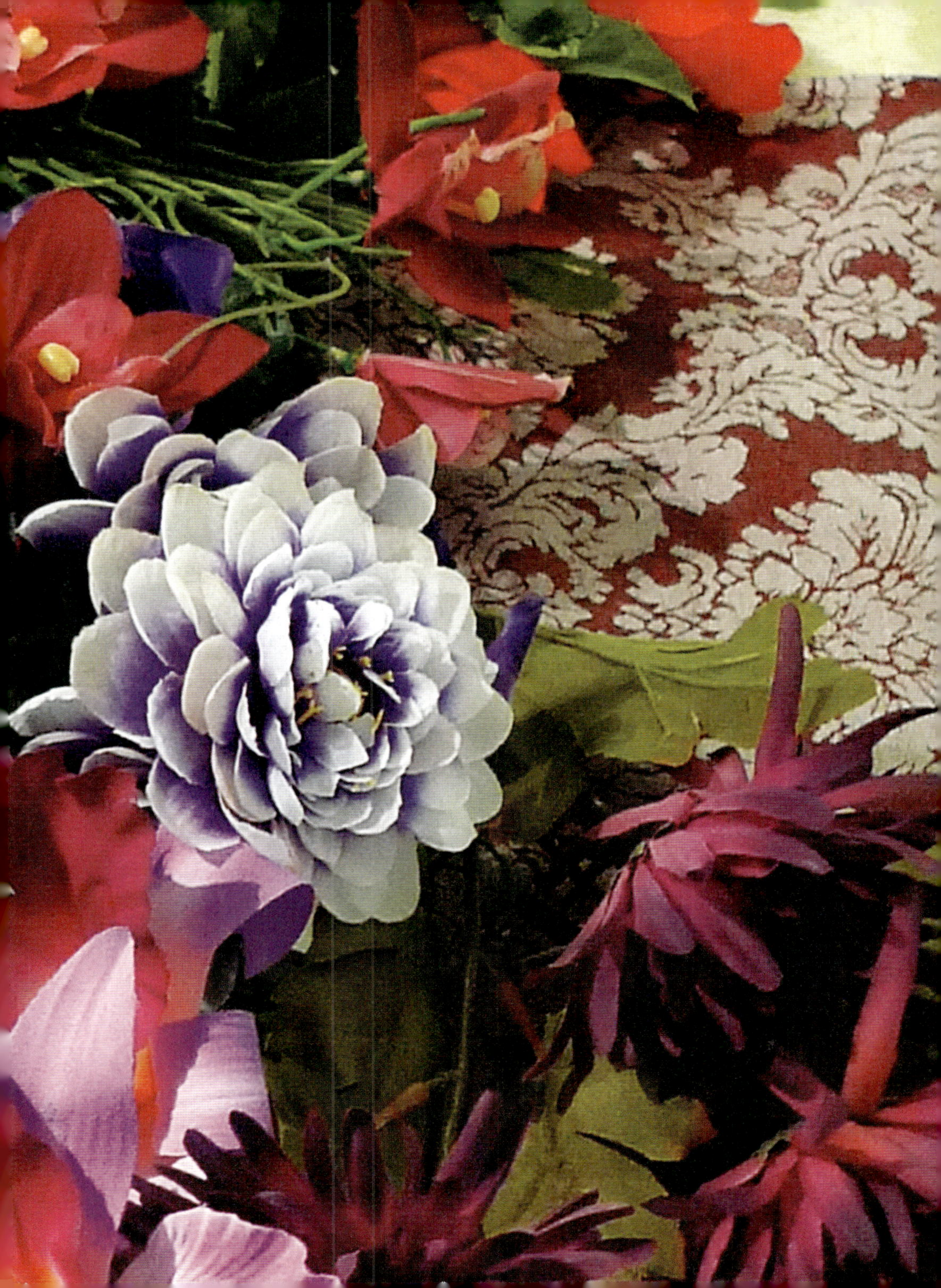

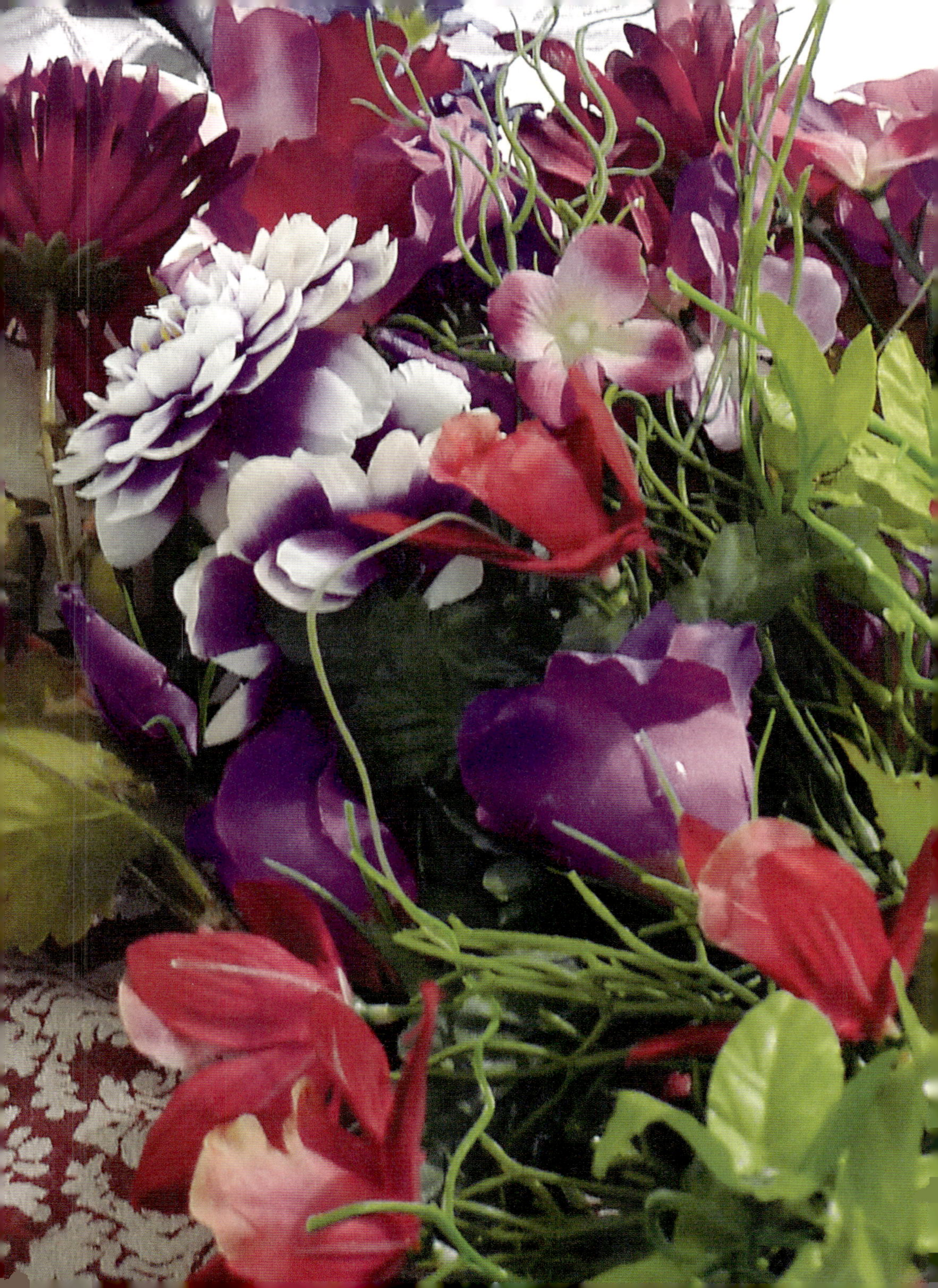